The Big Book of Blackjack

D0710126

The Big Book of Blackjack

Arnold Snyder

Cardoza Publishing

Cardoza Publishing is the foremost gaming and gambling publisher in the world with a library of more than 200 up-to-date and easy-to-read books and strategies. These authoritative works are written by the top experts in their fields and with more than 10,000,000 books in print, represent the best-selling and most popular gaming books anywhere.

Copyright © 2006, 2012 by Arnold Snyder

Library of Congress Number: 2012937190
ISBN 10:   1-58042-315-9
ISBN 13: 978-1-58042-315-1

Visit our website or write for a full list of Cardoza Publishing books and advanced strategies.

CARDOZA PUBLISHING
P.O. Box 98115, Las Vegas, NV 89193
Toll-Free Phone (800)577-WINS
email: cardozabooks@aol.com
www.cardozabooks.com

—for Karen—

About the Author

Arnold Snyder is the world's foremost authority on blackjack and one of its greatest players. Snyder is the author of nine books and advanced strategies on the game including *The Blackjack Formula*, the groundbreaking work which revolutionized the ways professional card counters attacked the games, and of course, the best-selling classic, *Blackbelt in Blackjack*. For 23 years, he was the publisher of the highly respected Blackjack Forum, a quarterly journal on gambling for professional players.

In January 2003, in recognition for his contributions to the game, Arnold was elected one of the seven charter members of the Blackjack Hall of Fame. Arnold is a high-stakes professional player who has been writing about casino blackjack for over three decades.

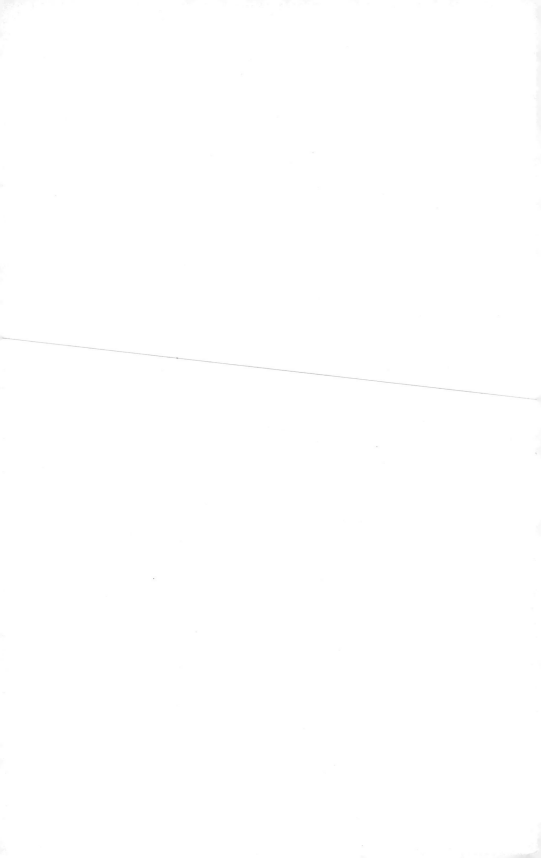

TABLE OF CONTENTS

INTRODUCTION

Blackjack: The War for the Money

> "The game is done! I've won! I've won!"
> —Samuel Taylor Coleridge, Rime of the Ancient Mariner

There's a war going on in the blackjack pits. The battle rages twenty-four hours a day, seven days a week, in every casino in the world where blackjack is offered. Both sides have their generals and their foot soldiers, their scouts and their spies, but—remarkably—most players are oblivious to it. If you are a blackjack player, this book will open your eyes to things that you never dreamed of that are going on at the tables, behind the tables, and upstairs in the surveillance room.

I am going to assume right from the start that you know nothing whatsoever about casino blackjack. We're going to cover it all, because every detail is so important. Let's say you just touched down on Earth from the planet Poindexter, attracted to Las Vegas by the dazzling lights. You stepped into one of the glittering palaces on the Strip, probably hungry, looking for something to eat. You walked up to one of the blackjack tables, eyeing the stacks of colorful chips scattered on the felt and nestled in the dealer's chip tray. . . Yummm!

Well, okay, maybe you're not that much of a beginner. Maybe you know that blackjack is a card game that people play for money. And you know they play this game in casinos, which are places that look to you pretty much like they look to that alien from Poindexter. The chips on the tables don't look particularly appetizing, but you do realize that those chips represent money, and that money is the object of this game.

Let me repeat that once more, because this concept is so important to this book:

Fact: The Object of This Game is Money.

I might also assume, since you picked up this book, that you know that casinos offer games that people play for money, and that there are some people who play blackjack well enough to make money playing—in some cases, a lot of money. And in the back recesses of your mind, you may wonder if perhaps you might not be able to make money playing this card game. And even if you're not thinking in terms of playing blackjack professionally, perhaps you think you might be able to play skillfully enough to supplement your income, or just well enough to break even—in addition to getting a lot of complimentary meals and show tickets for giving the casinos your action. And whether you are a rank beginner, or anywhere between rank beginner and full-time pro, I guarantee that you will soon know a lot of things about this game that even many seasoned professional blackjack players do not know.

To call casino blackjack a "game" is a serious misnomer. It may be a game to you now, and in fact, it may be a game to most of the players who take a seat to pit their luck against the dealer's. But for casino owners and a small number of skilled players, blackjack isn't so much a game as a money machine. No other card game in history has made as much money for the casinos as blackjack and...

Fact: No other card game has made as much money for the pros who know how to beat the casinos at their own game.

I realize that few who read this book are destined to become full-time professional gamblers. Most card counters are not professional gamblers. In many cases, winning players are doctors, lawyers, professors, and other upstanding citizens of their respective communities. Any person of average intelligence can learn to make money at the game of blackjack.

But I do want you to be aware that for the most serious and dedicated players, blackjack is a profession, a ticket out of the rat race. It's the reason they don't have to set their alarms to get up for work every morning; the reason they don't have to punch a time clock or wear a necktie five days a week; the reason they can make their own hours, choose their own days off, travel the world, and pick up their paychecks in cold hard cash without ever answering to a boss.

How is this possible?

This book will tell you exactly how.

In every bookstore, you'll find a dozen or more books on blackjack, and most of them say the same things. Here's how you play. Here's the basic strategy. Here's a simple card counting system. Good luck!

I'm going to give you all that information in this book—all of the basic technical information you need to beat the casinos at this game. But that's just the beginning. I'm also going to show you exactly how the pros think of this game—as a Way of Life.

We're going to go into a thousand things about this game that you won't find anywhere else. And we're going to illustrate every theory and practical technique with real-life stories of the players, though mostly unknown to the public, who have made the history of this game—the real history. I want to show you how the battle for the money has driven the development of this game and made it what it is today. I want you to see the ways the pros have beaten the casinos, the ways the casinos have fought back, and the ways the pros have overcome the casinos' countermeasures.

And you thought you were playing a simple card game? No way, Jose!

Welcome to the battlefield!

SECTION ONE:

THE MYSTERY HISTORY

THE LONG, SLOW BIRTH OF THE MOST POPULAR CASINO CARD GAME IN THE WORLD

There is almost as murky a scholarly dispute over the origins of Black Jack as there is over Poker and Gin Rummy.

— *John Scarne, Scarne's Guide to Casino Gambling*

John Scarne, gambling's most prolific author, had little to say about the origins of blackjack. In several of his books, he mentioned a number of the older European games that had similar structures, and vaguely concluded that the Italian game of seven-and-a-half was blackjack's most likely forerunner.

Most other gambling writers never went beyond Scarne. As Richard Epstein put it in *The Theory of Gambling and Statistical Logic*, "The exact origin of the game of Blackjack is rather murky." Epstein was not a historian, however; he was a mathematician. The attitude of most gambling writers was that if Scarne doesn't know the history of the game, who does?

In *Playing Blackjack to Win*, Baldwin, Cantey, Maisel, and McDermott said it this way: "The origins of the game have been lost in history." As we'll see, however, Roger Baldwin did turn up a sixteenth century Spanish game that sounded suspiciously like blackjack to him.

More modern authors never even gave it a shot. Thorp, Revere, Wong, Uston—all have little to say on the origins of the game. Others simply echo Scarne. Lance Humble and Carl Cooper, in *The World's Greatest Blackjack Book*, stated, "The origin of the game is unknown." And Olaf Vancura and Ken Fuchs, in *Knock-Out Blackjack*, agreed: "The exact origin of the game of blackjack is unclear."

So, for me, this is going to be a fun chapter to write because it gives me a chance to reveal a lot of information about the history of this game that I've learned through the years, but never really had an opportunity to disclose. I've never read about the origins of this game anywhere. And there is a reason for this.

In researching history, we must rely on the records of human beings—a species not particularly known for either accuracy or honesty—whose statements often contradict one another. When it comes to researching the history of gambling, we are even more confounded by the facts at our disposal. Gamblers have always survived by subterfuge and deception, and the movers and shakers in the microcosm of the gamblers' world include a vast array of scoundrels, liars, crooks, cheaters, braggarts, egomaniacs, and downright lunatics. But then, for me, that's why studying the history of gambling is a pleasure. The story is like a puzzle that you have to solve by figuring out which con artist was actually telling the truth. I might have actually enjoyed history class in high school if, instead of boning up on the naval career of John Paul Jones, I could have studied the three-card-monte career of William Jones, an Englishman who plied his trade on the Canadian railways throughout the mid-eighteen hundreds.

Most books that deal with the history of casino gambling are written by moral crusaders who want to expose the evils of gambling and the casino industry. Among the big sellers, *The Green Felt Jungle* by Reid and Demaris, *Temples of Chance* by David Johnston, and *The Luck Business* by Robert Goodman would all fall into this category. I'm not saying I disagree with these authors' conclusions, as the casino industry has always been controlled by some pretty slimy bastards. But these are one-sided histories. Just look at the subtitles printed on the covers of these books. In the same order as above, we have: How Politicians, Mobsters and Big-Name Talent Work Hand-in-Glove Running Las Vegas, Corruption Capital of the World; How America Inc. Bought Out Murder Inc. to Win Control of the Casino Business; and The Devastating Consequences and Broken Promises of America's Gambling Explosion. On the other hand, any gambling history penned by a casino owner—be it Donald Trump, Steve Wynn, or Harold Smith, all of whom have given us their two cents' worth—is just as one-sided, from the opposite perspective.

So, let's do something different. Let's look at the history of blackjack from the perspective of the player. Hey, I like to gamble. I make my living gambling. I don't want the casinos to be put out of business by morality crusaders.

THE BIRTH OF BLACKJACK

Gambling scholars have argued for decades about the origins of many modern gambling games. When it comes to the game of blackjack, the most popular house-banked card game in history, many modern texts tell us that the origins of the game are "uncertain." Hey, just about everything in this universe is uncertain, but the origins of blackjack are not. The game can be traced to a number of popular European card games from as far back as the fifteenth century. That's right around the time when Gutenberg invented the printing press, and cards themselves became popular (and cheap) enough to play games with. Prior to that, cards were hand-painted by artists and calligraphers for royalty only, and they were primarily used for religious, educational, or ceremonial purposes.

Virtually all card games are based on some specified number of cards being dealt, with a winner determined by some happenstance of rank, suit, match, sequence, or total. In the simple children's game of war—which in recent years has been modified into a house-banked casino game—the only determining factor of the winner is rank. In more complex card games, like poker, various combinations of rank, suit, match, or sequence may decide the winner. Blackjack is more complex than war, but much simpler than poker. The winner at twenty-one is decided almost entirely on the basis of total, with the cards' numerical values being added together.

IN THE BEGINNING... VINGT-UN, NAPOLEON'S FAVORITE GAME

There is little dispute that the first twenty-one games appeared in France in the early-to-mid-seventeen hundreds. The game was called vingt-un, or "twenty-one," when it was initially introduced, and was later more commonly called vingt-et-un. The name "blackjack" was not used until the twentieth century, when the game was being played in the mostly illegal casinos in America.

Because vingt-un first appeared as a private game, and was not banked by the casinos, we will never know in which French casino the game was first played. It was the custom of the time for the casinos in Europe to bank various popular games—notably roulette, hazard, trente-et-quarante, faro, and baccarat. Roulette was the most popular house-banked casino game in virtually all casinos where the game was legal. Hazard was a dice game that was the predecessor to craps. Faro was a variation of an older card game called bassette. But the casinos also allowed players who wanted to gamble in other popular card or dice games to do so if one of the players was willing to deal and bank the game, with the house taking a commission (usually 5 percent) on the banker's winnings. This was most common with baccarat, the player-banked variation being called chemin-de-fer.

Definition:

To bank a game is to take and pay all bets made by opponents. Poker is not a banking game because all players at the table are playing and betting against each other. All players' bets go into a central pot and one player will win that pot. Craps, baccarat, and roulette are games that the casino "banks" because all players are betting against the house, which takes and pays all bets. In banking games, there is no central pot with a single winner; the house/banker may beat some players, but lose to others. Modern casino blackjack is a house-banked game because players do not play against each other. Blackjack is always a banking game, with no central pot but all players playing against the dealer/house. In private home games, blackjack may be played with one player always acting as the house/dealer, and banking all bets, or it may be structured with players taking turns banking the bets and acting as the dealer/house.

According to historian Rev. Ed. S. Taylor (*The History of Playing Cards*, 1865, London), "Vingt-et-un appeared in about the middle of the eighteenth century and was to number amongst its early enthusiasts such unlikely bedfellows as Madame Du Barry and the Emperor Napoleon." Madame Du Barry was Marie Jeanne Bécu, a comtesse and mistress of Louis XV. She died in 1793. So, in seeking the origins of vingt-un, we must look for card games that predated the mid-to-late seventeen hundreds, with a similar structure in which the winning hand was determined by the total numerical value of the cards.

A Warning Issued on Professional Players at the Bath (England) Casino

"Those who love play must understand it in a superlative degree, if they expect to gain anything by it at Bath, where there are always ingenious men, who live by their great talents for play; for however great an adept a man may think himself at the games of whist, billiards, etc., will always find men, and women too, here, who are greater, and who make it a rule to divide the many thousands lost every year at Bath, among themselves only."

—*Captain Philip Thicknesse, 1778*

Before the Beginning... Quinze, Like Blackjack with Bluffing

One such game is a French gambling game called quinze, which means "fifteen." This game appeared sometime in the sixteenth century, and was popular in European casinos up until the mid-eighteen hundreds.

Here's how quinze was played:

As a casino game, quinze was not house-banked, but was banked by the player who dealt the cards. The house merely took a percentage of the dealer's win. All players bet against the dealer/banker, and bets had to be placed prior to the deal. A standard fifty-two-card deck was used, with each card counting as its face value. Aces counted as one, and all court cards counted as ten. The deck was shuffled, and each player and the dealer were dealt one card face down. Players had to play their hands before the dealer played his. Each player in turn had the option to hit or stand, and any number of hits was permitted. If the player achieved a total of exactly 15, he immediately turned up his cards, and provided the dealer did not also make a total of 15, the player would be paid off at 2 to 1 on his bet. If both the player and the dealer made 15, the hand was a push. The only exception was that a two-card 15, a natural 15, would beat a 15 total comprised of more than two cards.

Unlike blackjack, if the player busted with any total of more than 15, he did not have to declare his bust. He was permitted to simply tuck his hole card and wait for the dealer to complete his hand. And, if the dealer busted also, those players who busted before the dealer did not lose their bets. When both the player and dealer busted, the hand was a push.

Also, unlike blackjack, the quinze dealer was not bound by house rules in the play of his hand. Just like the players, the dealer could hit or stand at his preference, provided his hand total did not exceed 15. Still, as in modern blackjack, the house had an edge at quinze based on the dealer's not having to play his hand until the players completed their hands. Even though a player did not have to declare a bust in quinze, it was often obvious when a player had busted because the player's hit cards showed a total of 15 or more. The dealer could then stand without hitting, on any card, even a lowly ace, and assure himself a win.

This game had some interesting strategy features we don't find in blackjack. Consider...

In playing the game, any time the player had a hole card of 6 or more, he chanced busting. Also, if he had a hit card or cards showing that totaled 6 or more, he chanced revealing a bust to the dealer if he took another hit. For example, if a player had an ace in the hole, a total of one, and he hit it with a 6 for a total of seven, it was dangerous to take another hit because by standing he might convince the dealer that he'd made a strong total, in which case the dealer might risk a bust on his own hand. If the player hit his 7 total and drew a court card, the dealer would see the 16 total on the table, and know that regardless of what the player's hole card was, the player had busted. As you can see, quinze had definite psychological aspects to play, similar to poker, where the player would attempt to hide the strength or weakness of his hand from the dealer. In any case, the structure of this game is undeniably the same as blackjack.

If You Cut Quinze in Half... Still Bluffing

Sometime in the seventeenth century, an Italian card game appeared called sette e mezzo, or "seven-and-a-half." This game was remarkably similar to quinze, and is an obvious derivative of the same family of games as quinze. Seven-and-a-half was played with a forty-card deck, from which all eights, nines, and pip tens had been removed. The object of the game for the player was to achieve a total closer to 7 1/2 than the dealer's total, without going over 7 1/2. All cards counted their pip-values, except for the court cards which each counted as one-half. Unlike quinze, but similar to our modern game of blackjack, if the player's hand total exceeded 7 1/2, the hand busted and automatically lost. The player could not just tuck his hole card and hope the dealer busted also. One card, the king of diamonds, was wild, and could be counted as any value.

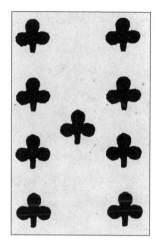 

> ### Definition:
>
> Pips are the suit symbols that indicate a card's value. A 9 of clubs, for instance, has nine club pips. A 5 of spades has five spade pips. The two cards above, a 9 of clubs and a 5 of spades, are from a French deck from the late seventeenth century, about the time that vingt-un was invented. Note that there are no index numbers in the corners of these cards to indicate the values. The cards' values were simply read by the number of pips.

As a casino game, seven-and-a-half was not house-banked, but was banked by the player who dealt the cards. All players bet against the dealer/banker, and bets had to be placed prior to the deal. The forty-card deck was shuffled, and each player and the dealer were dealt one card face down. Players had to play their hands before the dealer played his. Each player in turn had the option to hit or stand, and any number of hits was permitted, provided the hand total did not exceed 7 1/2. If the player busted with any total of 8 or more, he immediately turned up his facedown card, and the dealer collected his bet. If the player achieved a total of exactly 7 1/2, he immediately turned up his cards, and provided the dealer did not also achieve a total of 7 1/2, the player would be paid off at 2 to 1 on his bet. If both the player and the dealer made 7 1/2, the hand was a push. The only exception was that a two-card 7 1/2, a natural 7 1/2, would beat a 7 1/2 total comprised of more than two cards. As in blackjack, even if the dealer busted, those players who had busted before the dealer played his hand had already lost their bets. But similar to quinze, the seven-and-a-half dealer was not bound by house rules in the play of his hand. Just like the players, the dealer could hit or stand at his preference provided his hand total did not exceed 7 1/2.

Obviously, sette e mezzo was related to quinze. And like quinze, seven-and-a-half was based more on psychology than math. Since a player could have a very strong total without taking a hit with a hole card of 6 or 7, a dealer might be enticed into hitting his own hand if a player stood pat without a hit. And, since any hole card for the dealer other than a court card, valued at one-half, was in danger of busting, a player with a poor hole card, such as ace, deuce, or trey, might get the dealer to bust simply by standing pat. Because there was no fixed dealer strategy, both quinze and seven-and-a-half allowed trickery on the player's part conducive to getting the dealer to make wrong strategic decisions.

> Both quinze and seven-and-a-half are so close to the modern "home" version of blackjack, where dealers may usually draw or stand at their preference, that other than the target totals of 15 or 7 1/2, there is no major difference between these games and blackjack.

I will also note that the old Hoyles describe various methods of playing vingt-un that do not resemble modern twenty-one games. In most of the older descriptions of the game, there was no hit/stand requirement for the dealer. In some descriptions, vingt-un was played for a common pot, where all players played against each other. In another variant of the game, a natural 21 paid 2 to 1 regardless of whether it was dealt to a player's hand or to the dealer. In another variation, the jack counted as eleven, and a jack with any other ten-valued card was considered a natural 21. Doubling down and insurance—common options in the modern game—were not original features of vingt-un, and some old texts make no mention of twenty-one's pair-split option. In most of the older descriptions of the game, the dealer did not show an upcard to the players. About the only major difference between vingt-un and these older European card games was the target total of 21, as opposed to 7 1/2 or 15.

And as for Insurance...

One other older European card game probably contributed a single feature to our modern day game of blackjack. The French card game of trente-et-quarante, or "thirty-and-forty," which was introduced at the Spa Casino in Belgium in 1780, had the same card values as quinze, and a target total of thirty-one, but a structure similar to baccarat, where the players could bet on either of two hands dealt. But there was one curious feature of trente-et-quarante that later became a feature of modern blackjack. Trente-et-quarante was a house-banked game, and the house edge came from the house taking half of all bets when both hands totaled exactly thirty-one. But players were allowed to place an "insurance" wager against this possibility.

None of the descriptions of vingt-un in various old Hoyles mention anything about an "insurance" wager being allowed. This feature was added to the game of twenty-one much later in its history, most likely in the U.S. According to Steve Forte, the insurance wager was probably added in Nevada casinos sometime around the late 1950s. Photographs of casino blackjack tables from the 1950s do not show the familiar "Insurance Pays 2 to 1" signs on the layout, though photographs of tables from the 1960s usually do display this wording. I'll also note that in the 1957 analysis of blackjack by Baldwin, Cantey, Maisel, and McDermott, in their groundbreaking *Playing Blackjack to Win*, they state that most Nevada casinos offer insurance, and mention two forms of insurance available—insuring against an ace-up blackjack for 2 to 1, and insuring against a ten-up blackjack for 10 to 1. That ten-up insurance option has long since disappeared from any Nevada casino that ever offered it. The similarity of the insurance option at blackjack to the insurance bet at trente-et-quarante is undeniable, and as trente-et-quarante is still popular in the casinos of both France and Italy, I suspect the addition of this rule to blackjack started with someone familiar with trente-et-quarante.

But Before Quinze …Trente-Un, and a Sixteenth Century Card Sharp

An older game, however, that was a forerunner to both quinze and vingt-un was a game called trente-un, which was played throughout Europe back in the fifteenth century. Trente-un, which means "thirty-one," is believed to be of Spanish origin. The game was first mentioned in a sermon in 1440 by a famous French monk, Bernadine. We know the game was popular because there are recorded references to this game numerous times over the next two hundred years. Unfortunately, none of these references make any mention of the rules of play. Most of the commentary we have on this game came from medieval religious authorities, warning their flocks that trente-un was an evil game, and urging them to put their money into the church collection baskets and not into the hands of the profligate sinners who were running these games for Satan.

Are you getting a distinct feeling that we're getting close to the origins of blackjack?

One modern author who recognized that trente-un was the likely predecessor to vingt-un was Roger Baldwin, co-author of the first book with an accurate basic strategy, *Playing Blackjack to Win* (1957). Noting that trente-un was referenced by the famous sixteenth century Spanish novelist, Miguel de Cervantes, in a book titled *A Comical History of Rinconete and Cortadillo*, published around 1570, Baldwin quotes from Cervantes, where a professional trente-un player describes his skill at the game (and I love this quote): "I took along with me this pack of cards, for with these I have gained my living at all the publick houses and inns between Madrid and this place, playing One and Thirty; and though they are dirty and torn they are of wonderful service to those who understand them for they shall never cut without leaving an ace at the bottom, which is one good point towards eleven, with which advantage, thirty-one being the game, he sweeps all the money into his pocket."

Cervantes provides no details on the rules of One and Thirty, other than various facts we can surmise: 1) the game is played for money; 2) it is hand-dealt from a single-deck after a cut; 3) an ace can count for eleven; 4) making a total of thirty-one will win the money; and 5) the dealer's ability to control an ace to where he has easy access to it for his own or a confederate's hand is pretty much all it takes to be a professional thirty-one player.

This trente-un is sounding more like blackjack all the time!

If this were all we had to go on, we would likely conclude that vingt-et-un was derived from the older European games of quinze, sette e mezzo, and trente-et-quarante, all of which were preceded by the Spanish game of trente-un. The problem, however, is that there is a more modern game called trente-un, which is more like rummy, where players attempt to achieve a hand totaling thirty-one in a matching suit by taking and discarding cards from a common pile. The structure of this game is so unlike any of these other European banking games, however, that we would conclude that trente-un is probably not the forerunner of blackjack. That Cervantes quote from 1570 that Roger Baldwin provides, however, makes us wonder if the Spanish game of trente-un may itself have gone through some changes through the centuries, perhaps transforming as it did into sette e mezzo in Italy and quinze in France, finally becoming vingt-un, though trente-un itself no longer retained its initial structure. Digging a little deeper, we find that there was yet another old European game with the target total of thirty-one.

The Bone Ace Connection... where the Ace Equals One or Eleven

Walter Nelson, in *Games Through the Ages, Or the Merry Gamester*, says he suspects that trente-un was an early variation of a game called "Bone Ace," of which a very detailed description is provided in a book titled *The Complete Gamester* by Charles Cotton, published in 1674. As with quinze, the similarities to vingt-un are remarkable. In Bone Ace, aces may count as one or eleven, with court cards counting ten, and other cards counting their pip values. This is the oldest known game in which the card values are identical to vingt-un, including the otherwise unique double value of the ace as one or eleven.

Some features of this game are unlike vingt-un, but the main play of the hands consists of players attempting to draw to a total hand value of thirty-one. A total of exactly thirty-one is an automatic winner, and if a player's hand total exceeds thirty-one, the hand is an automatic loser. Bone Ace is obviously related to quinze, but we do not know if it predates quinze.

The question is: was the original game of trente-un, which we know to have been an older game than both quinze and Bone Ace, actually the same game as Bone Ace?

Answer: Yes. And our search for the origin of blackjack is over!

In David Parlett's *The Oxford Guide to Card Games* (Oxford University Press, 1990). Parlett quotes from the glossary of a book by the famous English lexicographer and translator, John Florio, titled *The World of Wordes*, published in 1611. Florio translates Trentuno as "One-and-Thirty... also called Bone Ace."

Although game historians insist we do not know where the French game of vingt-un came from, if any casino today started dealing quinze or Bone Ace, exactly according to the rules we know existed hundreds of years before vingt-un appeared, we would conclude that these games were merely derivatives of blackjack. That's how close they are in basic structure. Do we actually need to know the name of the Frenchman who first said, "Hey, how about twenty-one instead of fifteen or thirty-one?"

So, I will go out on a limb and state emphatically that the French game of vingt-un (twenty-one), which first appeared in the mid-seventeen hundreds, was simply a variation of a Spanish game called trente-un (thirty-one), which had been played since the mid-fourteen hundreds. Based on a passage in a book written by Cervantes in 1570, Roger Baldwin suspected this was so before anyone else, and he was right. Trente-un is where our modern game of blackjack came from.

But why has blackjack become so immensely popular? Is there something about the number twenty-one that is particularly appealing? In our twenty-first-century society, in most jurisdictions, twenty-one years is the age at which people can legally drink and gamble, but this is just a happenstance of the age we live in. Numerous other games, however, from beach volleyball to ping-pong, have 21 target totals, and for some reason possibly known to military history buffs, when a soldier dies he gets a twenty-one-gun salute. That magic just doesn't seem to exist for seven-and-a-half, fifteen, or thirty-one.

Vingt-Un Makes a Splash in Europe

At the time vingt-un was introduced in the casinos of France, neither quinze nor seven-and-a-half were being played as house-banked casino games. Trente-un and Bone Ace were long forgotten. The only popular house-banked casino card games prior to the eighteen hundreds were baccarat and trente-et-quarante. The game of faro, which had been the most popular house-banked card game in the European casinos throughout most of the nineteenth century, fell into disfavor by the late eighteen hundreds because of the ease with which a crooked dealer could cheat. There were many faro scandals in the casinos of Europe in which dealers were discovered to be cheating the players. Both baccarat and trente-et-quarante eased the gambling public's fears of cheating, since these games allowed the players to bet on either the bank or the player hand. Plus, both games were dealt from a shoe, allowing the potential sleight-of-hand artist less control over the cards.

So, when vingt-un was introduced in the casinos of Europe, as with chemin-de-fer, the casinos simply offered their tables and dealers for a commission from the banker. The precise rules and procedures probably differed based on private agreements between the players and bankers, and the game likely underwent many transformations in its early days. In addition to some of the game's early curiosities already mentioned, some old texts state that the dealer may take bets on ties. The dealer position, however, was not fixed, but automatically passed to any player who was dealt a natural (two-card) 21.

The major attraction of vingt-un to gamblers was that it was viewed as more of a game of skill. The casinos knew that players liked making hit/stand decisions because of the popularity of chemin-de-fer. Remember that the main difference between baccarat and chemin-de-fer was that chemin-de-fer was player-banked, with the house simply taking a percentage of the winning banker bets. In fact, this should have been a good deal for the house, since the house could not lose money on a game where no house money was ever at risk. The reason that casinos disliked chemin-de-fer, however, was that their potential winnings were always limited by the amount of money that the players banking the game had to risk. Often, the casino could afford to bank a much higher-stakes game than the visiting players, and if no wealthy gamblers showed up to play, then chemin-de-fer was not highly profitable to the house.

Many players, however, preferred chemin-de-fer to baccarat because in chemin-de-fer the players were allowed some hit-stand options, restricted to when a player hand totaled 5, which gave them a feeling of some control over their results. The chemin-de-fer banker had many more strategy options, but many players felt that some bankers made bad decisions. Those wealthy players who could afford to bank chemin-de-fer also often preferred banking the game to simply placing a banker bet at baccarat, because as bankers they felt they had more of an edge by making their own hit/stand decisions. The casinos did not allow players any hit/stand options on their house-banked baccarat tables for the house's protection. Based on baccarat's performance over its long history, the casinos knew that the bank hand had an edge on the player hand, provided the standard hit/stand rules were enforced for both hands, and the house took a percentage on the winning banker bets. But chemin-de-fer scared the casinos. Many times they saw bankers win money that seemed to stem from "wrong" player decisions, or correct banker decisions. And just as often, they saw players win money that seemed to stem from their "correct" decisions, and/or the banker's poor decisions. In fact, it is known today that the allowed strategy decisions at chemin-de-fer are fairly inconsequential.

In any case, when vingt-un appeared on the scene, players were being given an opportunity to make hit/stand decisions—and many more such decisions than were allowed in chemin-de-fer—in a game in which neither the bankers nor the players knew what the correct decisions were! But the game proved popular, and the casinos that offered it were making money. The early versions of player-banked vingt-un never overtook chemin-de-fer in popularity, but by the late eighteen hundreds it had become more popular than most of the other casino card games in Europe. In England, it was called "Van John," which is simply a pidgin-English pronunciation of the French name vingt-un. In German casinos, it became known as Ein-und-Zwanzig (One-and-Twenty), and in Australia it became "pontoon" (pidgin-Australian for vingt-un).

Players Like to Make Decisions

Some players simply want to gamble. The only decision most slot machines require is, "Which machine should I play?" After that, you just keep pressing the spin button and hope you hit a winning combination. The game of baccarat requires few decisions, primarily, "Do I bet on the player hand or the banker hand?"

Making decisions gives players a feeling of control over their results. Blackjack's popularity is due in part to the fact that player's always get to decide how to play each and every hand, with no restrictions on how many cards they can take. The first slot machines that allowed players to make decisions were the video poker machines introduced about fifteen years ago. In many casinos, these quickly became the most popular slots with players.

Games like roulette and keno allow players many decisions, giving the illusion of control, but these decisions have little effect on the house edge. Professional gamblers basically look for games with decisions that matter. Blackjack and poker stand out as the two games offered in most casinos where professional players can expect their correct decisions to earn them a regular income.

BLACKJACK IN THE WILD WEST, OR HOW TWENTY-ONE BECAME BLACKJACK

I think blackjack is a great profession. I get a lot of enjoyment out of it, not just because you can make a good living, but I think it's the perfect way to make money.

— *Tommy Hyland, from Gambling Wizards, by R.W. Munchkin*

HOUSE RULES CHANGE THE GAME FOREVER

It is not known precisely when the game of twenty-one entered the U.S., though it was not long after the invention of vingt-un in France. Various forms of gambling were either popular or tolerated in the original colonies on the East Coast. Lotteries were a popular method of raising money, and horse racing was common entertainment. But by the early eighteen hundreds, casino gambling was technically illegal throughout the U.S., other than in Louisiana and the Wild West, notably Nevada and California.

But something happened to the game in this country that made it hugely popular in the casinos—legal or not. Two new rules were introduced that eliminated much of the enormous edge enjoyed by the dealer, making the game attractive to players even when the house banked it.

In the popular European games of quinze, seven-and-a-half, and vingt-un, the players did not get to see a dealer upcard prior to making their hit/stand decisions. They had to play their hands with no information about what the dealer might be holding. Nor was the dealer bound by house rules in playing his hand in any of these games. The dealer could elect to hit or stand at his whim.

In the U.S. version of vingt-un, the basic structure of all of these games was retained but the players were also given an opportunity to see one of the dealer's cards prior to making their hit/stand decisions. And, just as important, the house dealer was required to follow a hit/stand strategy that was known to the players. Any dealer total of 16 or less required a hit, and any dealer total of 17 or more required the dealer to stand.

These two rules created blackjack as we know it today, and, as will be shown, made the game beatable for the first time by strategies based purely on mathematics, like card counting. A few other vingt-un variations also disappeared in the U.S. According to some of the old Hoyles, dealers had the same option as players to double down and take one card. How would you like to stand on your 16, have the dealer turn over a total of 11, and require you to double your bet against him? And consider the cheating possibilities—a dealer who was capable of saving a single card, say a 10, on the bottom of the deck could use it on his own hand when he wanted to double down against the players when his hand totaled 10 or 11.

Let the Games Begin...

In the 1820s, New Orleans passed legislation that required casinos to be licensed by city hall. This resulted in New Orleans having some of the poshest casinos in the country, with first class restaurants and a well-heeled clientele. As described by Herbert Asbury in *Sucker's Progress* (Dodd and Mead 1938), the Bourbon Street casino opened by John Davis in 1827 sounds comparable to some of the carpet joints in Las Vegas today:

> "The furnishings and appointments were nothing short of magnificent; the finest wines and liquors, and bountiful helpings from a well-stocked buffet, were served without cost to the players . . . In the public casinos were Faro layouts, Roulette wheels, and tables of Vingt et Un, all presided over by experts versed in the best methods of protecting the interests of the house."

HOW TWENTY-ONE BECAME BLACKJACK

A word here about the "experts versed in the best methods of protecting the interests of the house." The word is: cheaters.

Professional gamblers have historically been professional cheaters. It has only been in the past fifty years that the combination of government regulations and high-tech surveillance techniques has resulted in laws against cheating and the possibility of catching cheaters. In the U.S., especially, where the gambling public was unsophisticated, the original casinos were mostly bust-out joints, often using gaffed equipment. A gambling license in New Orleans in 1820, which made the casinos there legal, did nothing to ensure that the games were fair. The purpose of the license was to collect a tax for the city, not to protect the public. If a gambling syndicate wanted to do business in New Orleans, the proprietors of the casino essentially had to pay a bribe to city hall. Professional dealers were talented and charming sleight-of-hand artists.

Nevada did not officially become a state until 1864, by which time gambling already flourished in the saloons around the mining camps. The state lawmakers formally legalized gambling in 1869, though it remained entirely unregulated. Virtually every saloon had gaming tables, and many "casinos" were nothing more than tents. The most popular casino games were roulette, craps, and faro, though we do know that blackjack was also played in these saloons and casinos as a house-banked game. We know this because Nevada passed a law in 1910 outlawing all forms of gambling, but then modified this law in 1912 to prohibit only house-banked games, specifically naming roulette, faro, craps, and twenty-one among the outlawed games. Poker was allowed.

Blackjack likely returned to Nevada in 1915 as a player-banked game, when the law was modified to allow all card games in which the deal passed from player to player. But blackjack did not return in Nevada as a house-banked game until wide-open casino gambling was once again legalized in 1931.

> ### Carny Games
>
> Casinos know that serious players gravitate to games with a low house edge. In Europe, roulette is popular because two standard rules there—a single-0 wheel and the en prison rule—make the house edge just 1.3 percent. In the U.S., the double-0 wheel and no en prison rule makes the house edge 5.26 percent. Roulette is not very popular in the U.S. except with small bettors and tourists. In U.S. casinos, we rarely see $1000 bettors on roulette. Big money players in the U.S. are much more drawn to blackjack, craps, and baccarat, all of which have a house edge under 1.3 percent.
>
> Casinos offer many games that have a high house edge in order to attract tourists who don't know any better. Professional players call games like 3-Card Poker (3.4 percent house edge), Let It Ride (3.5 percent house edge) and Caribbean Stud Poker (5.2 percent house edge) carny games because the house edge is so high that playing games like these is like trying to beat a rigged carnival game that really can't be beaten. Players who bet big money, $500+, are rarely seen playing carny games.
>
> From the house's perspective, carny games make sense. They can afford to offer Caribbean Stud games with a $5 minimum bet, because players who bet only $5 at these tables will be losing at the same rate as a basic strategy blackjack player who's betting $50 a hand.

THE FIRST TWENTY-ONE PRO WAS A WOMAN

In the mid-eighteen hundreds, San Francisco's Barbary Coast district had more than one thousand gambling houses, most being saloons, brothels, or some combination of saloon, brothel, hotel, and casino. We know that twenty-one was being played in the wild western states during the eighteen hundreds, and we can assume that it had come from the more civilized East, where casino gambling was technically illegal in most states, but still widespread. Some of the professional gamblers who came west with the '49ers were likely Mississippi riverboat gamblers looking for fresh suckers.

The first steam-powered paddleboats had appeared on the Mississippi and Ohio rivers in 1811, and by 1833 there were more than five hundred boats in service. According to Alan Wykes (*The Complete Illustrated Guide to Gambling*, Doubleday, 1964), by the 1830s, approximately fifteen hundred professional gamblers were working the steamboats that ran between New Orleans and Louisville. That's an average of three cardsharps on every boat. Says Wykes: "At first the cardsharp was an outcast... but as the boats' officers became aware of the large potential income that lay at the tips of the cardsharps' fingers… they became his accomplices." The riverboat captains were soon competing with each other to attract not only the slickest cardsharps to their boats, but the wealthy travelers who were known to like a leisurely game of twenty-one or faro to pass the time on their journey. But with all the boats, and a growing army of cardsharps, the competition for suckers was getting worse every year. So, when gold was discovered in California in 1849, many of the gamblers went west to mine the pockets of the miners.

The most famous of the twenty-one dealers in California was a young woman named Eleanore Dumont, who later became known as "Madame Mustache." The unusual sobriquet might lead you to assume that she was something less than attractive, but early photographs of her belie this assumption. To the contrary, Madame Mustache was quite a dish. As described by historian Robert DeArment in *Knights of the Green Cloth* (University of Oklahoma Press, 1982), "She was small and delicate of feature, with dainty, dimpled hands, a mane of curly black hair, and doelike eyes. Soft down on her upper lip somehow enhanced the voluptuous curve of her mouth."

No one knows exactly where she came from. She may have come west with the '49ers, possibly having learned her trade in New Orleans or on the Mississippi riverboats. It is also possible that Madame Dumont had initially come to San Francisco as the wife, daughter, or paramour of an agent of one of the wealthy French gambling syndicates. Agents sent from France provided much of the investment capital used to build San Francisco's original Portsmouth Square gambling saloons during the Gold Rush.

Though no one knows exactly where the lovely Eleanor Dumont came from, she was, according to Henry Chafetz (*Play the Devil: A History of Gambling in the United States*, 1492-1955) "…perhaps the greatest professional woman gambler, certainly the most colorful…" She was not connected with any one casino, but like most of the professional gamblers of that time, she traveled with a deck of cards, would go into the saloons, and offer a game to any and all takers.

In 1854, she arrived in the California town of Nevada City, a few hundred miles northwest of San Francisco, a town that had sprung up from nothing when a rich vein of gold was struck in the Empire mine. Mining camps soon surrounded the town, and many of the town residents had a lot more money than brains. Within a few weeks of her arrival in Nevada City, she rented a place in the center of town, furnished it with rugs and chandeliers, and hung a sign out front that named her establishment, appropriately, the Vingt-Et-Un. Her saloon soon became the number one gambling establishment in the town, and it was the comely Madame Dumont that the gamblers came to play against. Again, according to Robert DeArment, "After closing her game, she would uncork bottles of champagne and treat the losers. More than one miner averred that he would rather lose to the Madame than win from somebody else." A few years after opening the Vingt-Et-Un, Madame Dumont joined forces with another gambling house operator to open a much larger establishment in Nevada City called Dumont's Palace. This was a full-fledged casino with roulette, faro, and chuck-a-luck games in addition to twenty-one. Eleanor Dumont, not yet thirty years of age, who had started out with nothing more than a deck of cards, had become one of the most successful twenty-one players in history.

In 1857, as the gold was petering out in the Nevada City area mines, she moved to Columbia where the gold strikes were plentiful. Despite prospering in Columbia, in 1859 she moved again, this time to Virginia City, and again in 1861 to Pioche, following the Nevada gold strikes. In Pioche, she began dealing twenty-one in a saloon owned by a man named Jack McKnight, fell in love, and married him. Shortly after their marriage, McKnight deserted her, disappearing along with all of her money.

Did "Madame Mustache" Really Have a Mustache?

According to Harry Sinclair Drago in *Notorious Ladies of the Frontier* (1969), Eleanore Dumont's nickname did not come into popular use until she was in her forties, no longer the beauty she had been in her youth, when the down on her upper lip darkened.

Eleanore Dumont went back to dealing twenty-one and following the gold strikes. She was always on the move, but now traveled with a pistol—not to protect herself from the gamblers whose money she won, but because she hoped to someday cross paths with Jack McKnight. She moved to Fort Benton, Montana, then to Helena, then to Salmon, Idaho, back to Nevada City, and finally to Bodie, California. On September 8, 1879 her body was found two miles from Bodie with an empty vial of poison in her hand.

Eleanore Dumont is the first known professional twenty-one player in history. She was widely respected by the miners and gamblers who played against her because she was believed to deal an honest game. For all we know, she may have dealt completely on the square, and simply beat her customers as a result of the "house edge." But most traveling card gamblers of that time did use sleight of hand, which was much more of an arcane art than it is today. Surely, there were other blackjack specialists before her, but none whose names are known and who specialized in the game of twenty-one exclusively. Throughout a gambling career of almost thirty years, Madame Mustache played only one game—twenty-one—and in the gambling dens of the old West, she became a legend in her lifetime.

THE CHEATERS THRIVED

Casinos flourished throughout northern California in the late eighteen hundreds until, in 1891, the California legislature outlawed many specific forms of house-banked "percentage games" by name, including faro, monte, roulette, twenty-one, and various other now-obsolete games like hokey-pokey and rondo. Also on the prohibited list was the old Italian game of seven-and-a-half, as well as the French game of trente-et-quarante under the name rouge-et-noir, as it was more commonly called in this country. Again, as in Nevada, poker was not banned. The reason for outlawing casino gambling at the time, as argued by the California state legislators, was primarily to "protect" the citizens of the state from cheats and swindlers. In most areas of the country, all forms of gambling were illegal; but even

The Expert at the Card Table

In 1902, an author writing under the pseudonym S.W. Erdnase self-published a 203-page book titled *The Expert at the Card Table*. This book contained the first comprehensive descriptions of gambler's sleights with cards. Erdnase was a professional card cheater, and he described for the first time in print the methods cheaters used for false shuffling, peeking the top card, dealing the second, dealing from the bottom, nullifying another player's cut, and more. The Expert at the Card Table is still in print and is still considered the classic text on this subject by both card magicians and card cheaters. Prior to the Erdnase exposé, sleight of hand with cards was an arcane art form. Card magicians' secrets were sold only to those in the "fraternity" of magicians, and cheater's secrets were virtually unavailable in print. Those who knew card moves were in a "secret society," much the same as pickpockets or forgers. The old traveling gamblers who worked the riverboats, the saloons, and the mining camps were rarely suspected of cheating because most people simply had no idea of the seemingly impossible feats that could be accomplished with sleight of hand.

where not illegal, the gambling was not legislated, but merely tolerated and completely unregulated.

A gifted sleight-of-hand artist could make a lot of money at that time. One of the most famous casino dealers in the 1870s, for instance, was Hamilton Baker, who dealt faro games in Virginia City, Nevada nine months of the year for a salary of $150 per night plus 15 percent of the profits from his table. His annual income was estimated at about $70,000, which in current dollars would make him a multi-millionaire, and Hamilton Baker was just a dealer! According to historian Alexander Gardiner (*Canfield: The True Story of the Greatest Gambler*, Doubleday, 1930), at one time Baker had seven of the greatest gambling houses in America bidding for his services. He was finally lured away from the legal casinos of Nevada to an illegal casino in Saratoga, New York where he was paid a salary of $4,500 per month to deal faro for four hours per night.

CANFIELD'S PROPHECY

In the mid-to-late-eighteen hundreds, the center of gambling in New York state was Saratoga Springs—a racetrack, spa, and resort area upstate where the wealthy vacationed. Though casino gambling was technically illegal throughout the state, the casinos paid off the local constabulary, who kept their noses out of the business of the wealthy. No one wanted scandals at the time, and many of the patrons of Saratoga's casinos were not only prominent civic leaders and businessmen, but also government officials. There were occasional "raids" on various of the casinos, usually at the behest of moralistic citizens who filed complaints with the police after having heard rumors of what went on in these places. A few fines would be levied, bribes would be paid, and the casinos would soon be back in operation.

The Saratoga Club-House, owned and operated illegally for more than twenty years by legendary gambler Richard Canfield, was widely regarded as the plushest casino on the East Coast, with a gourmet restaurant, expensive artwork adorning the walls, and a high-end clientele that included many of the prominent and wealthy citizens of New England. Canfield was the Steve Wynn of his time. He always dressed in the highest fashions, socialized with the rich and powerful, and insisted that his success as a gambler was due to the absolute honesty of the games he offered in his casinos. In addition to his Saratoga casino, he owned what was considered the poshest gambling house in New York City, as well as the Nautilus Club in Newport, Rhode Island. But after two decades of police raids and temporary closures, the police eventually shut down the Saratoga gambling house for good in September of 1907.

In a statement to reporters after announcing his retirement from gambling following the police closure of the Saratoga Club-House—and after dozens of arrests in his fifty-year career as a professional gambler—Canfield was no less than prophetic: "There will come a day, perhaps not in our lifetime, when gambling will be licensed... Gambling cannot be stopped... The best public policy is to regulate it and to obtain a revenue for the state. The license will be very expensive and it will involve strict regulations... The license will involve surveillance of some kind, including an examination of all the paraphernalia in use, and will be, to a certain extent, a certificate of integrity." The powers that be at the time thought he had gone batty in his old age.

TWENTY-ONE BECOMES BLACKJACK

According to Richard Epstein (*Theory of Gambling and Statistical Logic*, Academic Press, 1977), blackjack became popular during World War I, and was called "blackjack" from the practice of paying a bonus to a player who held an ace of spades with a jack of spades or clubs. John Scarne, (*New Complete Guide to Gambling*, 1961, Simon & Schuster), puts the year when this curious rule first appeared at 1912, when twenty-one tables appeared in horse-betting parlors in Evanston, Illinois. According to Scarne, by 1919 a Chicago gambling equipment distributor was selling felt table layouts emblazoned with the announcement: "Blackjack Pays Odds of 3 to 2." I believe Epstein's information is taken from Scarne, and Scarne states that he discovered the origins of blackjack in America as a result of his private discussions with old-time gamblers, not from any published texts that can be looked up today.

I am skeptical of much of what Scarne has written about blackjack, so I'll quote from Mickey MacDougall's *MacDougall on Dice and Cards* (Coward-McCann, 1944, NY), which was published prior to any of Scarne's books: "Many professionals dress up the game by giving prizes for certain hands. A favorite stunt is to offer ten times the size of the wager to anyone holding a natural twenty-one with a black jack. This adds interest to the game, but it also tempts a player to increase his stakes."

In an honestly dealt single-deck game, this gimmick bonus would give the player a substantial edge over the house, assuming the player knew basic strategy (an unlikely assumption). I would also assume that a gambling house that offered this bonus would be using any number of illegitimate methods to assure the house a healthy edge.

That curious bonus payout that gave blackjack its name, however, has long since disappeared. There may be some casino somewhere that pays a small bonus if a player is dealt a natural 21 which includes a jack of spades or clubs, but that is no longer a normal rule of the game. Today, a blackjack is simply any initial two cards that consist of an ace and any ten-valued card.

ED THORP VERSUS THE WORLD

Should I go to heaven, give me no haloed angels riding snow-white clouds, no not even the sultry houris of the Moslems. Give me rather a vaulting red-walled casino with bright lights, bring on the horned devils as dealers. Let there be a Pit Boss in the Sky who will give me unlimited credit. And if there is a merciful God in our Universe he will decree that the Player have for all eternity, an Edge against the House.

— *Mario Puzo, Inside Las Vegas*

If we were to ask most blackjack aficionados today—from the amateurs and hard-core gamblers who have tried every system under the sun, to the serious card counters, and even the full-time pros—what they know about the history of card counting, most would say that Ed Thorp wrote a book back in the '60s titled *Beat the Dealer* that had the first valid card counting system, and that a hundred books on card counting have been written since then with various refinements.

Close... but no Cohiba.

THE REAL STORY OF ED THORP'S ATTACK ON THE CASINOS

As a matter of fact, the first book with a valid though crude card-counting system was Baldwin, Cantey, Maisel, and McDermott's 1957 *Playing Blackjack to Win*, published five years prior to Thorp's *Beat the Dealer*. In a chapter titled "Using the Exposed Cards to Improve Your Chances," there is a chart that shows sixteen changes to their recommended hit/stand basic strategy, based on the last three, four, five, or seven cards being either ten-valued cards or low cards (2 through 6).

That book, however, never gained much popularity for various reasons. The publisher was small and did not have widespread distribution. It was cheaply produced, with a plastic spiral binding. And most importantly, the authors never claimed that their system would beat the house edge, only reduce it. The public was not all that interested in a gambling system that would simply help them to break even. One of the problems with Baldwin's card-counting system was that although he considered how the player's strategy might change as the make-up of the deck changed throughout the deal, he never considered how the house/player advantage might change. So, the book provided no betting strategy. And in blackjack, betting is where the money is.

Prior to the publication of an accurate basic strategy in 1957, blackjack was in the Stone Age. We will never know if there were crude approximations of a basic strategy in use when vingt-un was first introduced to the casinos of Europe two hundred-fifty years ago, or even if crude card-counting systems may have been employed at that time. Provided the dealer did not shuffle the cards between every round, even with a dealer-favorable rule like dealer takes ties, vingt-un would have been exploitable with card-counting systems since the deal passed from player to player equitably.

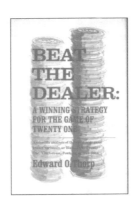

In *Beat the Dealer*, Ed Thorp tells us of various players he met in Nevada's casinos—players with colorful names like System Smitty and Greasy John—who had figured out not only close approximations of basic strategy on their own, using kitchen-table methods, dealing many thousands of hands to themselves and recording results, but even crude card-counting systems. So it's not so far-fetched to imagine that such savvy gamblers have always existed.

Julian Braun on "System Smitty"

I first met Julian Braun in 1981 when I interviewed him for Blackjack Forum. Over the twenty years until Braun's death in 2000, we had a lengthy correspondence and talked many times on the phone. I often asked him if he would write up the story of "System Smitty" for me, as he was one of the few old-timers who had known Smitty personally, and his stories about Smitty were amusing (and enlightening). With Braun now dead and gone, I'll take the liberty of describing the legendary Smitty myself, based on what Braun told me years ago.

Back in the early 1960s in Las Vegas, Braun met Benjamin F. "System Smitty" Smith, a character Ed Thorp mentions briefly in *Beat the Dealer* as one of the early card counters. According to Braun, Smitty was a professional gambler who got his nickname because he had "a system for every game." He had a regular clientele of out-of-town gamblers who would look him up when they came to Vegas, and he would act as a consultant for their play at the tables. In fact, Smitty was an excellent blackjack player, as he had devised a nearly perfect basic strategy by hand-dealing many thousands of hands to himself. But, according to Braun, Smitty was willing to play any game in any casino as per his client's wishes.

Smitty would use betting progressions, and based on the length of time his client wanted to play, or the amount of a win his client would be satisfied with, he would choose the betting system that he felt would most likely accomplish the desired result. He charged his clients no hourly fee, but simply took 10 percent of the total win at the end of their trip. If the client lost money, there was no charge for the consultation.

Because of the progression systems Smitty used, his clients won a lot more often than they lost, and Smitty made a good income from these arrangements. In fact, on the negative advantage games like craps and roulette, Smitty's clients lost more money overall than they won, but Smitty would bet wildly toward the end of a client's play if the desired win result had not yet been achieved, and he often pulled out a lucky win. It made no difference to Smitty whether his client lost a small amount or tapped out his entire trip bank, since Smitty only got paid when his client won. "It was a great scam," Braun said. "Smitty couldn't lose. He had a continual influx of other people's money to gamble with, so whenever he played he would either win or break even! All he could lose was his time."

There was the legendary Jess Marcum—at one time a highly paid consultant to Donald Trump—who had previously been a Rand Corporation nuclear physicist, but quit working for the government in the early 1950s to become a professional gambler. In *The Automat: Jess Marcum, Gambling Genius of the Century*, self-published in 1993 by the author, Sam Cohen, a lifelong friend of the Marcum's, Cohen relates how Marcum, bankrolled by millionaire friends, burned out his welcome at the blackjack tables not only in Las Vegas, but in Havana and throughout the casinos in the Caribbean islands. Marcum never published his blackjack system. Allan Schaffer, a gentleman introduced to me last year by Howard Schwartz at the Gamblers Book Shop as an old personal friend of Marcum's, told me that without using a computer, Marcum had pretty much figured out card counting at blackjack in 1949; he was barred from playing the game at one casino after another in Las Vegas, though the casinos had no idea how he was beating them. In a fascinating as-yet-unpublished autobiography by Jack Newton, one of a handful of pre-Thorp card counters from the 1950s, Newton says that it was Marcum who invented the first "point count" system for blackjack.

Other pre-Thorp card counters I've heard tales about through the years, in addition to Greasy John, System Smitty, Jess Marcum, and Jack Newton, include Joe Bernstein, a noted high-stakes poker pro, Manny Kimmel, who, along with Jess Marcum, beat the pre-Castro Cuban casinos out of $250,000 on a single trip, only to have the money confiscated at the Havana airport by Batista's mob bosses, Junior Gettings, who is possibly the "Junior" referred to by Thorp in *Beat the Dealer*, Glenn Fraikin, who beat the Vegas casinos for so much money he had his hands "broken," a common way the mob-run casinos dealt with card cheaters in the '50s, and Mel Horowitz.

In the July 25, 1953 issue of *Collier's* magazine, a now-defunct popular national weekly, there appeared an article by Joseph Wechsberg titled "Blackjack Pete," about a Las Vegas blackjack dealer by the name of Russell (Pete) Walker. Here's an excerpt from that article of what Pete told the author:

> The most dangerous opponents in blackjack are the ones who "case the deck." You recognize them by their tense look, their foreheads wrinkled in concentration. They memorize each card that is played out until only a few cards remain in my hand. Suppose that many of the low cards have been drawn after a few games and I'm still holding a relatively high number of face cards, tens and aces. Since the rule is that the dealer must hit 16 and stand on 17, the deck caser knows there is a better than even chance that the dealer will go bust. So the deck caser will stand on an unusually low hand... Sometimes I gather that something's up when players, after betting conservatively five or ten bucks, suddenly start to bet fifty and a hundred. Then I know it's time to shuffle the cards!

ED THORPE VERSUS THE WORLD

Betting big in ace-rich decks was probably the most popular pre-Thorp blackjack card-counting strategy. It's mentioned in Harold Smith, Sr.'s 1961 autobiography, *I Want To Quit Winners* (Prentice Hall, New York), which was published the year prior to *Beat the Dealer*. Harold Smith, Sr., was the founder and longtime proprietor of the now-defunct Harold's Club in Reno, which at one time was the biggest and most popular casino in Nevada. Harold's Club opened in 1935, followed shortly thereafter by Harrah's, when Las Vegas was just a dusty desert highway stop, and Reno was Nevada's biggest gambling town.

But when Thorp's *Beat the Dealer* hit the public, with a powerful counting system that had been mathematically proven to win, published by no less than Random House, one of the most reputable publishing houses in the world, blackjack history was made. *Beat the Dealer* hit the best-sellers lists, and Thorp became an instant celebrity. You must realize, however, that Thorp was bucking the common wisdom when he said he had developed a system for beating a casino game. Hundreds of charlatans before him had made similar claims about systems for beating not only blackjack, but roulette, craps, baccarat, the racetracks, the Irish Sweepstakes, you name it.

And although Edward O. Thorp is now a legend among blackjack players, widely recognized as the genius who finally put it all together and showed players how to win, it wasn't that smooth a ride for him after the publication of his groundbreaking book. In fact, he found himself accused of being a fake, a charlatan, and nothing less than a public menace. Today, all of this has been forgotten. For those who weren't around back then, let me tell you the inside story of what happened after *Beat the Dealer* was published. To my knowledge, this story has never been told, and it's a doozy. A more unlikely cast of characters couldn't be put together by Hollywood. So, let's start by introducing two prominent members of the cast, and explain how these characters got mixed up in this story.

> "Believe it or not, Professor Edward O. Thorp's unbeatable winning Black Jack system—which made him world famous because of the ignorance about gambling of the national communications media and various mathematicians—is really not a system at all.... The best thing this strategy can possibly do for the player is to cut down the house's favorable 5.90 percent to about 3.90 percent."
>
> — *John Scarne, Scarne's Guide to Casino Gambling*

MICKEY MACDOUGALL,
THE "CARD DETECTIVE"

Samuel Michael "Mickey" MacDougall was a former Nevada Gaming Control Agent who was hired by Thorp, prior to the publication of *Beat the Dealer*, to accompany him on one of his early trips to Nevada to test his ten-count system in live casino games. MacDougall was an expert on cheating, and Thorp wanted to be sure that the games he played in were being dealt honestly. MacDougall was fifty-nine-years old, and mostly retired, when Thorp hired him. MacDougall had authored three books on cheating at gambling twenty years earlier, but was currently living a quiet life in Newark, New Jersey and writing a newspaper column for the *Sunday Star-Ledger*.

What do we know about Mickey? He was born in 1903 in Philadelphia. He took an interest in magic at the age of fourteen, and began hanging around a local magic shop. He got a Russian stage illusionist by the name of Horace Goldin to hire him as an assistant, and spent many of his teen years traveling on tour with Goldin. Other magicians he met in these travels showed Mickey some sleight-of-hand moves. When he exhibited a knack for close-up magic, one shifty fellow tried to enlist him as a partner in cheating gamblers. MacDougall was fascinated by these gambling sleights and practiced incessantly, but rather than go the crooked route, he discovered that many well-heeled gamblers would pay him to observe their games when they suspected cheating, to help them "clean up" the games. So, he started hiring out his services as the "Card Detective," and even had business cards printed with this nickname.

As the eventual proprietor of his own magic shop, he made a lot of connections among sleight-of-hand aficionados and gamblers, honest and otherwise. He learned everything he could and soon found he was in demand for lectures and demonstrations on the art of cheating and how players could protect themselves from professional cheaters. In 1939, at the age of thirty-six, he self-published his first book, *Gamblers Don't Gamble*. It was primarily an exposé of card moves, complete with photos, and became so popular that a New York publisher, Garden City Publishing, took over the publication and distribution in 1940. MacDougall wrote two other popular books, *Danger in the Cards* (Ziff-Davis, 1943) and *MacDougall on Dice and Cards* (Coward-McCann, 1944).

During World War II, MacDougall worked for both the U.S. Army and the U.S. Navy, primarily in training GIs to recognize cheaters in their private games. Gambling was a popular activity for soldiers and sailors during the war, among themselves and in the juke joints that proliferated around the army bases and seaports. Following the war, MacDougall continued to lecture, occasionally doing consulting work on gambling cases for police departments, and eventually became an agent with the Nevada Gaming Control Board.

On top of this, MacDougall was one of the smartest gambling authorities on the scene. Although not a mathematician, MacDougall had a gut-level understanding of gambling games, and displayed an understanding of card-counting theory two decades before Thorp. In *MacDougall on Dice and Cards* (Coward-McCann, 1944, NY), the legendary "card detective" states that when blackjack is played in a gambling house, "the professional generally shuffles the entire pack after every deal, thus preventing the observant player from improving his chances by remembering the cards which have been played." So, obviously, the idea of keeping track of the cards at blackjack predated even the 1950s. In fact, MacDougall goes on to describe precisely how using this type of information might benefit a player who holds a total of 15 against the dealer's 4 upcard, with seven players at the table. "By the time the deal reaches the player, twenty-six cards are out, of which the player has seen nineteen ... Of the nineteen known cards, thirteen were sixes or lower. There are twenty-six cards left in the pack, of which only eleven can help the player. So the odds against him are 15 to 11 ... Why not let [the dealer] take the chance of being busted, since the odds favor that event? ... The twenty-one player who manages to win a few dollars now and then ... analyzes every hand in exactly the same fashion. The mathematical probability of helping his count determines whether he draws a card or stands."

This may not be advanced card counting by any means, but it does demonstrate that the logic of card counting was known to gamblers decades before *Beat the Dealer*, or even the Baldwin book, had appeared on the scene. In fact, Thorp never claimed to have invented the concept of card counting at blackjack. In his Acknowledgments at the beginning of *Beat the Dealer*, he states, "I owe a great deal to ... some of the old-time Nevada 'count' players." He also describes a crude ten-counting system, similar in many ways to his own ten-count system, but independently devised years prior to the publication of *Beat the Dealer* by a Las Vegas pro named Benjamin F. Smith, who was widely know at the time as "System Smitty."

In any case, Mickey MacDougall had all the necessary credentials, and he was the guy Ed Thorp hired in January of 1962 to accompany him to Nevada in order to verify that the games he played in were honest. Thorp's book was scheduled to come out in November of that year, and Thorp wanted to include some real-world casino experience, but he simply didn't trust the casinos. Many of the noted gambling experts at that time, just like today, said that the games in legitimate gambling casinos were all on the up-and-up. No cheating. For instance, in Oswald Jacoby's *How to Figure the Odds* (Doubleday, 1947), Jacoby's main advice was that if the casino has been in business for many years, it must be honest. "Only the honest gambling houses stay in business year after year... the odds are very high that your favorite gambling house is strictly on the level... It can well afford to be... Don't come to the conclusion that the gambling house is crooked just because you walk out a loser every time you play. You figure to lose." Well, Thorp didn't figure to lose, so he hired MacDougall to at least assure that the games were on the level.

Also along as an observer on that trip was gambling historian Russell Barnhart, who chronicled the entire adventure in the Spring 2000 *Blackjack Forum*, in an article titled "The First Counters: My Blackjack Trip in 1962 to Las Vegas and Reno with Professor Edward O. Thorp and Mickey MacDougall." According to Barnhart, although Thorp won a small amount of money on this nine-day excursion, MacDougall found cheating in almost every casino they played in. As a former Nevada Gaming Control agent, MacDougall was shocked to find that almost all of the casinos in Nevada, including the most respected carpet joints, were cheating. It was widely believed that following the Kefauver Committee Hearings in the U.S. Senate in the 1950s, which purportedly had removed organized crime from the casinos, that the games in all of the major casinos were now strictly on the level.

ED THORPE VERSUS THE WORLD

THORP'S WINS AND LOSSES IN 1962 TEST OF TEN-COUNT

According to Russell Barnhart's records, these are the wins and losses at each casino visited by Ed Thorp, Mickey MacDougall, and Barnhart during their nine-day blackjack trip to Las Vegas and Reno from January 23-31, 1962.

DAY	CASINO	HOURS	$ BET SPREAD	NET
1	El Cortez	1	1 - 5	-33
	Fremont	1	5 - 50	-100
	Horseshoe	.25	5 - 50	+40
2	Fremont	.75	5 - 50	+135
	Stardust	1	5 - 50	+145
	Dunes	.50	10 -100	+170
	Hacienda	1	5 - 50	-60
	Tropicana	.50	5 - 50	+60
	Sands	4	5 - 50	-235
	Thunderbird	1	10 - 100	+20
3	Fremont	1	10 – 100	+105
	Silver Palace	.50	10 - 100	+180
	Stardust	1.75	7 - 75	-176
	Desert Inn	.75	10 - 100	+260
	Riviera	1	7 - 75	+403
	Sahara	.50	5 - 20	+30
	Flamingo	.25	5 - 50	-64
4	Fremont	.50	7 - 75	-165
	Horseshoe	.25	5 - 20	-13
	L. V. Club	.25	5 - 50	-23
	Desert Inn	1.75	10 - 100	+570
	Riviera	1	10 - 100	+95
	Sands	1	5 - 50	-95
	Sahara	.50	10 - 100	+40
	Tropicana	.50	10 - 100	+190
	Flamingo	.50	5 - 50	-100
5	Stardust	1	5 - 50	-80
	Riviera	.50	20 - 100	+285
	Desert Inn	1	20 - 75	+305
6	Tropicana	.75	20 - 200	+325
	Desert Inn	1.75	20 - 200	-768
	Riviera	.05	25 - 200	+160
	Stardust	.75	25 - 200	-100
	Sahara	1	15 - 75	+245
	Sands	1.25	20 - 200	-5
7	Sands	1.25	5 - 50	+40
	Stardust	.50	5 - 50	-170
	Flamingo	.50	10 - 100	+40
	Dunes	.50	1 - 20	-20
8	Tropicana	1.25	5 - 50	-25
	(Reno) Holiday Inn	.25	25 - 75	-600
	(Reno) Golden Hotel	1	5 - 40	-215
	(Reno) Harrah's	3	25 - 200	-430
9	Harold's Club	1	1 - 20	-50
	Total Results:	**48.8 hours**		**+317**

Following the publication of *Beat the Dealer*, in which Thorp reported on the cheating he encountered at high stakes play (and Thorp had made other trips at higher stakes than he played on the trip Barnhart had witnessed), MacDougall apparently felt the need to inform the public himself of what he had witnessed. To quote from his newspaper column which appeared in the Sunday Star-Ledger in Newark, New Jersey, November 29, 1964: "At casino after casino, once Thorp's wagers hit the $500 maximum, skullduggery started. It was soon apparent that the hoodlums who control Las Vegas weren't going to give the sucker an even break."

But let's move on to the next character in this crazy drama…

JOHN SCARNE, "THE WORLD'S FOREMOST EXPERT ON GAMBLING"

Suffice it to say that John Scarne was the most prominent authority on gambling in the world at the time Thorp's book was published in 1962. He was the author of numerous best-selling books on games and gambling since 1945, and was widely respected by serious gamblers both for his analyses of games and his exposés of cheating methods.

What do we know about Scarne? He was a contemporary of Mickey MacDougall's in that he was born the same year, 1903. Instead of hailing from the Irish ghettos of Philadelphia, however, he came from the Italian ghettos of New York. Much of his early history was similar to MacDougall's. He took an interest in magic in his youth, became fascinated with sleight-of-hand artists, and also took an interest in carnival scams, hustlers, and cheaters of every stripe.

Scarne's professional career as an expert on cheating, however, began after MacDougall's. MacDougall had published three books by 1944. Scarne's first book did not appear until 1945. Although their paths may not have crossed physically, it is highly likely that Scarne knew of MacDougall's books, and it would not be too far-fetched to guess that he looked up to MacDougall's success as an author.

As Scarne and MacDougall were both pushing forty during WWII, neither man was about to be called into service. Like MacDougall, however, Scarne found a similar way to serve. In addition to doing lectures and demonstrations for GIs, describing how cheaters worked with loaded dice, marked cards, and various sleights to rob them, Scarne managed to get the official army magazine, *Yank*, to run a series of articles he wrote describing the most common cheating methods used by card and dice hustlers. These old Yank articles were John Scarne's first published works.

Scarne's first book, titled *Scarne on Dice*, came out after the war in 1945. Most of its 422 pages were dedicated to describing various forms of popular dice play, with all of the odds, the rules, and the methods used by hustlers to take unfair advantage of suckers in the games. It surely ranked as the most extensive treatment of craps ever to see print up to that point in time. But there is one very curious section of the book that appears incongruously in his chapter exposing the folly of betting systems, in which Scarne blasts off at Mickey MacDougall, essentially calling him an ignorant phony, a pretender.

The Scarne/MacDougall Feud

What was the cause of Scarne's acrimony toward MacDougall? Why did he fail to show any degree of respect for this widely acclaimed expert on cheating who, like him, was in the business of protecting the public from gambling scams? Scarne's vitriol is so over-the-top—he goes on about MacDougall for eight pages—that one can't help but wonder if this diatribe isn't based on something personal. As a matter of fact, it was based on something personal, and in Scarne's eyes, MacDougall took the first swing.

In his third book, *MacDougall on Dice and Cards*, published a year before Scarne's first book, Mickey MacDougall briefly describes how an article in Yank magazine, intended to protect GIs from being swindled, backfired and aided the crooked crap game operators. According to MacDougall, *Yank* published the "correct" odds payouts for craps—not the payouts that were traditionally paid by legitimate casinos, but the payouts that would make every bet fair—with no advantage to either taking or laying the odds. Legitimate casinos, of course, couldn't offer these odds, but the crooked bust-out joints—who didn't need a built-in house edge since they were using crooked dice—had no problem offering players the "correct" odds payouts. MacDougall stated in his book that "Crooked houses from coast to coast pasted a copy of *Yank* above the dice table, with the sign 'We pay official Army odds.'"

In telling this story, MacDougall does not mention John Scarne by name, but in fact, Scarne was the author of that Yank magazine article. In reading MacDougall's treatment of this incident, it's doubtful that MacDougall meant to criticize Scarne or *Yank*. He calls the Yank article "a laudable attempt to prevent servicemen from being cheated." He simply seems to be pointing out an ironic twist of events to show how crooks would capitalize on virtually anything, and how an attempt to protect players actually drove players away from the legitimate casinos and straight into the clubs run by the crooks.

Despite the fact that this fiasco was reported in newspapers at the time, and that *Yank* had to issue statements for publication explaining to the public that "correct" odds could not be offered in the legitimate gambling houses, it enraged Scarne that MacDougall would insinuate in any way that his Yank article had backfired and aided the cheaters. When it came to criticism of any kind, Scarne proved to be very thin-skinned, and he never forgave MacDougall for this jab.

Keep in mind that John Scarne was a nobody when *MacDougall on Dice and Cards* was published. Scarne's only published work was the collection of articles he'd written for *Yank*, and he was proud of his work. MacDougall was the nationally recognized authority in this field. So MacDougall could possibly have been more tactful in his treatment of this scandal. Had he mentioned Scarne's name in his book, and offered even one line of praise for the work Scarne had published in *Yank*, the two men might have become friends.

Instead, they became bitter enemies.

MacDougall attempted to sue Scarne and his publisher for libel, to no avail. As *Scarne on Dice*, co-authored with Clayton Rawson, was largely composed of articles Scarne had written for *Yank*, the book was published by the Military Service Publishing Company of Harrisburg, Pennsylvania. It may have been futile for MacDougall to try to sue a government contractor who had been publishing books for the U.S. Army since 1921, especially since the country's mood of patriotism in 1945 was at an all-time high following the victory of the Allied forces in WWII. In my opinion, Scarne's comments on MacDougall would probably not have passed the test of libel. As a public figure, MacDougall was a fair target. But we'll never know if MacDougall's libel suit had any merit, because the judge simply threw the case out of court.

Scarne Triumphs

From this point forward, John Scarne's career went gangbusters. By the mid-1950s, he had authored half a dozen books on gambling and games. He was a natural showman, a talented sleight-of-hand artist, and a tireless self-promoter. In 1961, the year before Thorp's *Beat the Dealer* came out, *Scarne's New Complete Guide to Gambling* was published, solidifying John Scarne's position as the world's premier gambling expert. This was Scarne's masterwork, the most comprehensive book on gambling in print, with sections on horse racing, sports betting, lotteries, sweepstakes, the "numbers" game, bingo, craps, blackjack, roulette, slot machines, baccarat, keno, backgammon, poker, carnival games, bridge, gin rummy, and dozens of other common and uncommon gambling games, with extensive coverage of cheating methods, hustles, scams, and game protection. In addition to his fame from his books, he was also by this time a highly paid consultant to the casinos, not only in Nevada, but in Puerto Rico, Panama, and even in Batista's Cuba prior to the Cuban revolution. He was a personal consultant to Conrad Hilton at the Caribé Hilton. He had also been called to testify as an expert witness in 1961 by the U.S. Senate Subcommittee Hearings on Gambling and Organized Crime, where he astonished the senators with card tricks, entertained them with jokes, and educated not only the senators, but the whole country, about the devious tricks employed by gambling cheaters and crooked casino operators. At the age of fifty-eight, John Scarne had become a living legend.

Enter Edward Oakley Thorp...

In 1962, the year after the publication of *Scarne's New Complete Guide to Gambling*, Random House published Edward O. Thorp's *Beat the Dealer: A Winning Strategy for the Game of Twenty-One*. This book, in which a mild-mannered assistant professor of mathematics was claiming to have developed via computer simulations a method for beating casino blackjack, made Thorp an instant celebrity. Newspapers and magazines all over the country were doing features about him and his discovery. And *Beat the Dealer* was soon topping the best-seller lists, surpassing the sales of every gambling title in history, including all of John Scarne's books.

In addition to this newcomer's instant fame as the national gambling guru, after Scarne had spent two decades achieving this status, there were two specific things that surely rankled John Scarne about *Beat the Dealer*. In his "Acknowledgments," Thorp wrote: "I owe a great deal to Michael MacDougall, special investigator for the Nevada Gaming Control Board." Scarne had been under the impression that he had all but buried MacDougall's credentials as a gambling expert.

And then, to rub salt into Scarne's wounds, on page eleven, Thorp criticized the blackjack analysis that was published in *Scarne's New Complete Guide to Gambling*. In his book, Scarne claimed that he was the first authority to figure out the house edge over the player at blackjack, which he calculated to be 5.9 percent. He came up with this result by figuring out what the house edge would be if the player used the same strategy as the dealer, always hitting 16 or less, and standing on 17 or more (with no accounting whatsoever for player double downs or pair splits). Scarne also provided his recommended blackjack basic strategy in his book, which Thorp mercifully ignored. Among Scarne's improper basic strategy recommendations were: players should stand on 16 if the dealer shows an ace or 10 up (while correct basic strategy is to hit); players should not split eights against the dealer's 9 or 10 (in fact, eights should be split); never split sixes or nines (very wrong); split tens versus a dealer 5, 6, or 10 (wrong versus 5 and 6, and absolutely idiotic versus 10); and soft double with A2 to A6 only against a dealer 6 up (there are many more proper soft doubling plays that should be made).

Thorp not only pointed out that Scarne's analysis was inaccurate, but also that it was not—as Scarne claimed—the "first" such analysis at all. Baldwin, Cantey, Maisel, and McDermott had not only used an accurate method for estimating the house edge, but they had also provided an accurate basic strategy for the player five years prior to the publication of Scarne's book.

As Thorp's fame spread, even the Las Vegas casino owners had to concede that Thorp's ten-count system was the real thing. On April 1, 1964, less than seventeen months after the publication of *Beat the Dealer*, the Las Vegas Resort Hotel Association changed the standard blackjack house rules for all of the casinos in Las Vegas. In the *New York Journal American*, a spokesperson for the Association was quoted: "In the last fifteen years there hasn't been one plane that landed without at least one person in possession of a [gambling] system. This guy [Thorp] is the first in Las Vegas history to have a system that works." The specific rules that were changed: blackjack players would no longer be allowed to split aces and double downs would be restricted to a two-card total of 11 only. Within three weeks, the Las Vegas casinos gave up on the new rules because they lost so many of their regular customers who refused to play the game with the poor rule set.

Scarne to the Rescue!

The Las Vegas casinos turned to John Scarne. What could they do to stop the system players? A plan was quickly hatched. Thorp and his ten-count system had to be discredited. So, barely a week after the attempted change in the rules had failed, on April 28, 1964 John Scarne, in collaboration with the Sands Hotel and Casino in Las Vegas, issued a press release challenging Thorp "and his millionaire backers" to a $100,000, winner-take-all, blackjack freeze-out, to be publicly staged at the Sands Casino in Las Vegas. Scarne claimed in his challenge that, contrary to Thorp's claims, Thorp's strategy would lose at the rate of 3 percent. Scarne's challenge provided that Thorp could specify the rules, as well as the minimum and maximum bets allowed, provided they were in accordance with current conditions in Nevada's major casinos. Newspapers all over the country printed the challenge.

But there was one catch. The terms of the challenge specified that John Scarne would act as the dealer!

Needless to say, Thorp declined to accept the terms. Scarne, after all, was one of the world's foremost sleight-of-hand artists, and this did not appear to be a test of the ten-count system so much as a test of Scarne's ability to hoodwink Thorp with a deck of cards in his hand.

So, Thorp simply repeated the challenge that he had made to the casinos in *Beat the Dealer*. He agreed to put up $10,000 if a casino would play against him in a single-deck game, with minimum and maximum bets of $25-$500, dealing each deck until no more than ten cards remained in the undealt portion of the deck, and that after shuffling the deck, the deck would not be hand-held to deal, but placed on the table to eliminate the possibility of card manipulation during the deal. Thorp specified that the play would continue until he either lost his entire $10,000 stake, or won $10,000 from the casino.

No Las Vegas casino, or any casino anywhere, ever accepted Thorp's challenge.

So, Ed Thorp's fame, and the casinos' fears of card counters, continued to grow. Blackjack by this time had replaced craps as the most popular casino table game, and despite the handful of capable card counters, the casinos were making more money than ever from the incapable amateurs who were attempting to count cards without spending the necessary time with practice and memorization.

In 1965, Random House announced that the following year, a second, revised edition of B*eat the Dealer* would be published by their paperback division, Vintage Books, with a newer, simpler, card-counting system that could be mastered by "average" players. Again, the casinos began freaking out, and again, they turned to their long-time advisor, John Scarne.

So, in 1966, when Thorp introduced the "Simple Point Count," now more widely known as the High-Low Count, in the new edition of

Beat the Dealer, John Scarne came out with his autobiography, *The Odds Against Me* (Simon & Schuster)—one of very few books he authored that did not have his name in the title. In this book, Scarne again attempted to discredit Thorp, again claiming that Thorp's blackjack strategy would not beat the casinos, and describing how Thorp had refused his challenge to play against him at the Sands with Scarne dealing the cards. But, Scarne dropped an unexpected bomb in this book. He wrote that in 1947, at the then-new Flamingo Hotel and Casino in Las Vegas, he told Bugsy Siegel, manager of the Flamingo, that he could beat the game of blackjack fair and square by using a "card casing" system. He then describes how he demonstrated to Siegel how easy it was to keep a ten-count by using a stack of chips to count the cards.

This was an astonishing revelation in light of the fact that up until this time, Scarne's position was that Thorp's ten-count system would not work, and that Thorp was a fraud. Now, Scarne was claiming that he knew about the ten-count system fifteen years before Thorp, had used it himself, and had even demonstrated it to a famous, though now long-dead, casino manager. What was most curious about this revelation was that in none of Scarne's previous books, including his 1961 masterwork, *Scarne's New Complete Guide to Gambling*—in which he had claimed to provide the first accurate analysis of casino blackjack—had he ever mentioned the concept of card counting, let alone the ten-count system specifically. But in various places throughout this new autobiography, he referred to knowledge of card counters, whom he called "cheaters" or "card casing mobs," as if counting cards were illegal.

The Downfall of John Scarne

Scarne's fans were beginning to question his credibility. After years of maintaining that Thorp's ten-count was a sham, and in a book where he continued to insist that Thorp's system was a loser, Scarne was now claiming that he knew about card counting years before Thorp, that he had demonstrated the power of the ten-count to Bugsy Siegel, and that card counters were actually cheating! None of it made sense to players. Whose side was Scarne on? And did card counting work, or not?

Scarne also claimed in this autobiography that he had met the mysterious "Mr. X" and "Mr. Y," the anonymous backers who Thorp claimed in *Beat the Dealer* had put up the money for his casino tests of the ten-count. Scarne said that Mr. X and Mr. Y were actually known casino cheats and hustlers, that they had informed him that Thorp had lied about the casino tests, and furthermore, that—contrary to Thorp's claims—no cheating at all was discovered in the casinos of Nevada! According to Scarne, "I do know from my own investigations of Nevada casinos that operators earn money with their favorable percentages and not by cheating. In all my years of investigating gambling in Nevada, I found two minor cases of casino cheating, which I immediately reported to the Nevada Gaming Control Board."

Scarne was making a huge mistake. By this point in time, dozens of reputable and independent mathematicians had verified the accuracy of the Baldwin basic strategy, and Thorp's ten-count system, along with other card-counting systems, were being tested via computer simulations by programmers at universities all over the country.

Jacoby Claims the Credit!

Even Oswald Jacoby, the stodgy old bridge expert, who had totally ignored blackjack in his 1940-47 book that covered casino gambling, *How to Figure the Odds* (Doubleday), converted to the Baldwin basic strategy and a crude ten-count system following the publication of *Beat the Dealer*. In his 1963 book, *Oswald Jacoby on Gambling*, Jacoby reproduces the Baldwin basic strategy, including the few modifications that Thorp made in *Beat the Dealer*, and then explains that players should make big bets when the cards remaining to be dealt have a "higher ratio than normal" of ten-valued cards, and reduced bets when the pack is "light" of these high cards.

To his discredit, Jacoby never mentions Thorp or the Baldwin group for having already published these discoveries! No, Jacoby presents the tables that he personally drew up "using desk calculators and some simple basic assumptions," and presents his strategy as if he were the genius who finally figured out blackjack! What can I say? Too many gambling writers are egotistical blowhards, and even the established and respected authors fail to give credit where credit is actually due. It is almost a tradition in the field of gambling literature for an author to put his name on another writer's discoveries and claim them as his own. What John Scarne and Oswald Jacoby were doing forty years ago has continued ever since through the writings of many more recent authors, including a number of reputable experts as well known and respected today as Scarne and Jacoby were in their time.

But Oswald Jacoby only has a bit part in this tragicomedy. If Scarne would have challenged Jacoby to a contest, and if Scarne and Jacoby would have started public battles over which one of them invented card counting, then we would have had a rip-roaring farce. But it didn't happen. Scarne ignored Jacoby. Everyone ignored Jacoby. I only mention Jacoby because he was more-or-less "Scarne Lite" at the time, a bridge, poker, and gambling authority who was widely known primarily through his long-running syndicated newspaper bridge column. You'd think that with even Oswald Jacoby picking up the basic-strategy and card-counting torch, Scarne would have seen the writing on the wall.

Meanwhile, Back at the "World's Foremost Gambling Expert"

Absolutely nobody believed John Scarne when he said that in twenty years of consulting for the casino industry, and specifically as an expert on cheating at gambling, he had only found two minor incidents of casino cheating in the entire state of Nevada. He was a cheating expert! What the hell were the casinos paying him for if they didn't need his services? In fact, Scarne contradicts this claim himself in his updated and expanded 1974 edition of his 1949 classic, *Scarne on Cards*, where he states, "Nevada casinos are fleeced of millions of dollars yearly by agents... in collusion with crooked Black Jack dealers and pit bosses...I doubt there is a casino anywhere operating Black Jack tables that is not taken for a bundle each year by outside and inside cheats."

But Thorp had already become a hero to players, and there was only one conclusion to be drawn about his main detractor: John Scarne was simply catering to his casino cronies, spouting whatever they wanted him to say.

Thorp's system doesn't work!

Anyone who attempts to use Thorp's system is a cheater!

The casinos are squeaky-clean honest!

John Scarne, a players' advocate for three decades and the most respected authority on gambling in the world, became just another crybaby for the casinos. The industry couldn't accept the fact that any player, no matter how smart, could beat the odds that had always been rigged in the house's favor. Thorp beat the odds.

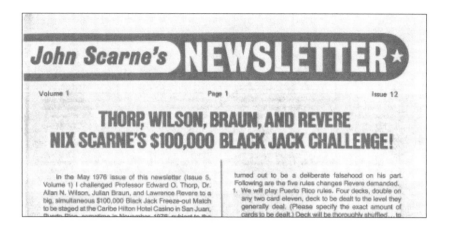

John Scarne's NEWSLETTER★

Volume 1   Page 1   Issue 12

THORP, WILSON, BRAUN, AND REVERE NIX SCARNE'S $100,000 BLACK JACK CHALLENGE!

In the May 1976 issue of this newsletter (Issue 5, Volume 1) I challenged Professor Edward O. Thorp, Dr. Allan N. Wilson, Julian Braun, and Lawrence Revere to a big, simultaneous $100,000 Black Jack Freeze-out Match to be staged at the Caribe Hilton Hotel Casino in San Juan, Puerto Rico, sometime in November 1976, subject to the

turned out to be a deliberate falsehood on his part. Following are the five rules changes Revere demanded. 1. We will play Puerto Rico rules. Four decks, double on any two card eleven, deck to be dealt to the level they generally deal. (Please specify the exact amount of cards to be dealt.) Deck will be thoroughly shuffled . . . to

The $100,000 Challenge

From this point on, it simply got worse. In book after book for the next decade, John Scarne never backed down from anything he said, no matter how contradictory to other statements he had made. In the mid-1970s, Scarne revised his $100,000 challenge to Thorp, this time adding the names of other card-counting experts who had appeared on the scene—Julian Braun, Allan Wilson, and Lawrence Revere—to his list of challengees. Again, Scarne found little interest among those challenged to put up their money. A few letters were exchanged. Various rules and procedures were proposed, but nothing could be agreed upon.

John Luckman, founder and proprietor of the Gamblers Book Club in Las Vegas, acted as a go-between in the challenges and counterproposals. Although Scarne was not insisting on dealing the cards himself this time, there was a major disagreement over the location. In his new proposal, Scarne said that he had arranged for the contest to take place at a Puerto Rican casino, using Puerto Rican rules and a Puerto Rican dealer, in a game supervised by a Puerto Rican casino manager, who was a longtime personal friend of his. According to Luckman, the challengees said they would only agree to a contest at an impartial Las Vegas location. John Luckman told me that Thorp et al. felt that Scarne, being an acknowledged master of cunning, could too easily "fix" a Puerto Rican game. Lawrence Revere was the only one of those who had been challenged who said he would be agreeable to the match. As an ex-dealer, ex-pit boss, and longtime player, Revere felt that he could recognize a cheating scam. He didn't think Scarne could outsmart him, and if Scarne tried something, he relished the idea of exposing the trickery. But the other challengees—Thorp, Wilson, and Braun—were all math guys, not savvy gamblers. They were all too aware of Scarne's reputation as an expert on scams to trust him, and they apparently did not have enough faith in Revere's abilities to gamble $100,000 on the prospect of being cheated.

Throughout 1976, in his self-published "John Scarne's Newsletter," Scarne railed against the "blackjack wizards" who would not accept his challenge. He claimed that he attempted to set up the game in Nevada, but was told by the Gaming Control Board that such an event would require a special license. According to Luckman, the challengees felt that Scarne would simply not agree to the challenge at a location where he did not have complete control over the conditions.

Scarne's Mysterious WWII "Ten-Card Count" Pamphlet

In 1978, Scarne published a revised version of his 1961 book, changing the title (slightly) to *Scarne's Guide to Casino Gambling*. In this book, Scarne still holds fast to his analysis showing that the house advantage in casino blackjack is 5.9 percent, though he concedes that the Baldwin, Cantey, Maisel, and McDermott basic strategy could lower the house advantage by "about 2 percent." Card counting, he maintains again, is a virtual waste of time. By this time, of course, the world of gamblers and gambling experts completely ignored Scarne's book as irrelevant. It was illogical for him to claim that card counting did not work, and at the same time qualify card counting as "cheating."

In this new book, Scarne's incomprehensible stand on card counting became even more confounding. He claimed that during World War II he wrote a pamphlet, which he says the army distributed to "millions of GIs," titled, "Beware of the Ten-Card Count Blackjack Strategy." He even "reprints" a long section of this alleged U.S. government pamphlet, in which he warns GIs that if they are dealing blackjack to a player who continually increases his bet size toward the end of the deck, to shuffle up the cards, as this player may be a "vicious ten-card counter who is out to steal every GI's monthly pay."

But did John Scarne really write this pamphlet during World War II? Or was he just taking another desperate shot at Ed Thorp, the man who had dethroned him? In this mystery pamphlet, Scarne claims that "ten-card counting" was a common talent for casino blackjack dealers in the 1940s, and that hundreds of these ex-dealers/counters were now in the armed services fleecing their fellow soldiers and sailors by masquerading as common players.

Is this true? Why had Scarne never mentioned this in his 1949 book, *Scarne on Cards*, or mentioned it in the hugely expanded (535 pages) 1974 edition of this book, or in any of his other books prior to 1978? Were Nevada dealers counting cards two decades before Thorp? And if, as Scarne alleges, the ten-count was commonly known to casino dealers in the '40s, why were the casinos so amazed when Thorp's ten-count proved to actually work? Was John Scarne, long America's most beloved and revered gambling expert, trying to pull one last scam to discredit the man who said the great Scarne had made a mistake? Was Scarne trying to rob Thorp of his invention and claim it for himself?

In many years of collecting gambling books and systems, I've never run across anyone who's ever seen John Scarne's alleged World War II pamphlet on card counting. Even Howard Schwartz, resident know-it-all at the Gamblers Book Shop in Las Vegas, tells me he's never seen a copy of Scarne's card-counting pamphlet. Nor have I ever found any published pre-Thorp ten-count referred to by any other book or author.

In 1992, in an attempt to solve this riddle, I wrote articles for the two most widely circulated gambling magazines in print, *Card Player* (Las Vegas) and *Casino Player* (Atlantic City), in which I appealed to the readers to contact me if anyone had ever seen a copy of John Scarne's alleged U.S. government published pamphlet, which Scarne claimed had been distributed to millions of GIs during WWII. As a result of these articles, I was contacted by a number of collectors of gambling ephemera, some of whom had all of the old *Yank* magazines from WWII with Scarne's articles. As a matter of fact, these old Yanks are still widely available over the Internet, and can be purchased inexpensively on eBay and other collectibles auction sites. I have yet to find anyone who has ever seen a copy of this mysterious Scarne pamphlet on card counting however. In my opinion, it does not, and never did, exist.

In 1985, at the age of eighty-two, John Scarne passed away. At the time of his passing, the world of gambling had long before left him behind. It was a sad end for a man who for decades was the most respected authority in the world on casino gambling. What was most sad about it was that it probably didn't have to end that way. Had Scarne looked at Thorp's work objectively, accepted Thorp's polite criticism, then praised Thorp for his discoveries, Scarne would likely have remained in his revered position as the Grand Old Master of Gambling.

And what is saddest about Scarne's fall from grace is that we must now question everything he wrote about gambling. Since it appears that he simply made up stories about Thorp when his own expertise was in question, did he make up other stories in his books for similar reasons? Did he really amaze Fidel Castro with his card tricks in Cuba while Castro was in the process of "liberating" the Havana Hilton in 1959? Did he really teach Bugsy Siegel how to count cards in 1947? Did he really astound the great Harry Houdini with his card tricks? And did Scarne really learn that the name "Black Jack" first appeared in an Evanston, Illinois horse betting parlor in 1912? When it comes to the history of gambling, John Scarne left us with more questions than answers.

The late gambling historian and magic buff Russell Barnhart, who knew both Mickey MacDougall and John Scarne, accompanied Ed Thorp on his 1962 trip to Nevada to test his system, and, in fact, introduced Thorp to Mickey MacDougall, told me that John Scarne was not fully to blame for the vitriol toward Thorp that appeared in Scarne's books following the publication of *Beat the Dealer*.

"John Scarne couldn't write," Barnhart told me. "Not professionally. All of his books were actually written by Clayton Rawson, whose name only appeared as co-author on Scarne's first book in 1945. Scarne was just a performer and a brilliant close-up magician, among the best ever, but he wasn't a writer. Rawson ghost-wrote a lot of Scarne's stuff, and he took great liberties with putting words into Scarne's mouth."

John Scarne, Mickey MacDougall, John Luckman, Clayton Rawson, Russell Barnhart, Lawrence Revere, Julian Braun, Allan Wilson, and many of the others who figured into this drama forty years ago, have long since passed away.

We do know that John Scarne was the author of some twenty-eight books on games and gambling that were published between 1945 and 1983, making him one of the most prolific authors in this field in history. Yet, despite the incredible amount of detail in his books, he almost never provides a reference for where he obtained his information, and not one of his books contains a bibliography. Whether Scarne or Rawson are to blame, to discover that Scarne appeared to make up facts as he needed them is disturbing. All we can do at this point is move on. With the publication of Thorp's book, John Scarne had been left behind, not so much by Thorp, as by the age of technology. Once Thorp had shown the way, the world followed. Mathematicians and computer programmers became the new gambling gurus.

LET'S GET READY TO RUMBLE!

> It was widely believed that the desert around Las Vegas was amply sprinkled with the makeshift graves of dealers from the old days—dealers who'd tried hidden pockets, accomplices posing as lucky players, and all manner of other tricks to smuggle chips from mob tables.
>
> — *Ivan G. Goldman, Where the Money Is*

There are many players who do not believe that card counting at blackjack could work simply because it makes no sense that the casinos would ever create such a game in the first place. And if the casinos had such a game, then why wouldn't they just change the rules in some way so that players could no longer beat the game? The casinos, after all, are the ones who make the rules.

The fact is that blackjack was never supposed to be a game that players could beat. The casinos had always had to deal with a few wiseguys who had found various ways of getting an edge on them. But not every college kid that got off the bus.

To understand why this crazy situation, this never-ending cat and mouse game, exists in the casino blackjack pits today, let's look at the way it came down way back when.

HOW DID IT GET THIS WAY?

With the publication of Ed Thorp's *Beat the Dealer*, the casino industry was at a crossroads. They literally did not know what to do about the "card counter problem," and as they were raking in more and more money due to the popularity of Thorp's book, they were not really sure that it was a problem. Let's look at the politics.

The casino industry in the U.S. in the 1960s was 100 percent a Nevada industry. There was no other state where casino gambling was legal, so there were no federal laws regulating it. Nevada was also the only state with legal brothels, and Nevada's laws on alcoholic beverage consumption were less strict than any of the other states. For instance, Nevada had no laws against drinking on the public streets, or even while driving a vehicle, and the bars and liquor stores were open 24/7. Tens of thousands of couples entered the state each year for the sole purpose of getting married, on the spot, without blood tests; and cheap and easy divorce was also available without lengthy court proceedings. Nevada was not a child-friendly state in the 1960s. This was a playground for consenting adults. Much of Las Vegas had been built with mob money, and the judges and politicians throughout the state needed casino backing to get elected. There were no theme-park family casinos at that time. People came to Nevada for wide-open gambling, sex, and booze at all hours.

As Thorp had discovered, even the major casinos had "mechanics" on duty who could cheat players when ordered to do so by the house. This was accepted procedure within the industry. The only players who were beating the casino games with regularity were wiseguys. Many of the early card counters had a lot of other tricks up their sleeves. Jess Marcum, for instance, was considered unusual by other Vegas gambling pros in the 1950s because he wouldn't have anything to do with cheating. He simply wanted to beat the games with math. According to Sam Cohen, Marcum's biographer, poker pro Joe Bernstein attempted numerous times to get Marcum involved in poker scams, but Marcum never took him up on the offers. It was how the gambling pros of that era viewed their world. At the poker tables, the local pros colluded with each other to milk the suckers who showed up on the weekends. In the casino games, many of these players had no qualms with colluding with dealers to take off the house. To be a professional gambler on either side of the tables was to be a scam artist—that was the life, and all involved in it knew it.

Thorp changed all that. Suddenly, college kids and businessmen who could beat the

> **Definition:**
>
> A mechanic is a professional gambling cheat who can skillfully perform sleight-of-hand moves with cards, dice, or chips.

game of blackjack were showing up in the casinos. The casino bosses had never seen anything like this. Out-of-towners had never been a worry before; these were the rubes who had always been the easy money.

But many of those who were trying to count cards in the casinos simply couldn't do it. Thorp's ten-count was difficult. It required not only a better than average memory and a lot of time spent memorizing charts of strategy data, but also a better-than-average ability to do math at the tables, and very quickly. So, although the casinos were worried, they kept adding more and more blackjack tables because most of these new players were unable to use Thorp's system with any accuracy. In addition, on the advice of their main consultant, John Scarne—despite his public insistence that card counting didn't work—the casinos started adding two-deck, then four-deck games, in an attempt to foil card counters.

MORE MATHEMATICIANS GET INVOLVED

In 1963, a computer scientist from New York, Harvey Dubner, participated in a panel discussion on blackjack at the Fall Joint Computer Conference, which was being held in Las Vegas that year. Dubner revealed a point counting system he had devised, using +1/-1 values, that was much simpler to use at the tables than Thorp's ten-count. Dubner's count values would go on to become the most popular card-counting system in the history of the game, now popularly known as the Hi-Lo Count.

Julian Braun, an IBM computer programmer from Chicago who was on the same panel discussion, took an interest in Dubner's simple system, and began to work out a program for optimizing the strategy.

Then, in 1965, another participant at that same panel discussion, Allan N. Wilson, a nuclear physicist with General Dynamics in San Diego, no doubt inspired by Dubner's approach, published a book titled *The Casino Gambler's Guide*, which contained a point count system he had devised. Wilson's counting system was weak compared to Thorp's ten-count, but other counting systems were being devised by players inspired by Thorp's book. Newspapers all over the country had classified ads appearing from blackjack system developers with "new, easy" ways to count cards. Thorp had shown that blackjack could be beaten, but players wanted an easier way to count cards.

BEAT THE DEALER, SECOND EDITION

By 1966, just four years after the initial publication of *Beat the Dealer*, the changes that had taken place in the Las Vegas casinos were incredible. Although the game of blackjack had boomed, and by now far outstripped craps as the casinos' number one table game, many casinos had also switched from the traditional single-deck games dealt to the bottom, to four-deck games in which only three to three and a half decks were being dealt out.

That's when Ed Thorp dropped another bombshell. Under the auspices of their Vintage Paperback division, Random House published a revised and expanded edition of *Beat the Dealer*. And the most important addition was Harvey Dubner's Hi-Lo counting system, which Thorp called the Complete Point Count, with a computer-optimized strategy devised by Julian Braun. To the casinos' frustration, this was a system that could more easily be applied to multiple-deck games.

Thorp was keeping the casinos on the run.

Still, the casinos' fears were mostly unfounded. The Complete Point Count was easier to use than the ten-count, but it was not a lot easier. It required players to keep two separate counts. In addition to the running count of the cards' point total, the player had to keep a count of the exact number of cards remaining to be played. And in order to play his hand, he had to memorize a chart of 158 different strategy changes to be made according to the count.

Thorp also included a Simple Point Count in this new edition of his book, but at the time that strategy seemed way too simple to most players to gain much of an edge, or to be taken seriously by players who wanted to beat the game. Later, the power of Thorp's simpler method of adjusting the running count, without keeping a separate count of the exact number of cards played, would be shown.

Should You Read Thorp's Book Today?

Many players see Thorp's *Beat the Dealer* on the bookshelves, but put it down when they see the latest revision was in 1966 because they think they want a more current book on card counting. I agree that the counting systems in Thorp's book are cumbersome by modern standards. But every blackjack player should read *Beat the Dealer*. This is the historic text that started it all, and you can feel the excitement that Thorp felt as he was revealing secrets to players for the first time, secrets that would ultimately change an industry. So, don't read it for the system; read it for the adventure. On top of that, Thorp is marvelous in describing the mathematics of the game for non-mathematicians, and he is passionate in his stance against the casino cheating that was so prevalent in Nevada at the time. This book shaped the way professional players thought about games for decades to come.

THE GRIFFIN AGENCY IS BORN

Every card counter quickly learns about the dreaded Griffin books. Initially, it was just a single book. Now, in its fifth "volume," the Griffin books are a virtual library of photos and information about professional casino gamblers. In fact, the mug books of card counters' photos that are published by Griffin Investigations in Las Vegas have become so well known among professional blackjack players that they often don't even use the proper name when referring to them. One counter might ask another, "Are you in the book?" And the other will immediately know what he's talking about.

The book.

An annoyance for every advantage player.

To be fair, it's not all card counters' photos. There are some actual cheaters and thieves, purse-snatchers, and slot machine "sluggers" in the Griffin books. But it's more card counters than any other category, and for a good reason. There just aren't very many real crooks in the casinos. And casinos aren't scared of purse-snatchers. The security guards will take care of them. The casinos fear the players who can blend into the crowd and legally take money from their gaming tables simply by playing with intelligence.

Intelligence is not a trait any casino is looking for in its customers. And the Griffin books are essentially mug books of the intelligent players, the customers the casinos definitely do not want playing their games.

But where did "the books" come from? How did the concept originate? Most counters today have no idea. It seems the Griffin books have been around for as long as card counting itself.

Well, almost…

The timing of their arrival was perfect.

It was 1967 when a young Las Vegas private detective, Robert Griffin, first got the idea for the books that have plagued card counters now for almost thirty years. Ed Thorp's *Beat the Dealer* had just gone into its second (1966) edition, and the casinos were frantic to find an answer to the growing problem of getting rid of this new crop of professional players.

They had tried changing the rules of blackjack in 1963, but it didn't work. Their main consultant, John Scarne, was valiantly trying to convince the public that Thorp's system was a fake and that card counting didn't work, but the public wasn't buying it. In fact, it was ruining Scarne's reputation as a player advocate, which he clearly no longer was.

So, throughout 1964 and 1965, Scarne began advising the Las Vegas casinos to stop dealing single-deck games and start dealing blackjack from four-deck shoes, which he believed would be far more difficult for card counters to keep track of. At the same time, Scarne was warning players that the single-deck blackjack games were too "dangerous" for players because skilled card mechanics could cheat too easily in a hand-held game.

Many of the Las Vegas casinos did, in fact, switch from single-deck games to four-deck shoes. And it was nearly impossible for any player to use Thorp's ten-count in a shoe game. But when Thorp's 1966 edition of *Beat the Dealer* came out, with the new Hi-Lo counting system that could be used to count cards with any number of decks, the casinos knew they were in trouble. Thorp was not letting up—more and more books and counting systems were being sold, and John Scarne had no solution.

Robert A. Griffin did.

In 1967, Griffin started a company called Griffin Investigations, Inc., "for the purpose of providing surveillance and investigative services to casinos," according to their promotional brochure. Prior to the Griffin Agency, casinos had always provided their own surveillance, and they had rarely shared information with each other. But now, casinos had a common enemy—card counters—and Griffin's main product was a mug book of names and photos of counters who had been identified and barred.

Most card counters learned about Griffin the hard way, when they found themselves being ejected from casinos where they had never played before, shortly after arriving at the blackjack tables for an initial play. Elaborate disguises and fake IDs soon became a necessity for high-stakes pros once they were "in the book." Some players who were not card counters also found themselves being identified as counters in the Griffin book, as they had been misidentified to Griffin as such by paranoid pit bosses. Other non-pros had their names and photos entered into the Griffin book as "associates" of card counters simply because they had been seen socializing in the casinos with other players who were already in the book.

The casinos' fear of counters, and the failure of John Scarne to provide any workable protection from the threat, opened a huge market for Robert Griffin's services. Griffin was essentially telling the casinos that they did not need card-counting experts on their staffs to identify counters at their tables. Griffin would compile the names and photos of counters from all of the casinos in Las Vegas, updating his mug book monthly, and the casinos simply had to subscribe to his service to get the book. Just about every major casino in Las Vegas subscribed.

The "Weirdest" Blackjack Book Ever Published

In 1968, a mathematics professor at the University of California in Berkeley, writing under the pseudonym, "Jacques Noir, Ph.D.," wrote one of the most important books in blackjack's history, yet most blackjack players never even saw it! Noir had done some serious studies of the game using the University's computer, and he had developed a unique ten-count system. It was one of the easiest-to-use counting systems ever developed, because it required nothing more than a simple running count. Because of the way in which the count was "unbalanced," it made perfect insurance decisions, and also was very accurate in estimating when the house edge had turned to a player edge, all by running count with no math or extensive memorization required.

Unfortunately, the publisher, a small Berkeley print shop publishing under the name Oxford Street Press, didn't think a book on casino blackjack would sell as well as a book on slots. They wanted a chapter on playing the slots. So, the author made a trip to the casinos of Lake Tahoe, Nevada and put together a twenty-two-page chapter on the slot machines that were available, complete with photos and charts showing the payout tables. But the rest of this two hundred-page book is a serious study of blackjack and card-counting systems.

Oxford Street Press published the book with the title *Casino Holiday* and a dust jacket that featured a full-color photo of high-kicking Vegas showgirls. Beneath the lovely legs of the showgirls, the book's subtitle reads, "Lake Tahoe Slot Machine Guide."

Incredibly, the word "blackjack" does not even appear on the cover!

So, it's no wonder that this book was not a big hit with blackjack players, most of whom never even picked it up to browse its pages. Two other authors, Stanley Roberts and John Archer, in different books, later popularized the Jacques Noir unbalanced ten-count system. The system was also my inspiration for the unbalanced Red Seven Count.

Today, *Casino Holiday* is a collector's item among gambling buffs, if you can find one with that showgirl dust jacket intact.

ENTER LAWRENCE REVERE

In 1969, a former casino pit boss, Eugene Griffin, AKA Paul Mann, AKA Griffith K. Owens, AKA Leonard Parsons, also known as "Spec," writing under the name Lawrence Revere, self-published *Playing Blackjack as a Business*. You know that anyone with that many names had to be a card counter. His first edition was not much more than a self-published pamphlet, thirty-six pages and spiral bound. But this book made blackjack history. Revere had taken the simple method Thorp had suggested for his Simple Point Count of estimating the "true count" simply by dividing the running count by the number of remaining decks, and applied it to a full set of strategy indices he'd hired Julian Braun to produce.

This was the advance that made professional level play accessible to players with average math abilities. By 1971, Revere's book had grown to 172 pages, and in 1973, Lyle Stuart became the publisher. *Playing Blackjack as a Business* was one of the most influential books in card-counting history, and it's still in print. Revere's counting systems, at the time of their publication, were the strongest systems ever developed. Revere had done the impossible: he not only simplified Thorp's methods, but he increased the advantage a player could gain by card counting.

Revere's self-published, 1969, 36-page Playing Blackjack as a Business

Should You Read Revere's Book Today?

Although Lawrence Revere died in 1977, his book, *Playing Blackjack as a Business*, is still in print. Remarkably, Revere's card-counting systems are still as powerful as any counting systems ever developed. Revere was probably more responsible than any other author for the number of professional players that plagued the casinos in the early 1970s. His book is a classic "how-to" text. He spends very little ink describing the theory of card counting or telling personal anecdotes. He simply presents the material that must be learned and the ways to practice what you need to win. No fluff, no filler. I believe any card counter could benefit from Revere's book, if for no other reason than to acquire more of his no-nonsense approach to getting the edge.

Revere had one message for those who wanted to be card counters. You must be perfect. Practice, practice, practice. A single mistake per hour can kill your edge.

While he was alive, Revere taught lessons in his Las Vegas home to aspiring card counters. Many players from that era tell a similar story about Revere. At the end of each lesson, he would require his student to count down a deck of cards without error. Inevitably, the student would fail. Unbeknownst to the student, Revere had surreptitiously removed a card from the deck, and actually caused the student to fail.

Enough reliable old-timers have told me they witnessed such a scene that I figure there must be some truth to it. Some say Revere did this solely so that the student would have to pay for another lesson. One professional player who knew Revere disagrees. "He didn't charge that much for lessons, especially considering his reputation. He was about as close to a legend as an author could be at that time. And he didn't really need the money. I think he did this just to keep them on their toes, always thinking they weren't yet perfect and had to improve." This pro feels that Revere took on students mainly because he enjoyed having company around he could tell his stories to.

THE BIRTH OF TEAM PLAY IN THE 1970'S

In the early 1970s, card counting became big business. One of the most creative and successful players from that time (or any time) was Al Francesco, who had been playing since 1963 and had traveled with Lawrence Revere for a while. As a poker player, Al knew that the best way for a player to make money was to disguise his strength from his opponents, but he couldn't figure out a way that a card counter could do this at a blackjack table. Then, in 1971, it hit him. That year, Al started his first blackjack teams, using the Big Player (BP) approach. It was the method he'd been seeking for eight years.

Here's how it happened. Al was in a casino with his brother, who was also a card counter, and his brother was playing dollar blackjack, spreading from $1 to $5 while they were killing time before dinner. Al wasn't playing, but was standing beside the table talking to friends. On a whim, whenever he noticed his brother had a $5 bet on the table, Al would shoot out a $100 bet, knowing that the count must be high, but otherwise paying no attention to the game. He did this for about half an hour. As he was walking out of the casino, however, the pit boss chased him down. To Al's amazement, the boss had caught up with him in order to offer him dinner or a room, telling Al that he was the type of player the casino wanted to cultivate as a customer.

Within weeks, Al was training three players to count cards and signal him when the count was high. He was the first Big Player. The strategy proved to be a huge success, and within a year, Al Francesco had more than twenty players trained as spotters, and three BPs that he could mix and match with his spotters in different casinos on playing trips. This team approach was a major advance in professional blackjack strategy. Blackjack teams today still use Al's BP approach with great success.

ELECTRONICS ENTER THE PLAYERS' ARSENAL

During this same time period, Keith Taft began developing the first concealed blackjack computer, and by 1972, Keith had started using a computer in the Nevada casinos to play "perfect" blackjack. Nevada had no laws at that time prohibiting the use of devices at their tables. Keith's first computer weighed fifteen pounds. He went on to develop dozens of concealable computers and other electronic devices over the next two decades, ever smaller and more powerful. By the mid-'70s, Keith and his son, Marty, had met Al Francesco, and they would be putting together teams of players using computers to beat the blackjack tables.

Keith Taft with his first blackjack computer, circa 1972

How Do You Use a Concealed Blackjack Computer?

In 1984, when it was still legal to use computers in the casinos, Keith Taft hired me to write an operating manual for his "David" computer, which was the computer Ken Uston later referred to as "George." Here's how it worked:

In the toe of each shoe there were two "switches," or buttons—one above each big toe and one beneath—for a total of four switches. Each switch conveyed a different code to the computer, which was a small epoxy-encased device that was strapped to the calf beneath the trousers. The computer itself was about the size of a pack of cigarettes, but thinner. By using a series of toe taps, kind of like Morse code, the player could relay to the computer everything it needed to know in order to make a decision in a blackjack game—which cards had already been dealt, what cards the player held, and the dealer's upcard.

This computer communicated its decisions to the player with buzzes and taps on the sole of the player's foot. It was not easy to use one of these devices. It essentially entailed learning to "type" with your big toes. Even once you had memorized the codes, inputting them via the toe switches was a chore. It took weeks or even months of practice to get to the point where you could use the device at casino-dealing speed without foot cramps stopping you.

ENTER STANFORD WONG

In 1975, Stanford Wong came out with **Professional Blackjack**. Wong had a Ph.D. in economics from Stanford University, hence his pseudonym. This book was the next big advance for card counters. Wong described his playing style, which included table-hopping shoe games to avoid playing at negative counts. As four-deck shoes were the most widely available games in Las Vegas by that time, this original approach was brilliant. The casinos looked for card counters by watching for their betting spreads. It had never occurred to the casinos that a counter might be watching a table from the aisles, waiting for an advantageous count before jumping in to bet.

The counting system Wong published was the Hi-Lo Count, and like Revere's count, used the easy divide-by-remaining-deck(s) approach to running count adjustments. So, at last, some twelve years after Harvey Dubner had proposed the Hi-Lo count values, his system was available in a format both fully optimized with strategy indices, and presented with a simple methodology of play. Wong's table-hopping approach to shoe games was in many ways similar to Al Francesco's Big Player (BP) team approach, but allowed a

DEALER SLANG

Snapper: a blackjack.

solo card counter to attack shoe games invisibly, and without a team of spotters. This playing style has since become widely known as wonging.

DID KEN USTON BETRAY HIS MENTOR?

Then, in 1977, Ken Uston's first book, *The Big Player*, became a best seller for Holt, Rinehart, and Winston. Co-authored with professional writer Roger Rapaport, this was the book that taught the public at large, and casino industry insiders, how Al Francesco's blackjack teams got away with winning huge amounts of money in casinos all over the world.

Many of Uston's teammates, however, and especially Al Francesco— the man who had invented the team concept and taught Uston how to play—felt betrayed. Al had been using his BP teams since 1971, racking up huge wins at all of the major casinos in Las Vegas and Reno, without any inkling of suspicion within the casino industry of what he had been doing. And for three and a half years, Al had been doing this with a twenty-one-man team that included three BPs and eighteen spotters. By playing in three different casinos, and continually rotating spotters and BPs in and out of all of them, Al felt that the casinos would never be able to make the play by putting together his spotters with his BPs. Al Francesco felt certain that the only way his BP strategy could ever be discovered would be by someone on his team spilling the beans. And he had two team policies that he required all team members to adhere to: complete honesty and absolute secrecy.

Ken Uston, in fact, initially got a position on one of Al's teams in 1974 as a result of another player's violation of the honesty policy. Al had a brother-in-law at that time acting as a Big Player, and he discovered his brother-in-law was stealing money from the team. So Al fired him and started looking for another BP. He was introduced to Ken Uston, and he felt Uston would be the right man for the job. As a vice president of the Pacific Stock Exchange in San Francisco, Uston had the credentials to fool the casinos into thinking he was a man with a lot of money. And, Uston was obviously smart and ambitious, and knew how to play the part of a millionaire who could throw money around at whim. Al trained Uston to count cards, and later to act as a BP. Al later commented wryly, "I probably should have stuck with my brother-in-law; at least he wouldn't have written a book about it!"

Al did not find out about Uston's book until a week before the book was published. And the way he found out about it devastated him. For the first time, at the Sands Casino in Las Vegas, Al's team was busted by casino security. Uston was the Big Player on that play, and he was putting on a show for a representative of his publisher who was at the casino to watch him in action. The publisher subsequently used the team's bust to promote the book and make Ken a media star. And it worked. Ken Uston and the big bust at the Sands made the news, and Uston was soon widely viewed as the mastermind Big Player who had made it all happen.

Though Uston always denied it, Al has always felt that Uston set up the bust simply to promote the book. According to Al, Uston was not a winning BP with his teams. He was aggressive and flamboyant, but he never really won any money. The fact that Uston had spent more than a year writing a book about Al's teams, without ever mentioning to Al that he was doing it until it came out in the news, drove a wedge between the two men that would last for years to come.

But there is no denying that Ken Uston's *The Big Player*, published in 1977, influenced and educated many other card counters about the team approach. Al Francesco had been betrayed, but it was no coincidence that the Tommy Hyland Team, the Czech Team, and the MIT Team were all initially formed in 1978, the year after the publication of *The Big Player*. This book, filled with exciting stories of subterfuge and incredible wins, ushered in the Age of the Blackjack Mega-Team. It is one of the blackjack classics that probably created more professional players than any book since Lawrence Revere's *Playing Blackjack as a Business*.

And what happened the year after *The Big Player* was published? In 1978, Resorts International, the first East Coast casino, opened in Atlantic City. Now, the game really gets crazy...

BIG BOOM ON THE BOARDWALK

No one had anticipated the tidal wave of humanity which surged into Atlantic City after Resorts opened its doors in 1978. Gross profits at this one casino averaged over $600,000 per day, far higher than any one of the larger Las Vegas casinos.

— *C. R. Chambliss & T. C. Roginski, Playing Blackjack in Atlantic City*

The phenomenal growth in the casino industry that occurred in Nevada throughout the 1960s and '70s as a direct result of the popularity of Ed Thorp's *Beat the Dealer*, had the East Coast politicians and business leaders buzzing with plans to get casinos legalized in New York, New Jersey, and elsewhere on the East Coast. So much gambling money was flying west to Vegas and Reno every day, a plan had to be hatched to keep those dollars closer to home.

In 1974, a referendum to legalize gambling in New Jersey failed, but a similar referendum that would limit the casinos to Atlantic City passed in 1976. Atlantic City had been chosen as the first East Coast gambling venue because the politicos felt, and rightly so, that the public would accept it. It was well located and had once been a popular vacation resort town, but had long since fallen on hard times. The once-famous boardwalk was in disrepair, and the surrounding residential neighborhoods had become slums of broken-windowed tenements.

No one in the state could make an argument that casinos might destroy the neighborhood. The neighborhood was a pit of poverty and despair. Instead, the hope was that casinos might revitalize the town.

THE COPS VERSUS THE ROBBERS

There were some who predicted that if New Jersey legalized casino gambling in Atlantic City, the town would soon dwarf Las Vegas as the country's gambling mecca because of the relative proximity to all those big East Coast cities—New York, Philadelphia, Baltimore, Boston, and Washington, D.C. Everyone figured Nevada would likely keep the California trade, but Florida was closer to New Jersey than Nevada, as were many of the big Midwestern cities—Detroit, Chicago, and Cleveland.

Obviously, these seers have been proven wrong. There is a lot of gambling in Atlantic City today, and a lot of blackjack, but in the nearly three decades since casino gambling was legalized, no one today could imagine Atlantic City making much of a dent in Las Vegas's status as the gambling center of not only the U.S., but the world.

What is most striking to players who gamble in both Nevada and New Jersey, however, is the totally different "feel" of the casinos in these states. The difference is based on the way the two states entered the gambling industry. Nevada's casinos grew out of mob money. The whole state was wild and loose and dangerous. New Jersey's casinos, on the other hand, came out of a corporate environment. High-powered business tycoons, politicians, and lawyers were behind every casino that opened its doors. With the state requiring a five hundred-room hotel as a prerequisite for even applying for a casino license, the types of punks and hoods who set up bust-out joints in Las Vegas back in the 1930s, '40s, and '50s, didn't even dream of opening a casino in New Jersey.

Today, despite the corporatization of Nevada's casinos in the past few decades, the difference between the Nevada and New Jersey casinos—and it's a palpable difference that you can feel, even if you can't quite put your finger on it—is the difference between the cops and the robbers. Nevada makes us think of what the world would be like if the robbers ran the show, made the laws, and owned everything, while New Jersey gives us the feeling that the cops are in charge. Most of us don't really care much for either cops or robbers. But we can't deny that if we're looking to let loose on vacation, robbers are a bit more fun to party with.

ATLANTIC CITY, HERE WE COME!

In 1978, Resorts International opened in Atlantic City, the first legal East Coast casino in the twentieth century. Their four- and six-deck blackjack games offered a new form of surrender, dubbed by card counters as "early surrender," since the casino allowed players to surrender half a bet even when the dealer showed an ace or 10 up, and before the dealer checked for a blackjack. This rule gave basic strategy players a small edge over the house right off the top, without any card counting whatsoever! And the advantage to card counters was even greater. From opening day, card counters had a field day at Resorts' tables. Ironically, as word spread through the gambling community that card counters found the Resorts' blackjack game to be the most lucrative game for players in the country, gamblers from all over the world—most of whom knew nothing about basic strategy or card counting—flocked to their tables. And, ironically, Resorts International was soon the most profitable casino in history, winning an average of $650,000 per day.

A team of professional blackjack players whose founders were from Czechoslovakia that had been playing in Las Vegas flew all of their members to Atlantic City to take advantage of this new surrender rule. This team, which later became known in the casino industry as simply the Czech Team, found the Resorts' game to their liking and stayed for months.

A New Jersey college student named Tommy Hyland, who had just turned twenty-one, started going to Atlantic City in 1978 when he heard about the favorable blackjack game at Resorts. Within a year, he had organized about twenty of his college and golfing buddies into a team of blackjack players. Hyland's team continues to this day as one of the most successful casino gambling operations in history.

It was also in 1978 that the first MIT blackjack team was started. This team actually consisted of students from MIT, Harvard, and other East Coast colleges. Johnny C., now a legendary player who joined the team in 1981, plays high-stakes blackjack to this day and continues organizing teams of professional players. The Czechs, the Hyland teams, and the MIT teams would be the scourge of the casino industry for decades to come. Many believe these teams owe their existence to the Resorts' game with its early surrender rule that made the game so easy to beat. College kids found that they could pool their money, play blackjack with a modicum of intelligence, and get rich quick.

In fact, it was a combination of that easy-to-beat early surrender game and Ken Uston's *The Big Player* that had just been published in 1977 that worked together to create an environment where new teams of smart young kids could make millions playing blackjack.

John Scarne's Last Gasp

1978, the year Resorts International opened its doors in Atlantic City, also proved to be John Scarne's last gasp as a gambling expert. At the age of seventy-five, his final book was published, *Scarne's Guide to Casino Gambling*. The book was released prior to the opening of Atlantic City's first casino, but Scarne had managed to get hold of the New Jersey Casino Control Commission's authorized blackjack rules in time to offer his analysis. He wrote that the Commission "made a shambles of the Black Jack rules by adding the unfavorable-to-the-player 'Surrender Bet' with its monstrous 22.5 percent house advantage. The surrender bet is an Asian importation which is the biggest Black Jack sucker bet." Boy, did he have it wrong. I have spent hours trying to figure out how Scarne ever calculated that this rule, which is one of the most favorable blackjack rules for players ever to appear, had a 22.5 percent house edge. I am at a loss.

THE "EXPERIMENT"

In January of 1979, after fighting for a month with both card counters and the Casino Control Commission over how to handle card counters at their tables, Resorts International began what came to be known to card counters as "The Experiment." For a two-week period, the Casino Control Commission required the casino to allow all card counters to play unhindered at their blackjack tables without any betting restrictions or shuffle ups. All games had to be dealt out two-thirds—67 percent of the cards—between shuffles.

Although the Experiment had started out with a festive atmosphere, that atmosphere quickly degenerated to bitter acrimony. Ken Uston, who was a media star by this time as a result of his first book, *The Big Player*, and subsequent TV appearances, and on the outs with Al Francesco, was now running his own blackjack team. In some of the local press reports on the Experiment, dealers accused Uston of being cheap. One dealer claimed that Uston only toked him $1 after a big win at his table. Uston responded that he always tipped the dealer $5 after a winning session, which did not go very far in reversing his cheapskate image in the town.

One member of the Czech team, Walt, was arrested for cheating. He had a $500 bet on the table and won his hand. Before the dealer paid him, he allegedly "capped" the bet with another $500 chip. The dealer did not see him cap the bet and paid him $1000. But the surveillance camera saw it, and Walt was arrested. The Czechs claimed that Walt had been "set up" for the bust by a pit boss. This implied that the boss and Walt had arranged for Walt to cap his bet when the boss wasn't looking. Then the Czechs said that Walt's bet cap was an "accident," that Walt had simply put out a $1000 bet for the next hand, not having noticed that the dealer had not yet paid his $500 win for the prior hand, then collected the $1000 payoff, having forgotten that the $1000 bet was supposed to be for the next hand. As bet capping was the most common method of player cheating at shoe games, and since Walt's cap was a textbook example of how it was generally done—cap the winning bet at first base while the dealer is busy settling with third base —the Czechs' arguments were falling on deaf ears. The story was spreading among casino personnel that these card counters were cheaters and had to be watched closely. Based on the Czechs' complaints, the card counters were circulating rumors that the pit personnel were trying to set up counters for bogus cheating arrests.

Meanwhile, the Czechs started spreading rumors that the casino was planning to pay off counters with counterfeit chips, so that counters could be arrested for fraud when cashing out. This rumor had some counters examining chips at their tables and questioning bosses about chips that had been paid to them that "looked funny." As this rumor spread in the pit, some pit personnel felt that the Czechs, in fact, might be planning to introduce counterfeit chips. Now both sides of the tables were examining chips. The paranoia throughout the casino was high.

The Experiment ran for two weeks, from January 16 through January 30, 1979. No counterfeit chips ever surfaced. Ken Uston's small team won $145,000 in the nine days that they played, and Uston, as was his style, made a big media event of his team's success. There were articles about him in *Time* magazine, the *New York Times*, and many other newspapers across the country. The Czech team reportedly won much more than Uston's team, though it appeared they would have an expensive court battle looming over Walt's arrest. In an interview years later, Tommy Hyland also acknowledged that his newly formed team was at Resorts for the Experiment, stating simply that, "We crushed them."

THE PARTY'S OVER

But on January 31, with the blessings of the Casino Control Commission, Resorts International began ejecting professional blackjack players from their tables. The casino had no problems identifying many of them, as during the Experiment most of the team players openly discussed what they were doing, some going so far as to taunt the casino dealers and bosses who were powerless to remove them from their tables. Many experts now believe that if the card counters had gone quietly into Resorts, had refrained from boasting about their wins while still at the tables, and not dragged the media into the event to brag about their skill and their winnings as Uston had done, the Casino Control Commission may never have buckled under to the casino's pressure to allow them to bar card counters.

The fact is that during that two-week experiment, Resorts' overall win from their blackjack tables was not reduced one iota. In fact, the casino win had substantially increased during that time, as their tables were so crowded with players who were trying to count cards but could not. The counters, however, thoroughly embarrassed the casino, and in the midst of the counters' bragging about their huge wins, the dealers felt they had been stiffed.

By the end of 1979, two new casinos had opened in Atlantic City, with half a dozen more in planning or under construction. The Boardwalk Regency, operated by Caesars, opened in June, and the Park Place, operated by Bally's, opened in December. All three were averaging about $500,000 per day in winnings from their table games, more than any of the Las Vegas Strip casinos at that time. Card counters were being barred from the tables daily, but Ken Uston was in the process of suing the Casino Control Commission for its decision to allow the casinos to prohibit counters from playing. Meanwhile, the casinos—worried that Uston's lawsuit might succeed—were petitioning the Commission for numerous proposed changes to their blackjack games. They wanted the right to deal blackjack from eight-deck shoes, to eliminate the early surrender option, and to deal out only 50 percent of the cards in a shoe at their discretion. Where this battle would end was anyone's guess.

In June of 1981, based on a report filed by ECON, Inc., the New Jersey Casino Control Commission gave the Atlantic City casinos permission to remove the surrender option from their games. ECON was an accounting firm hired by the Atlantic City casinos to make a case for them. According to ECON's report, Atlantic City card counters enjoyed a win rate of 4.38 percent! Counters knew that this was three to four times their actual win rate, but the New Jersey Casino Control Commission had no blackjack experts, or even mathematicians, on staff to refute this inflated number.

To this day, the attitude of the Atlantic City casinos toward card counters and all big money players at their blackjack tables remains one of mistrust. Players who are used to the friendliness of Nevada casino personnel, especially toward high rollers, are often taken aback by their treatment in Atlantic City. Big money blackjack players are immediately suspect in Atlantic City's casinos, and compared to Nevada, comps are often hard to come by. The negative effects of that two-week Experiment have lasted more than twenty years.

But the huge media interest in card counting on the East Coast continued unabated. The expansion of casino gambling in Atlantic City, with half a dozen new casinos approved and under construction, was eclipsed in the news by the public interest in Uston's lawsuit against the Casino Control Commission. There had also been a 1979 *Sports Illustrated* article about Keith Taft's at-that-time legal concealable blackjack computer, which, naturally, featured Ken Uston modeling the device. Everywhere you turned you saw Ken Uston.

USTON CONTINUES HIS MEDIA HYPE

Ken Uston's *Million Dollar Blackjack* was published by SRS Publishing in 1981. This was Uston's best book, and it soon became a best seller. In it he revealed just about everything he had learned from Al Francesco about card counting, training methods, and team play structures.

Then in 1982, Ken Uston won his lawsuit in New Jersey, which required the Atlantic City casinos to allow card counters at their tables. Card counters rejoiced at first, but the Atlantic City casinos reacted by switching from six-deck games to mostly eight-deck games and dealing out only four decks between shuffles. Most card counters gave up on these games as a waste of time.

Despite this, throughout the early 1980s, card counting continued to grow. Keith Taft continued to run computer teams in both Nevada and Atlantic City, and now had a shuffle-tracking version of his concealable computer, which he called "Thor." This computer had no problem beating eight-deck games with poor penetration. Some of the big teams started using Keith's computers. Both Al Francesco and Ken Uston had computer teams with Keith. Tommy Hyland was also using computers with his team. In Las Vegas, Steve Forte had added computer play to his arsenal of weapons against the casinos, and other entrepreneurs, like Mickey Lichtman, were designing their own shuffle-tracking computers. At this time, the big teams were also starting to track shuffles mentally. Atlantic City had managed to kill the profit-potential of their games for the average players and weekend-warrior card counters, but the pros had quickly reacted by adopting new tactics.

AN EXPERT GOES DOWN THE TUBES

In 1982, a hitherto reputable blackjack author and expert, Jerry Patterson, co-authored and published a worthless blackjack system called TARGET with a newspaper writer named Eddie Olsen. Patterson had previously authored two books on card counting, and in 1980 had founded a blackjack "clinic" in New Jersey to train players to count cards. He had been using Stanford Wong's Hi-Lo Count from Wong's *Professional Blackjack*, as well as my *Blackjack Formula*, as the texts for his card-counting course. With the explosion of blackjack in Atlantic City, his school had become so successful that he began franchising branches in other states. But with the sudden death of early surrender in Atlantic City, and the Atlantic City casinos' switch to eight-deck games with poor penetration, public interest in card counting on the East Coast died quickly. Patterson's blackjack clinic fell on hard times. It appeared to most experts that with TARGET, Patterson was grasping at straws to keep his school alive. Despite pleas from both Stanford Wong and myself, Jerry would not budge from his determination to sell TARGET.

I analyzed the system and exposed it as nonsense in *Blackjack Forum* in September of 1983, and many other experts, including Stanford Wong, Peter Griffin, Julian Braun, and Ken Uston, soon joined me in this opinion.

Patterson was not only losing the support of other experts, but some of his franchisees were abandoning him, refusing to sell the TARGET course unless Patterson could produce mathematical or computer simulation proof that it worked. Many believed that Patterson had simply made a mistake and would soon see the light. If the Atlantic City casinos found that they had to offer better games in order to keep their customers, then perhaps Patterson's blackjack clinics could thrive again, without this TARGET nonsense.

By the end of 1983, however, all of the Atlantic City casinos were dealing eight-deck games only, though they had quit the practice of cutting off four decks from play. Most were now dealing out six decks. The casinos had apparently found that they needed to offer beatable games in order to bring back their players. So, the games were beatable again with card counting, though they were no longer the best games in the country. In fact, without the early surrender rule, those eight-deck shoes made the Atlantic City games among the toughest games in the world for card counters to beat. The big teams had the bankrolls necessary to beat them, but average players couldn't do it. Patterson stuck with TARGET and lost his credibility with many of his former associates.

THE INSIDE SCOOP ON
THE CAMPIONE CASE

In 1994, a player by the name of Anthony Campione filed a lawsuit against the Tropicana Casino in Atlantic City. This turned into a major fiasco, and it had far-reaching repercussions for blackjack players in New Jersey. Here's what happened.

I got a call from Anthony Curtis, publisher of the Las Vegas Advisor, asking me if I had any interest in doing some consulting work for the Trop in Atlantic City. I told him no. Curtis had been a long time friend, and I knew him to be a staunch players' advocate. He said a player was suing the Tropicana and the casino was looking for an expert to refute testimony by the players' experts, Doug Grant and E. Clifton Davis. Curtis said the player was claiming he should have won hundreds of thousands of dollars at the Trop, but that the Trop was discriminating against him and wouldn't let him play.

I found this to be incomprehensible since the New Jersey Casino Control Commission's regulations forbade the casinos from barring players, even if they were card counters. Curtis had no explanation, as he had only talked briefly with one of the Trop's attorneys, who was asking him to recommend an expert witness.

Curtis contacted me because some years back I had published *Blackjack Forum* reviews of the blackjack systems being sold by both

Grant and Davis, and I had criticized both systems as worthless and invalid approaches. (My published opinion, in brief, was that these system sellers were either hucksters or idiots.) Curtis said it sounded to him like these phony system sellers were behind this lawsuit, and were trying to pull a scam on the Trop. He said that this might turn into a big case in New Jersey, and it could be an opportunity to publicly expose these phony systems in the mass media. I told him that I would be willing to stick by my published opinions on these systems, not to aid the casino, but to publicly expose the folly of these systems that were being sold to naive players.

I was then contacted by one of the Trop's attorneys. I provided a deposition in Las Vegas. The attorney provided me with the written statement of Campione's expert, E. Clifton Davis, in which Davis stated that he knew that Mr. Campione had taken Jerry Patterson's TARGET course, was a capable TARGET player, and that based on his skill he should be able to win hundreds of thousands of dollars annually playing blackjack. This floored me, because Campione was not using Davis's system, but Patterson's TARGET system, another system I had trashed in print years earlier. I was happy to provide the Trop attorney with my written opinion that the TARGET system was worthless, and that any player using the system would have no advantage over the casino.

My work was done. I had simply stated an opinion I had published years earlier.

I heard nothing more about this case for many months. Then an East Coast player called me and told me that he had just read a newspaper article that said that Stanford Wong had testified in court in a lawsuit against the Tropicana in Atlantic City, a suit brought by a player named Campione, and that Wong had testified on the side of the casino. I knew that the Trop's attorneys had also spoken with Wong back when they'd talked to me, so I assumed they had decided to use Wong as their expert in this case. Fine by me. Wong had also come out against the TARGET system as nonsense.

A couple of days later, I called Stanford and asked him about the trial. He told me that if he had known the facts in the case, he never would have testified. As a matter of general legal procedure, expert witnesses are never provided with the facts of a case. He said that it turned out the casino had refused to pay a bet by the player, then had the player forcibly removed from their blackjack table by security guards.

I asked Wong if he had refuted the validity of the TARGET system in his testimony. He said that he knew nothing about the use of the TARGET system in this case, but that he was simply shown a standard card-counting system with strategy charts, and was told that this was the system Campione was using. He said he simply acknowledged in court that it appeared to be a valid counting system. He also told me that Peter Griffin had provided a written analysis of the system, and had agreed that it was a valid counting system.

This was getting downright weird.

I called Peter Griffin and asked him if the Trop's attorneys had informed him that Campione was a TARGET player. He said he was not told that. He was simply given a typical card-counting system to analyze, which he had done. Griffin had also published statements years earlier expressing his opinion that TARGET was baloney.

I found this whole thing inexplicable.

Why would the Trop have dropped me as an expert, swept the TARGET system and E. Clifton Davis's statement under the rug, and instead supplied Wong and Griffin with a valid card-counting system as Campione's method of play?

Kind of strange, huh?

In discussing this bizarre turn of events with various legal experts, I've only heard one theory that makes sense. The Trop's defense rested on the casino's right to take countermeasures against professional players. They had gone way overboard in their mistreatment of Campione, and appeared to have violated both the state's gaming regulations and the player's civil rights. But if it came out in court that the player was not, in fact, a professional player capable of beating them at the blackjack tables, then they should not have been taking any countermeasures against him. If the Trop had presented my opinion of the TARGET system in the case, then it would appear that the Trop could not even tell a skillful player from a player using a worthless system. Which, I suspect, they couldn't. Nor could they inform Stanford Wong or Peter Griffin that Anthony Campione was a TARGET player, because both Wong and Griffin had publicly disavowed the TARGET system as a valid approach to beating blackjack in the past.

So, the judge and jury were led to believe that Campione was a capable professional card counter, and awarded him more than a million dollars in compensatory and punitive damages!

The Trop appealed the case to the New Jersey Supreme Court, however, and the judgment was reversed. According to the state supreme court, a player in New Jersey has no right to bring charges regarding a gaming violation against a casino in any civil court. The matter must be settled by the Casino Control Commission, and the Commission has no authorization to award monetary damages.

So, Campione got the shaft.

I have always wondered two things about this case.

One: how did the Trop's attorneys get Campione's attorney to discard E. Clifton Davis's signed statement that Campione was a TARGET player?

And two: what would have happened if Campione's case would have been presented to the jury with the actual facts, and it came out in court that Campione was not a professional player, but was an amateur using a worthless system? Would the court have viewed the incident as a violation of a regular customer's civil rights, and not as a "gaming violation" that occurred when a casino was attempting to protect its profits from a professional gambler? I suspect Campione may have been able to keep that million bucks had the facts come out.

But, sadly, Campione died shortly after the Supreme Court reversed its judgment.

So, my involvement in this case was peripheral. I provided the Trop attorneys with a written opinion of the TARGET system, to refute the written opinion by E. Clifton Davis. But I never appeared in court, and my opinion was never used in court.

But this case did have far-reaching effects on the Atlantic City casino industry. The newspapers had been comparing this case to the case Uston won decades earlier. The media believed that Campione was fighting for the rights of professional players, and some went so far as to state that Campione's initial victory was the most important victory for card counters since Uston. All of the actual facts of the case had been suppressed.

So, where did this lead?

THE ATLANTIC CITY CASINOS FIGHT FOR THE RIGHTS OF THE STUPID

The Campione case gave the Atlantic City casinos a lot of ammunition in their fight against card counters' rights. The prospect of professional players suing the casinos for money they "should have won," assuming they had the right to play, was frightening to the casinos. They stepped up their lobbying efforts to get the Casino Control Commission to approve stricter countermeasures against suspected professional players.

The CCC members, however, still felt that their hands were tied by the Supreme Court's 1982 Uston decision. The court had specifically ruled that players who were merely using intelligence to make their playing and betting decisions could not be discriminated against. The casinos felt that this was not fair. According to federal laws against discrimination, intelligence was not "protected." It was a violation of federal law to discriminate on the basis of race, religion, nationality, sex, age, or handicap. Discrimination against intelligence was not contrary to federal laws, and such discrimination was widely practiced by the casinos in other states. Nevada, for instance, could bar smart players under the innkeeper's "right to refuse service to anyone."

Finally, the Atlantic City casinos came up with a new argument. Since a portion of the state tax imposed on the casinos—albeit a small portion—was used for social programs for the elderly and infirm, then professional players' winnings from the casinos were reducing the funds that went for these social programs. By allowing blackjack players to play intelligently, the CCC was indirectly discriminating against the elderly and infirm, which are federally protected classes. The casinos claimed that the CCC was violating federal anti-discrimination laws. Simply put, their case was that letting smart people play blackjack discriminates against the old, the handicapped, and the infirm. The CCC bought this argument.

So, in 1999, the New Jersey Casino Control Commission passed a regulation that allowed the Atlantic City casinos to restrict the bets of suspected card counters, while allowing other players at the same tables to bet according to the posted limits. This is how the law reads:

> "The casino may attempt to reduce the suspected card counter's earning potential by lowering the posted maximum wager at the table, but waiving the limit for all other players at the table except the suspected card counter... Such measures are authorized by the Commission to protect... the continued funding of beneficial social programs for the senior citizens and disabled citizens of New Jersey."

To say nothing of the beneficial social programs for Donald Trump...

Did I mention that blackjack is the craziest, nuttiest, looniest game on the planet?

INDIANS, RIVERBOATS, LAWSUITS, AND LOOT

> There is nothing new about the business of separating a sucker from his money. That is what gambling is about. Legal larceny.
>
> — *Ovid Demaris, The Boardwalk Jungle*

Within a few years, the legalization of casino gambling in Atlantic City was already being viewed as a massive failure. The promise of rebuilding the city and restoring it to its former status as an attractive resort destination had virtually died. The city itself remained a slum. The only development that had taken place was the development of the casinos. The fat cats were getting rich, but the poor stayed just as poor. No neighborhood development had taken place. There were no restaurant or entertainment venues springing up in hopeful communities around the casinos. All of the dreams about the revitalization of an American town that had been talked about so excitedly as the lawyers drew up the thousands of pages of documents that would make the dream possible had died. It turned out that the lawyers were being paid by the men who wanted to own the casinos, and the documents, it turned out, gave the money that was pouring into the casinos to the casino owners, with scant few crumbs left for the community.

Funny how nobody had considered that the lawyers might actually be serving the clients who paid them. Funny how the clients who paid those attorneys were raking in loot by the wheelbarrows full, yet somehow had managed to make the whole thing come off as a failure, so that no other community anywhere could get the public support, or the votes they needed, to give Atlantic City competition. It appeared there would never be any competition for Atlantic City other than Nevada, and Nevada was a long way away.

All the talk of legalizing gambling elsewhere, in fact, had died with the dream in Atlantic City. Businessmen and politicians had no leg to stand on in any argument that casinos would be a good thing for their communities. Everyone pointed to the shameful fiasco of Atlantic City and said, "Not here."

The gambling "boom" might have died right then and there, not so much a boom as a little pop and fizzle. But something occurred that took everyone by surprise. The businessmen, the lawyers, and the politicians all knew that they could never again get the public support they would need to expand gambling operations anywhere else in the country. But there was a small group of people who were living in poverty, who had no lawyers, no politicians, and no bankers, who saw Atlantic City in a way that no one else did. With no public referendums, or marketing campaigns with media blitzes, or any concern whatsoever for what the local authorities might think of their legal right to have a casino, they pooled their modest resources and said, "Screw you, Donald Trump. We'll be your competition."

THE MICHIGAN INDIANS LEAD THE WAY

In 1985 the Indians in Michigan decided to expand their bingo operations into full-scale casino gambling. The Chippewas began adding blackjack tables on their reservations, and state and federal authorities immediately stepped in to close them down. But to the astonishment of the government authorities, the Indians kept reopening the games. It had been quite a number of years since the feds had been fighting with Indians anywhere, and this was a development that had the authorities in a quagmire.

The Indians were claiming a legal right as sovereign nations, according to various treaties with the U.S. government, to operate casinos on their reservations. What's more, the citizens of Michigan were supporting the Indians. They wanted to play blackjack. The state and federal cops realized they couldn't arrest the players for gambling, since they didn't have this kind of jurisdiction on Indian reservation lands, but they could not believe that the Indians had the right to just start opening casinos out in the Michigan woods! It was preposterous.

I was publishing *Blackjack Forum* at the time, and my Michigan subscribers were saying the games were good for card counters, mostly four- and six-deck shoe games with deep penetration and betting limits from $1 to $100. For blackjack players in the Midwest, this was exciting news. With the only other legal games in the country located in Nevada or New Jersey, the midwestern players wanted a venue closer to home.

Within a few years, Indians all over the country would follow the Chippewas' example, resulting in massive busts, confiscation of gambling paraphernalia, and lawsuits and counter-suits until the feds stepped in to solve the issue in 1987.

Because the Indian reservation casinos were not covered by any state gaming regulations, high-stakes players had to be very cautious about cheating. If there were no state laws that required that cards not be marked, for instance, or that honest shuffling and dealing procedures be used, what could prevent a crooked dealer from cheating players? In fact, without laws specifying precisely what constitutes a "lawful" game, cheating is not a crime. And since both the state and federal authorities were attempting to shut down the Indian reservation casinos, players in such casinos had to view these games as "every man for himself" as far as the honesty of the games was concerned.

The Feds Put the Law on the Indians' Side

In 1987, the Indian Gaming Regulatory Act was passed in Congress, settling court disputes all over the country and basically allowing Indians to operate full-scale casinos on their reservations

> **Tip for All Players:**
>
> Whenever a new casino opens, be extremely careful in watching for dealer errors. Most new casinos have many green dealers, who frequently make errors on payouts.

in states that allow gambling of any type. The IGRA paved the way for Indians to go full-steam ahead with their casino operations. But this law still did not provide any gaming regulations. In fact, it pretty much left the regulations up to the individual tribes. The law simply told the states to keep their hands off the Indians' affairs. The Indians could have their casinos.

Many casino industry analysts today question the wisdom of the federal government in giving the Indians carte blanche on their casino operations. But this was an entirely different political climate for casinos than we have today. At that time, only two states in the country had legal casinos.

Many, if not most, Indians on reservations were living in abject poverty. Alcoholism was rampant, and many were receiving welfare, food stamps, and other government assistance. The initial Indian casinos in Michigan and elsewhere were relatively small operations, basically extensions of the Indians' bingo halls where a few blackjack tables had been added. The feds had no doubt noticed that these bingo and gambling operations were getting many of the Indians who lived on these reservations off the government dole. How could that be a bad thing?

Although there were always religious and moral crusaders in every community who opposed gambling, it was obvious that the majority of the people in the states where the Indians opened their gambling operations supported the Indians' casinos, and many were their customers. Also, the Indians were standing on very firm legal ground in claiming the right to open casinos on their reservations. By federal law, the Indians were "sovereign nations" and not bound by most state laws on their reservations. To deny the Indians' rights to casinos as a form of free enterprise would require that the U.S. government break yet another treaty with the Indians.

The Indian Casino Expansion Begins

At the time the IGRA passed, there were already Indian casinos operating in Michigan, North Dakota, South Dakota, and Washington.

In 1989, the Mohawks opened three casinos on their reservation in upstate New York with four- and six-deck blackjack games and betting limits up to $200. Despite the IGRA, local authorities and the FBI immediately closed them down. The state had no argument with the blackjack games, but insisted the casino had no right to operate slot machines. The casinos immediately reopened and prepared for a long legal battle over their rights as a sovereign nation. It got ugly. There were shootings and vandalism. But in the end, as had been the case everywhere else, the Indians won.

In 1990, both Minnesota and Wisconsin Indian reservations began opening casinos with little opposition from authorities. State officials were beginning to realize that it was useless to fight the Indians on this issue. The public supported the Indians and the media made the outside officials look bad if they attempted to interfere with the Indians' peaceful casino operations. Today, both Minnesota and Wisconsin have more than a dozen Indian reservation casinos.

Bye-Bye Welfare, Hello Wealth!

In 1992, after a long battle with federal and state officials, the Mashantucket Pequots opened the Foxwoods Casino in Connecticut. The casino had eighty-five blackjack tables—more than any casino in Atlantic City at that time. This casino has a very funny history—funny, that is, as long as you're not a banker who refused to give the tribe a loan when they were seeking start-up capital.

The Mashantucket Pequots had fewer than three hundred members. The governor, Lowell Weicker, was staunchly opposed to the Indians having a casino in his state, and he fought tooth-and-nail in the federal courts to keep it from happening. Despite his best efforts, the Indians finally won their battle with the state authorities to open a casino. But Governor Weicker continued his media campaign against the proposed Foxwoods Casino. He pointed out that the Pequots' reservation was 120 miles from any major population area (Boston or New York), and that federal law prohibited any bank from accepting Indian reservation land as collateral for a loan, making such a loan an enormous risk for a lender. As all of the big U.S. casinos' profits were primarily driven by slots, and as slots were not specifically allowed by the feds' agreement with the Pequots, Weicker vowed that he would never allow slots in his state.

According to Kim Isaac Eisler (*Revenge of the Pequots*), after the tribe won the right to open a casino with Vegas-style table games on their reservation, the tribe "...approached twenty-four northeastern banks and lending institutions..." and "...all turned them down..."

This small band of Indians went on to change the face of gambling in America.

A group of Malaysians read about the plight of the Mashantucket Pequots, and felt that because this reservation in Connecticut—even out in the woods—was closer to New York City and Boston than Atlantic City, it would be a great location for a casino and a sound investment. So, to the chagrin and shock of all the U.S. banks that had turned down the tribe's loan applications, the Malaysians fronted the Indians $58 million to build a casino. From opening day, the Foxwoods Casino became the highest grossing casino in history. The Indians cleaned up, the Malaysians cleaned up, and a lot of U.S. banks missed the boat. Every formerly poverty-stricken Indian on that Connecticut reservation is a multi-millionaire many times over today.

The Danger of Crooked Games

In 1994, a player named David Smith filed a federal lawsuit against the Sycuan Casino near San Diego, claiming that he had been cheated. In California's Indian casinos at that time, the casinos were not allowed to bank the games. They provided the dealers and cards, but the games had to be banked by players, with the casino simply taking a commission on all bets. Smith claimed he had lost hundreds of thousands of dollars banking a game at the Sycuan Casino before he discovered that the casino was providing marked cards. To Smith's dismay, the federal court judge dismissed the suit. As "sovereign nations," Indian reservations are not within the jurisdiction of the U.S. court system. Smith had to take his case to the Sycuan's tribal court.

Smith's case was strong. He had obtained a deck of the casino's cards and had them examined by marked-card experts. The marks were undeniable. Furthermore, when the tribal chiefs checked more of the decks in the casino's stock room, they discovered that all of the house cards were similarly marked. It appeared to be an open-and-shut case. Someone who worked in the casino at a management level had to be involved.

Smith wanted his money back. The casino knew the amount of his losses, which had occurred over a period of weeks, and he demanded that the tribe make reparations to him. Unfortunately for Smith, the tribe had no gaming regulations requiring them to restore his losses. They insisted that the tribe itself was not guilty, as the tribe knew nothing about how their cards got marked. They agreed to fire one of the casino managers who may have been involved in the scam, or at least should have been more careful in guarding the casino's card stock, but other than that, they washed their hands of the matter.

Had this occurred in Nevada, where state laws govern the casinos, Smith would have had his losses restored in full, most likely with additional punitive damages. In addition, the casino would have been subjected to a substantial fine, and quite likely would have lost its state gaming license. All Smith had gotten from the Sycuan tribe was an apology.

But the Indians Keep Coming

Indian casinos in New Mexico also won in court in 1995, and were allowed to start banking blackjack games on their reservation casinos. They immediately opened tables with mostly six-deck shoes and betting maximums of $100 or $200.

In 1996, the Mohegan Sun Casino opened in Connecticut, the first real competition for Foxwoods since Foxwoods had opened four years earlier. Like Foxwoods, it opened to huge crowds that have never subsided. And contrary to what many experts predicted, the Mohegan Sun did not seem to diminish the crowds at Foxwoods.

In the year 2000, despite an opposition campaign heavily financed by the Nevada casinos, California legalized house-banked casino blackjack in the Indian reservation casinos. I was living in California at the time, and the Nevada casinos' tactics were hilarious. There were billboards all over the highways in the state urging citizens to "Vote No on Casino Gambling," all with messages about the evils of gambling, the inevitable destruction of communities, blah blah blah. It came out in various local newspapers that the anti-gambling billboard ad campaign was sponsored by Nevada casinos! Californians didn't buy it. By a huge margin, the people voted to allow Nevada-style casino blackjack on the state's Indian reservations. Within a month, dozens of California's Indian casinos dropped their "commission" games and started dealing Nevada-style blackjack. And just as quickly, Nevada's casinos started investing in these Indian reservation operations. Hey, if you can't beat 'em, join 'em!

In 2003, Arizona legalized blackjack in Indian reservation casinos. All games are mandated to be six decks and machine-shuffled. The rules include dealers hitting on soft 17, with limits ranging from $5 to $500. Within six months, more than a dozen Indian casinos were open throughout the state.

Today, there are Indian reservation casinos offering blackjack games in seventeen states: Arizona, California, Colorado, Connecticut, Indiana, Iowa, Kansas, Michigan, Minnesota, New Mexico, New York, North Carolina, North Dakota, Oregon, South Dakota, Washington, and Wisconsin.

Where Atlantic City had failed to generate the spread of casino gambling in the U.S., and in fact had hindered the growth of the gaming industry, the Indians had succeeded. Other communities could ignore the Atlantic City fiasco in their attempts to legalize gambling and point to the Indians' successes. It was possible for a casino operation to restore a community, generate income for thousands of local residents, build neighborhoods, and reverse trends of poverty and hopelessness.

The Cowboys Challenge the Indians

Seeing the huge profits the Indian casinos were generating, many state lawmakers around the country started asking themselves why they couldn't just license non-Indian casinos in their states. What it really boiled down to was that businesses on Indian reservations were not subject to the same state tax laws that private enterprises within a state were subject to. Except by way of special negotiated "compacts" allowed by the federal government, the states could not profit from the Indians' gambling winnings.

The casino gambling industry suddenly found friends within various state governments. It started out slowly, as if the waters had to be tested by first just dipping a toe, but it soon turned into a nationwide pool party. Come on in! The water's fine!

In 1988, just one year after the feds had passed the IGRA, Deadwood, South Dakota legalized blackjack in bars, but with a $5 maximum bet. Card counters did not rush the town, but locals and tourists were happy with the new law.

FAST FUN IN PHOENIX

Also in 1988, "social gambling" was legalized in Arizona, and dozens of bars in Phoenix and Tucson opened blackjack and crap tables for the public to use. The Arizona law was meant to help keep the locals at home, not turn the state into a gambling mecca. Because the state was literally next door to Nevada, every weekend tens of thousands of Arizonans piled into their vans and headed for a weekend of gambling in Las Vegas or Laughlin. The town of Laughlin, in fact, seventy-five miles from Las Vegas, and about one minute from Arizona, was built for the sole purpose of extracting gambling dollars from the residents of that state. Built on the banks of the Colorado River across from Bullhead City, Arizona where no Nevada town had even existed, a Nevada entrepreneur named Don Laughlin bought a chunk of land, built a casino, got the new "town" named after himself, and soon had competition from nine other casinos, including some of the biggest Vegas and Reno properties—Harrah's, the Hilton, the Ramada Hotel, and the Mandalay group. The Arizona lawmakers felt that most of the state's citizens who were hopping over to Nevada every weekend were just low-stakes casual gamblers who wanted to play a little blackjack or shoot some dice. No big deal. Why not allow them to stay right here at home and gamble in the local bars and night clubs? Why should all our citizens' entertainment dollars be leaving the state every weekend?

So, with little fanfare, "social gambling" was legalized. No minimum or maximum betting limits were placed on the games, as these were intended to be "friendly social games" run by the players themselves. In fact, the bars and night clubs were forbidden from banking the games or even from taking a percentage on the games. Furthermore, to keep these games "friendly," the players themselves would supply their own cards and dice, deal the games themselves, and set their own rules and regulations. All the club owners could do was supply the tables and sell drinks to their customers.

Yeah, right…

Cheaters of every stripe immediately invaded Arizona since there were no laws regulating gambling. What had been an exodus from Arizona to Nevada every weekend had literally been reversed. I visited Phoenix with Anthony Curtis and we found crooked games everywhere we looked. Marked cards, false shuffles, dealer/player collusion scams— and there were no laws against operating games like these! The games lasted for about a year before the state legislators revoked the law—too much bad press.

> Gamblers' sleights always impress magician-trained manipulators tremendously because, between ourselves, they are usually far slicker than anything a magician knows.
> —*Mickey MacDougall, Gamblers Don't Gamble*

It was many years before Arizona would try legalizing gambling again, and when they did, it was with some of the strictest regulations of any state, stricter than even Nevada or New Jersey.

BUT MORE CASINOS OPEN IN OTHER STATES

In 1990, Washington state legalized blackjack in card rooms, providing the deal passed equitably from player to player and a player/ dealer banked the game. Betting maximums were placed at $25. Colorado also legalized blackjack in bars in three small tourist towns with $5 maximum betting limits. And in 1991, Iowa legalized riverboat gambling with $5 maximum bets at blackjack.

Then it happened… To the dismay of the Iowa riverboat owners, nearby Illinois legalized riverboat gambling with $500 maximum bets allowed at blackjack. The fight for those gambling dollars was getting serious. Illinois was looking to tap the huge midwestern market—

Chicago, Cleveland, Milwaukee, Detroit, St. Louis, Indianapolis—the Midwest gamblers would no longer have to fly to Las Vegas or Atlantic City to play a little blackjack, or drive out into the woods to find an Indian casino.

In 1992, Louisiana and Mississippi both opened their first riverboat casinos and Mississippi approved "dockside" gambling to create even larger casinos on the gulf. Mississippi would allow bets of up to $1000, and Louisiana up to $500. The South was now up for grabs. Soon Missouri would join the competition.

In April of 1994, the Casino Windsor opened, just across the bridge from Detroit. It was immediately packed with gamblers day and night. The huge Detroit, Flint, and Toledo gambling market now had a more convenient gambling option than driving to Illinois or visiting Michigan's out-in-the-woods Indian casinos. Detroit's politicians got casinos legalized by arguing that the struggling city needed to keep their gambling dollars from going to Canada.

THE WACKINESS IN WINDSOR: HYLAND'S TEAM ARRESTED

Just a few weeks after the opening of the Casino Windsor, three members of the famous Tommy Hyland blackjack team were arrested for cheating in Canada. Despite the fact that they weren't cheating, but only using a legal shuffle-tracking strategy, they found themselves awaiting trial for more than a year.

Initially, the players were charged with using illegal "devices" to count the cards. The devices in question were strings of beads that the two women at the table were discovered to be wearing beneath their clothing. Then the prosecution discovered that there were no laws against players using devices—even computers—in the Canadian casinos! So, they formulated a new charge. They claimed that since the two women at the table were actually keeping track of the aces, then signaling the BP to increase his bets when they thought an ace was about to be dealt, this constituted "fraud," since the signals were secret and the women appeared to just be casually observing the game.

I was the expert witness for the defense, which involved explaining to the judge how card counting, shuffle tracking, and ace-sequencing work. After a four-day trial and months of waiting for the verdict, the players were found not guilty. Shuffle tracking and card counting were now officially legal in Canada. Many found it incredible that a casino would attempt to prosecute players for mentally beating the game. How could thinking be illegal? The case proved to be an embarrassment for both the casino and the provincial authorities that had pursued it. It again came down to attempting to prosecute players for thinking while they play, then using intelligence to make decisions. I spent a day and a half on the witness stand, and it was truly bizarre. The DA had no comprehension of blackjack, card counting, or gambling. He kept trying to get me to state that card counting and shuffle tracking would make the other players at the table lose more. He thought card counters were somehow winning money from the other players at the table, and not from the house!

But there was a reason why the casino was pursuing this case. The Casino Windsor had three Las Vegas casino conglomerates—Caesars, MGM, and Circus Circus—as financial partners, and these casinos were the instigators and pursuers of this trumped up cheating charge. They never would have attempted such a charge in Nevada or New Jersey, but they wanted to test the possibility of pursuing this type of case in a location where gambling law was not so established. So, they took the tact that because the players were using secret signals at the tables, this in itself constituted a conspiracy to defraud the casino. If they could get signaling defined as fraud in Canada, then it might be worth pursuing such a case in the U.S.

But it didn't work. This case, therefore, not only established that card counting and shuffle tracking were legal in Canada, but that it was also perfectly legal for players to work in teams and to use secret signals at the tables, provided that whatever they were doing to get their edge over the house was not in itself illegal.

OPTIONS, OPTIONS, OPTIONS

Nothing slowed down the expanding casino industry. Politicians and businessmen in every state were fighting over the right to open casinos, the jurisdictions where casinos would be allowed, the licensing procedures, and the taxes that the various states and local communities could collect from the casinos. It was all about the money, the money, the money.

Casinos opened in Kansas and Oregon, Massachusetts and Texas. Cruise ship casinos were running out of Florida and other eastern seaboard states.

While Windsor, Illinois, and Indiana were raking in the bucks from midwestern gamblers, it took five more years before the powers that be in Michigan could agree to casinos in downtown Detroit. The MGM Grand opened Detroit's first non-Indian casino in 1999. The joint was packed night and day from the moment it opened. It became and remains MGM's most profitable property, winning more money per square foot in its casinos annually than the MGM Grand in Las Vegas, the Mirage, or even Bellagio. By year's end, the MotorCity Casino, mostly owned by the Mandalay group, opened to overflowing crowds to provide competition for the MGM.

AS THE INDUSTRY GREW, SO DID THE OPPORTUNITIES TO EXPLOIT IT

Throughout the 1980s and '90s, many of the secrets of professional blackjack players were revealed to the casinos in books and periodicals aimed at players. Many hole-card techniques, shuffle-tracking techniques, and card-counting approaches for solo players, partners, and whole teams of players had been published. The casinos were using various countermeasures to deal with these problems. They were employing more decks and shuffling earlier to keep counters from obtaining the large advantages available from end-play. They were disallowing mid-shoe entry to foil table-hoppers and BP teams. They had "auto-peek" devices to eliminate some potential opportunities from hole-card strategies. They had developed more complex shuffles to foil the trackers. They now had extensive video camera surveillance, replacing the awkward mirror and catwalk system that had been used for decades. They kept photos of known professional players in the pits and surveillance rooms, either taken by their own cameras or provided by the Griffin agency. And they had formed informal surveillance information networks, or SINs, to inform other casinos in the area via emails and faxes of card counters discovered in their casino. Counters who were backed off at a casino often found that they could not play at any casino in town that night because of a SIN fax that had gone out on them.

It would seem that by this time it would be virtually impossible to count cards and get away with it in the casinos, but that was not the case. Because of the Indian Gaming Regulatory Act and the expansion of casino gambling on riverboats and everywhere else in the country, the base of experienced casino management personnel was not deep enough to keep up with the growth. Casino bosses and managers in Las Vegas and Reno were being lured with big bucks to points all over the country, considerably thinning the talent even in those traditional gambling towns. In many new casinos, bosses and managers with no casino experience whatsoever were getting jobs on the basis of their having managed department stores or business offices. Thousands of new dealers and hundreds of new floor persons, pit bosses, shift bosses, casino managers, and surveillance monitors had to come from somewhere. So, they came fresh out of high school or college, or in some cases from the local Radio Shack or K-Mart. They knew nothing about casinos or card counters or gambling. And it was their job to protect the games. This is where the cat-and-mouse game gets really fun.

The New Game Protectors

For more than half a century, game protection in Nevada had been simple and straightforward. Every casino had old-timers on staff who had seen it all, and many had done it all. Some worked in the pits as bosses, and some walked the catwalks and watched the games unseen from behind overhead mirrors. They looked for suspicious players, known professionals, and unusual moves at the tables. It was not easy to con an old con.

There was a big demand for experienced game protection personnel, but the talent pool was thin. This opened a whole new market for the high-tech whiz kids who believed that computers could do anything a human being could do, but faster, better, and cheaper.

In 1996, at the Fall Gaming Show in Las Vegas, a new surveillance product was unveiled to the industry. "Blackjack Survey Voice," developed by an entrepreneur named Oliver Schubert, was sold as a computer program that could identify card counters when an operator simply input the cards dealt, the players' bets, and their playing strategy decisions. The idea proved popular with casinos, and soon numerous similar competing products, with names like "BJ Tracker" and "Shuffle Guard," were on the market.

The job of game protection had shifted completely from the pit and floor personnel to the surveillance department. Pit bosses were no longer expected to watch the games so much as the money—the payouts, the buy-ins, and the cashouts. They were no longer expected to identify card counters so much as to check the IDs of suspected minors and call hosts to make sure any high rollers were taken care of. The surveillance agents, in fact, were often just as unskilled and inexperienced as the floor crews, but they had technology at their service—expensive camera systems, video recorders, and computer software.

For professional players, this was ideal. It was much easier to fool a computer than an experienced human being, especially when the computer was being monitored by a human being with little experience.

The new millennium rang in with Nevada-style casino gambling legal in more than two dozen states. Every province in Canada had legal casinos. There were casinos in Montreal, Vancouver, Winnipeg, Calgary, Edmonton, and even up in the Yukon Territory. Casinos had likewise spread throughout Western Europe and Asia, Africa and Australia, New Zealand, and the Caribbean. Throughout Eastern Europe—Russia, Czechoslovakia, and Yugoslavia—casino gambling became a huge industry, and here, as everywhere, blackjack was offered.

Card counters were no longer limited to choosing between Nevada and New Jersey. They had a whole world of games to choose from. But, as some players discovered the hard way, the danger of being cheated in a casino had grown just as rapidly as the industry had expanded.

SECTION TWO:

THE GAME, THE RULES, THE STRATEGIES

PLAYING THE GAME

> There's skill and there's luck and we hold both traits almost as dearly as life, liberty, and the pursuit of happiness.
>
> — *John L. Smith, On the Boulevard*

So, you're here from the planet Poindexter, and the weird human concept of money has been explained to you. You now realize that in order to buy enough rocket fuel for your long trip home, you're going to have to make some. You look at the options. Get a job at Starbucks. Rob a bank. Or play blackjack. Hmmm… This card game looks enticing.

Lucky for you, this is an easy game! For a human being, already familiar with the concept of a deck of cards, the game is even easier to learn. If you sit down at a casino blackjack table, having never played blackjack in your life, within twenty minutes you'll understand all of the rules, options, and procedures. This is not chess or backgammon. It's not even Old Maid or Crazy Eights. Blackjack is as simple as a card game can be. You place your wager, the cards are dealt, you've got to make one or two quick decisions, and bang—you either win or lose. That round is over.

Or, so it should be.

But the fact is I've seen literally hundreds—no, thousands—of errors by dealers through the years, and in most cases, the players do not catch the error. I've seen dealers overpay and underpay hands. I've seen dealers take the money from players whose hands have won, and I've seen dealers pay players who have lost. I've seen dealers explain rules and payouts incorrectly, and I've seen pit bosses observe all of these types of errors without stepping in to correct the dealers.

Since dealers are actually being paid to do this job, and have presumably been trained in all of the rules, payouts, and procedures, I must conclude that perhaps this game is not so easy. Since players have their money on the line, sometimes substantial amounts of money, and presumably care about whether or not they win or lose their wagers, but often do not catch these errors, perhaps this game is not so easy. And since the pit boss is there as the "protector" of the house bankroll, and is being paid a high salary to make sure the dealer does everything correctly, perhaps there is something about this "simple" game that makes it not so simple.

DEALER SLANG

Audition: to deal in front of a supervisor to try out for a job.

Break-in: a rookie dealer.

Clerk: a good, accurate dealer.

Lumpy: a poor, incompetent dealer.

The house makes its money at blackjack by having a small mathematical edge over the players—and a smaller edge than at any of the other casino games. Blackjack dealers are trained to deal and resolve the hands quickly. The speed of play, inevitably, leads to dealer errors.

THE DEAL

As you face the dealer, the seat at the far right of the table is referred to as first base. The seat at the far left is referred to as third base. Don't go looking for "second base" or "home plate." Wrong game! There's no shortstop either.

The table has five to seven betting spots for players (some cruise ships have nine spots!). There is usually a "betting limits" sign posted on the table, which states the minimum and maximum bets allowed. Some casinos also post the rule variations for their games on the table.

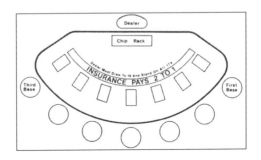

Blackjack is played with anywhere from one to eight decks of cards. If more than two decks are used, the shuffled cards are placed into a specially designed box on the table called a shoe, from which the dealer deals the cards.

Starting at first base, the dealer deals one card to each player, then one to himself, then a second card to each player, and then one more to himself. One of the dealer's cards is turned face up as his upcard.

DEALER SLANG
Anchor: the last player to play his hand.

THE BASIC STRUCTURE AND OBJECT OF THE GAME

You look at your two cards and total the value of your hand. Card denominations of 2, 3, 4, 5, 6, 7, 8, and 9 count exactly at their face value; that is, a deuce counts as two points. Card denominations of 10, jack, queen, and king each have a value of ten points. The ace counts as eleven, unless this would push your hand total over 21, in which case the ace counts as one.

Suits make no difference.

The object of the game is to get the total of your hand to beat the total of the dealer's hand without going over 21. You must play your hand before the dealer plays his and if the total of your hand goes over 21, you "bust"—an automatic loss, no matter what happens to the dealer's hand.

You have a variety of options on how to play your hand, depending on the posted rules—typically including hitting, standing, splitting a pair, or doubling down.

You may split a pair if your first two cards are the same value and you wish to convert them to two hands instead of one, in which case you add another bet so that each hand has the same bet amount.

Definitions:
Hit means to take a card.
Stand means to decline a card and stay with your current total.

To double down is to add an amount equal to your initial wager to your bet in return for agreeing to accept only one more card. This is done only when you believe you have an advantageous starting hand.

Most casinos allow doubling down only on your first two cards, and some have other restrictions. We will discuss all doubling options in detail later.

All players play against the dealer, who must follow house rules on whether to hit or stand on his total, and may not split or double down. If the player and dealer hands tie (both equal the same total), it is called a push, and neither wins nor loses.

Any two-card hand that consists of one ace and one ten-valued card is called a blackjack, or a natural, and is an automatic winner, paid off at the rate of $3 to every $2 bet, or 1.5 to 1. If both the dealer and player get a blackjack, it's a push. No money changes hands.

> IMPORTANT: In Nevada, many single-deck games now pay only 6 to 5 on a blackjack, and a few pay only 1 to 1. In the traditional game, naturals pay 3 to 2, and unless I specify that we are talking about a game where naturals pay less than 3 to 2, assume I am discussing the traditional game. We will discuss these other games in depth later, but let's start with the traditional game. Lower payouts on naturals greatly increase the house edge and cost players a lot of money.

"Hard" Hands and "Soft" Hands

Tip for Beginners:

Always look for the traditional game. The six-deck or eight-deck game with the full 3 to 2 payout is a better game for players than the single-deck game paying 6 to 5.

Any hand in which the ace can be counted as eleven, without busting, is a soft hand. Example: You hold an ace and a 6. This is a soft 17. Another example: You hold an ace, a 9, and a 7. This is a hard 17. In this case, if you counted the ace as eleven, your total would be 27—a bust. It's important that you be able to read your hand's value—hard or soft—quickly and effortlessly. If you are dealt a hand with five or six small cards, including a couple of aces, you will be confused. Notice I didn't say you may be confused; I said you will be confused. Just stop and take the time to total it up, one card at a time, counting each ace as one. If you finish with a total of 9, then you've also got a soft 19 if you total one of the aces as eleven. If you finish with a total of 13, then this is a hard 13. Your aces have to stay counted as one each.

BLACKJACK QUIZ #1

Here are some practice hands. See if you can tell which ones are hard hands, and which ones are soft hands, and what each total is. Example: The answer to Hand # 1 = Soft 17. Now you fill in the other seven answers. The correct answers are on the following page.

Hand # 1:	A♥ + 2♦ + 4♦ = ?
Hand # 2:	K♠ + 2♠ + A♦ = ?
Hand # 3:	A♥ + 7♠ + 5♠ = ?
Hand # 4:	A♣ + 3♠ + A♦ + 6♦ = ?
Hand # 5:	5♠ + 2♠ + 4♥ + A♣ = ?
Hand # 6:	8♦ + 6♣ + A♥ = ?
Hand # 7:	4♠ + A♦ + 5♥ = ?
Hand # 8:	A♥ + A♦ + A♣ + 2♠ + 2♥ + 2♦ = ?

ANSWERS TO QUIZ #1

Here are some practice hands. See if you can tell which ones are hard hands, and which ones are soft hands, and what each total is. Example: The answer to Hand # 1 = Soft 17. Now you fill in the other seven answers. The correct answers are on the following page.

Hand # 1:	A♥ + 2♦ + 4♦ = **SOFT 17**
Hand # 2:	K♠ + 2♠ + A♦ = **HARD 13**
Hand # 3:	A♥ + 7♠ + 5♠ = **HARD 13**
Hand # 4:	A♣ + 3♠ + A♦ + 6♦ = **SOFT 21**
Hand # 5:	5♠ + 2♠ + 4♥ + A♣ = **HARD 12**
Hand # 6:	8♦ + 6♣ + A♥ = **HARD 15**
Hand # 7:	4♠ + A♦ + 5♥ = **SOFT 20**
Hand # 8:	A♥ + A♦ + A♣ + 2♠ + 2♥ + 2♦ = **SOFT 19**

Before you go on, make sure you understand every answer, and that you are in agreement with every answer. If you disagree with any of them, you are making a mistake! The answers are correct. Reread the explanation of how you total and determine whether hands are hard or soft until you discover your error. These are the hands that players misplay most frequently, and that even dealers make mistakes on.

A big mistake beginners make is to let the dealer total their hand values for them. Most dealers are helpful, honest, and competent and will always give you the correct total, hard or soft. But this game is fast. The house makes its money by getting a piece of the action—casino slang for all the money bet—and dealers are first and foremost trained to keep the game going at a good clip.

Dealers get into a mechanical groove, on automatic pilot so to speak, and as with any tedious assembly-line job, their minds wander. Also, some dealers are crooked and some are just downright dumb. They can't add any better than you can. So take your time and do it yourself. Don't feel pressured to hurry up. That's your money on the table.

> "Dummy up and deal!" is the dealer's self-mocking work slogan. It means keep your mouth shut, your eyes on the layout and the cards flying. The game must go on, no matter what.
> — *David Spanier, Easy Money*

A crooked dealer will very quickly learn which players don't take the time to add up their hand values. They'll get a lot of opportunities to sweep your money off the table while you're letting them do all the adding.

> **Professional Gambler's Rule #1:**
> Never trust a human.

Playing the Hands

The dealer shuffles the deck(s), then offers the shuffled cards to be cut by a player. In all shoe games and in most hand-held games, a cut card is used. This is a colored plastic card that a player inserts into the deck to indicate the cut point, where the dealer then completes the cut. After the cut, the dealer burns a card. This means that he removes the top card from play.

Before any cards are dealt, all of the bets must be placed. The dealer then deals two cards to each player. In hand-held games, the players' cards are usually dealt facedown. In shoe games, the players' cards are usually dealt face up. If the players' cards are dealt face up, players are not allowed to touch their cards. If dealt facedown, each player must pick up his two cards in order to see his hand and make his playing decisions.

Card Handling Etiquette

Most casinos strictly enforce a rule that in games dealt facedown, where players must pick up the cards to play, the players may only touch their cards with one hand, and must leave their cards in sight at all times. This is to prevent cheating by players and is a legitimate concern. Players have been known to "muck" cards in and out of a game, switch cards with each other in order to make better hands, mark cards, bend cards, scratch cards—all kinds of sleight-of-hand moves designed to get them an advantage. The way the casinos see it, if you're willing to risk a prison sentence in order to beat them at a blackjack table, you're going to have to be crazy enough to try it one-handed! My advice... Don't even think about trying it!

Insurance

If the dealer shows an ace for his upcard, the first decision you will have to make is the insurance decision. Before you ever decide on whether you want to hit, stand, double down or split any pair, if the dealer shows an ace, he will ask, "Insurance?"

What does this mean?

To understand this option, you must know that if the dealer's first two cards are an ace and a ten-valued card—that is, a blackjack—he will automatically beat every player hand on the table except for a player blackjack, which would push his hand.

By offering insurance, the dealer is offering the players a side-bet that he has a natural—that is, that to go with his ace upcard, he has a ten-valued card in the hole. The dealer's unseen card is called his hole card. Most table layouts have a bar running across the length of them that says, "Insurance pays 2 to 1." If you are willing to bet that the dealer does have a ten-valued card under his ace, then you may place an amount of money equal to up to one-half of your original bet in the insurance space. That is, if you have a $10 bet on your hand, you may make an insurance wager of up to $5, but no more.

When you place an insurance bet, you are betting that the dealer has a blackjack. More specifically, you are simply betting that his hole card is a 10.

After all insurance bets are placed, the dealer usually peeks at his hole card. In some casinos, dealers wait until all of the players have acted on their hands before peeking at his hole card, but in most U.S. casinos, the dealer checks to see if he has a blackjack immediately after all insurance bets have been placed, and before the players make any decisions on their hands. This can be done either by bending up a corner of the hole card to visually look at the value (the old-fashioned method), or by inserting the corner of the card into a peeking device built into the tabletop (now more common). If the dealer has a natural, he immediately turns it up and proceeds to pay off insurance bets and to collect all original wagers placed by the players.

Since insurance bets are paid at the rate of 2 to 1, a player with a $10 original bet and a $5 insurance bet would lose his original $10 (since the dealer's natural is an automatic win), but would be paid $10 (2 to 1) for his $5 insurance bet. Thus, the player breaks even on this hand.

If a player has a blackjack when the dealer has an ace up, instead of offering insurance to this player, the dealer may offer even money. This means that, before the dealer checks his hole card, the player may accept an even money win for his blackjack. Many players do not understand that an offer of even money is identical to an offer of insurance when a player has a blackjack.

This is because a player who takes insurance when he has a blackjack will ultimately be paid even money whether or not the dealer has a 10 in the hole. Consider: You have a $10 bet on your blackjack hand and a $5 insurance bet. If the dealer does not have a 10 in the hole, then you will lose your $5 insurance bet. But you will win $15 (1.5 to 1) for your $10 blackjack hand. This is a net win of $10, or even money.

On the other hand, if the dealer does have a 10 in the hole, then you will win $10 (2 to 1) on your $5 insurance bet, but push on your $10 blackjack hand, again for a net win of $10—even money. So, if you have a blackjack, an offer of even money is the exact same thing as an offer of insurance.

Tip for All Players:

If you want to insure a blackjack, always turn your cards over and say, "Even money." Do not just place an insurance bet. Even though the results are identical in a traditional game, many dealers do not understand how to pay insurance on a blackjack. Some will just call it a push, and you will have to summon the pit boss to the table in order to get paid. Even dealers who have been dealing for many years will make this error. So, make it easy on yourself and the dealer. If you want to insure a blackjack, just say, "Even money."

Nevada casinos that now offer "Blackjack Pays 6 to 5" games allow insurance, but do not offer "even money" to players who have a blackjack. The reason for this is that "even money" is the correct net payout only when blackjacks pay 3 to 2. Imagine a 6 to 5 game where you have bet $10 and gotten a blackjack, only to look up to see that the dealer has an ace showing. If you take a $5 insurance bet and the dealer does not have a natural, you lose the insurance bet of $5. The dealer then pays you $12 (6 to 5) on your $10 blackjack bet, for a net gain of $7 ($12 - $5 = $7). If the house gave you even money ($10) instead for your insured blackjack, they'd be paying you an extra $3 for your blackjack on this 6 to 5 game.

What if you take insurance and the dealer does not have a natural?

If the dealer does not have a 10 in the hole, you lose the insurance bet. All insurance bets are immediately collected by the dealer and the play of the hands resumes, starting with the first base player and working clockwise.

Note: In some casinos, dealers do not check their hole cards or settle insurance bets until after the play of the hands. In these casinos, you will play out the hands first, then settle any insurance wagers. So, let's get into the play of the hands.

Hitting and Standing

The player's most common decision is whether to Hit or Stand. Again, hitting means to take another card. Standing is leaving your hand as is.

Example: A player holds a 5 and a 2 for a total of 7. Although I have seen players stand on a total of 7 in a casino blackjack game, there is no intelligent reason for doing this, as it is impossible to bust this hand with a hit. This is a hand that can only improve. So, the player signals the dealer for a hit. In a faceup game where players are not allowed to touch their cards, the player signals for a hit by scratching or tapping the tabletop with his finger next to his cards. In a facedown game where the player must pick up his first two cards, the player signals for a hit by scratching or tapping on the tabletop with the edge of his cards.

All casinos require players to use hand signals for their decisions. If you say, "Hit me," to the dealer, he will not deal you another card, but will instruct you to give the proper hand signal. Casinos require hand signals for their own protection. Since blackjack games are videotaped, a player who uses a hand signal to take a hit cannot later claim that he said "stand" and the dealer "misunderstood" him. Dealers are forbidden to follow verbal signals from players.

After a player signals for a hit, the dealer then deals the player another card face up on the table. The player may not touch this or any subsequent cards dealt to him. Let's say this card is a 10. The player may now decide to stand (not take any more cards) or hit again. The player may hit as many times as he chooses, so long as his total does not exceed 21.

A player signals he wants to stand by either waving his hand sideways (palm down) in a faceup game, or, in a facedown game, by simply sliding his original two cards facedown beneath or beside his wager. This is called "tucking" your hand.

Busting

If through hitting you achieve a total of hard 22 or greater, you have busted. Hand over. Wager lost. In a facedown game, if a player hits his hand to a total of more than 21, he should immediately lay his original two cards face up on the table. The dealer will collect the player's wager and sweep his cards off the table. In a faceup game, the player need do nothing as the dealer will see the bust, sometimes remarking, "Too many," as he collects the player's bet.

> One more time: if your hand has lots of cards and multiple aces, do not let the dealer take away your cards or your money until you have added up the total yourself. Always remember the Professional Gambler's Rule about humans.

Doubling Down

A player may also elect to double down on his first two cards. Again, this means that the player doubles the size of his initial bet, in exchange for giving up the right to receive more than one hit card. In the faceup game, this is signaled by placing an amount of money on the table beside the original bet that is equal to the amount of the original bet. In the facedown game, the player places his original two cards face up on the table behind his bet, then places an amount of money equal to his original bet beside it in his betting spot.

> Do not place the money on top of your original bet. Never touch your original bet. If you do, you will be warned by the dealer to keep your hands off your bet. There is a good reason for this rule. Players have been known to attempt to increase the original bet after seeing that they have a strong hand. This is cheating. If a dealer or pit boss sees you touching your initial bet, they will be suspicious of you because the casinos always adhere to the professional gamblers' rule about humans. They don't trust you any more than you trust them, and this is exactly as it should be.

A casino may have restrictions on when a player may double down. Some allow doubling down on any two original cards. Some restrict the doubling down option to hard totals of 9, 10, and 11 only, some to 10 and 11 only. There are even a few casinos that allow doubling down on more than two cards, but this rule variation is rare in the traditional (BJ Pays 3 to 2) game.

Many casinos allow players to "double for less" than the original wager, but none allow players to double down for more. It is very rare for a player to double for less, and usually only occurs when a player has insufficient chips to double down for the full amount of his bet.

Splitting, Resplitting, and Doubling After Splits

If a player holds two cards of the same value, he may split the pair into two separate hands. For example, let's say you are dealt two eights. You do not have to play this as a single hand totaling 16. By placing an amount of money equal to your original bet on the table, you may play each 8 as a separate hand. Again, in the faceup game, you do not touch the cards, but simply take this option by putting your money on the table. In the facedown game, you separate each of your cards face up on the table, and add the bet for the second hand beside one of the cards.

Most casinos allow any pair, other than a pair of aces, to be resplit up to four hands. If, for instance, you split a pair of eights, and receive another 8 on one of the hands, most casinos would allow you to resplit and play a third hand, or even a fourth hand, should yet another 8 fall.

But aces are handled differently. When you split aces, most casinos do not allow more than one additional card on each ace, nor do they allow you to resplit if you are dealt another ace on one of your split aces.

Also, if you receive a 10 on one of your split aces, this hand counts as 21, but is not a blackjack. You will not be paid 3 to 2 (or 6 to 5) on this hand, nor is it an automatic winner. It is simply a total of 21. The dealer will complete his hand, and if he totals 21 also, it is a push.

Most casinos allow you to split any ten-valued cards. For instance, you may split a jack and a king. Some casinos, however, require that only identical ten-valued cards, such as two kings, may be split. As with split aces, if you split tens and draw an ace on one of them, it is not counted as a blackjack, but merely as a total of 21.

Unless informed otherwise, assume the standard pair-splitting rules:

   1. Any pair may be split.

   2. Any pair, except aces, may be resplit.

   3. Split aces receive only one card each.

There are also many casinos that allow you to double down after splitting. For example, you split a pair of eights and on one of the hands you are dealt a 3 for a total of 11. Some casinos will allow you to double down on this hand if you so desire.

Surrender

In a few casinos, the player may surrender his first two cards and give up only half his bet. This means that the hand will not be played out. The dealer will collect the player's cards and exactly one half the amount the player had wagered. The other half of the wager is returned to the player.

Most casinos have no hand signal for surrender. This is the one verbal play allowed in most casinos. If you want to give up your hand, and half your bet, you simply say to the dealer, "I surrender." He will do the rest.

Surrender is not allowed if the dealer has a natural, in which case the player loses his whole bet. When the Atlantic City casinos first opened in the late 1970s, they did allow players to surrender before the dealer checked for a natural. This rule is called early surrender. It is not currently available in Atlantic City, but has occasionally been offered at other casinos. The original surrender rule is now often referred to as "late surrender." Some casinos in Europe and Asia allow early surrender versus a 10, but not against an ace.

No Hole Card

In some casinos, the dealer does not check his hole card until after all of the players complete their hands. In some casinos, the dealer does not even deal his hole card until the players' hands are completed. This means that the dealer may ultimately get a natural and beat the table. If a player had doubled down or split a pair, he would lose only his original bet in any U.S. or Canadian casino. But the European no-hole-card rule is different. In most European casinos, if the player doubles down or splits a pair, he will lose all double and/or split bets if the dealer gets a natural. In Europe, it is therefore more dangerous to double down or split pairs when the dealer has a 10 or an ace upcard.

Multi-Action

Some casinos use special table layouts that allow players to place up to three simultaneous bets. In these multi-action games, the player will play his hand once, but the dealer will play out his hand three times. The dealer will use the same upcard for all three of his hands, but will draw a new hole card, and new hit cards if necessary, against each successive player bet. In these games, all other blackjack rules and options remain the same.

The Dealer's Hand

The dealer completes his own hand only after all players have completed their hands. The dealer has no options. He is not allowed to double down or split any pair. He is not allowed to surrender. He must hit any hand that totals less than 17 and stand on any hand that totals 17 or more. The only exception to this is that some casinos require the dealer to hit a soft 17 (such as ace, 6). In these casinos, the dealer stands on hard 17 or over, and soft 18 or over.

In no casino does the dealer have any choice about how to play his hand. He must follow house rules. If, for example, you are playing in a faceup game and the dealer sees that you have stood on a total of 15, he does not automatically win if his total equals 16. He must hit his hand when his total is less than 17, and he will only win your bet if he does not bust. These are good rules for players. The fixed rules for the dealer's play of his hands, we will show, are the key to beating casino blackjack.

Uncommon Rules, Bonuses, and Side-Bets

There are some less common rules you may encounter that do not affect the game significantly. A few casinos offer bonuses for certain player hands, such as a holding of three sevens, or 6, 7, and 8 of the same suit.

A few casinos also offer various side-bet options. Over/Under, Royal Match, Lucky Ladies, Twenty-One Madness, and Super Sevens are among the most common. These types of options allow the player to place a separate bet, usually in a specially marked area of the table layout, and do not affect the play of the regular blackjack hand. We'll discuss these weird options later, and even tell you which ones can be beaten and how to beat them.

Many casinos today also offer games that look like blackjack, but are not blackjack, or at least, they are not the traditional game. Some casinos offer a blackjack variation called "Double Exposure" in which both of the dealer's first two cards are dealt face up, but the dealer wins all ties. This is a relatively rare game, requiring a different strategy from standard blackjack. In one common single-deck variation of blackjack, called "Super Fun 21," blackjacks pay even money, though there are many other doubling down, splitting, and surrendering options. In another game, called "Spanish 21," all of the tens have been removed from the eight-deck shoe. That is, the jacks, queens, and kings are all there, but no pip (or numeral) tens. Like Super Fun 21, this game also allows more options than the traditional game. We will describe these games in more detail later, but for now, let's stick with the traditional game.

> **Professional Gambler's Rule #2:**
> Information is money. More information is more money.

Does It Matter Where You Sit?

For professional players, seating position is often important and sometimes crucial. For card counters in single-deck games, the third base seat is quite a bit more advantageous because the counter will be able to see and count more cards before playing his hand. In faceup shoe games, it's much less important, but third base still has a bit more value for counters.

To determine the effect of seating position on basic strategy players who were not counting cards, I ran computer simulations of fifty million hands with seven players at the table. The sims showed that seating position has no effect whatsoever, regardless of the number of decks in play. So, unless you're counting cards, or using some other professional technique to get an edge, don't worry about where you sit.

But here's a weird fact. Some years back people started peddling bogus blackjack systems based on the "non-random" shuffles used in casinos. They claimed that these poor shuffles tended to "clump" the high cards with high cards, and low cards with low cards, and that this effect was very detrimental to the players—unless they used a special "trend" system that took this clumping effect into account.

To evaluate these claims, in 1987 I ran computer simulations of blackjack games with non-random casino-style shuffles. The poor shuffles had no effect on the players' results. So, I tested worse shuffles. Finally, I tested a shoe game in which the dealer did not shuffle the cards at all! He just took the cards from the discard tray and started dealing. This produced some very strange results!

PLAYING THE
GAME RIGHT

But it soon became quite clear that while losers flourished everywhere, winners were a rare and reticent breed with preferences for camouflage and anonymity.

— *Jon Bradshaw, Fast Company*

Thirty years ago I heard there was this card game that a person could play in the casinos, and make a living at it. That sounded like a great way of life to me.

But I was skeptical. I had a lot of questions.

If these "card counting" systems really worked, what made them work?

How well did they work? How much money could I really make?

And if these systems worked, why did they even exist? Why didn't the casinos just change the rules so no one could beat the games anymore?

I wasn't looking for some fly-by-night "system." There are a lot of con artists out there who are more than happy to sell someone a "guaranteed" scheme for how to make a million bucks. But I'm a skeptic. If someone tells me a certain strategy will win money in a casino, I want to know why it will win or I'm not interested. And he'd better have a simple, logical explanation. If I need a degree in statistics to comprehend a strategy, I'm not buying it.

And then, assuming you can convince me that a gambling system works, as far as I'm concerned, that just means it works on paper. Can I really go into casinos day after day, week after week, year after year, and just keep walking out with their money?

How could this situation ever have developed in the first place?

Casinos are in the business of extracting money from players. They offer games that are proven to keep their chandeliers lit and their owners swimming in champagne. Am I supposed to believe that Donald Trump is just a dummy that got lucky?

THE BASIC STRATEGY

Contrary to what many gamblers may think, blackjack is not just a guessing game. Most casino games are guessing games. But with any blackjack hand there is a correct strategy and an incorrect strategy. Basic strategy is the correct strategy. The correct strategy is the mathematically optimal strategy—that is, it will maximize your wins and minimize your losses on each hand over time.

> **Definition:**
>
> The mathematically optimal set of rules for playing each blackjack hand is called Basic Strategy.

You may have noticed that many other popular card games have no basic strategy. There is, for example, no basic strategy for poker. A poker player plays his hands according to whether or not he thinks his opponent is actually holding a strong hand or may be bluffing, and whether he himself is holding a strong hand or may want to attempt a bluff.

A basic strategy cannot exist for any card game as long as your opponent can make decisions, whether those decisions are good or bad, on how to play his hand. For hundreds of years, there was no basic strategy for blackjack because it was not a casino game where the dealer had to show one card and play his hand according to house rules. Instead, it was more of a poker-style game where both of the dealer's cards were hidden, the dealer could play his hand however he wanted, and players could attempt to bluff the dealer with their own play.

When the American casinos changed the rules of twenty-one to expose one of the dealer's cards and require the dealer to adhere to a strict hit/stand strategy, an important thing happened. They fundamentally changed the game from a poker-style game based more on psychology, to a purely mathematical game—as far as the player's strategy was concerned.

PLAYING THE GAME RIGHT

Why Basic Strategy Works... The "Odds"

For our purposes in this chapter, we're going to start with an assumption that today's dealers are dealing an honest game. No sleight-of-hand, no chicanery. We're not going to forget the First Rule of Professional Gamblers, but we're going to momentarily disregard it so that we can deal with the logic of the game, and reveal the basic strategy that will kill most of the house's mathematical edge. The fact is that most of the games you find in casinos these days are dealt honestly, and if you bump into a game that's not on the level, you're not even going to try to beat it. We'll discuss the suspicious telltale signs of a crooked game later so you know when to make a quick exit.

For the honestly dealt game, mathematicians—using high speed computers—have analyzed every possible hand you might hold versus every possible dealer upcard to devise the correct basic strategy for the game. One thing that likely shocked some of the first mathematicians to do these computer analyses was that a nearly perfect basic strategy had actually already been figured out and published by four GIs who had desk jobs and a lot of time on their hands in the mid-1950s. They had no computers, but they'd spent three years using old-fashioned mechanical adding machines to run through all of the possible outcomes of the hands dealt. This may have been the best value Uncle Sam ever obtained from four GIs' salaries!

We also know that some pretty good approximations of correct basic strategy had been figured out by various professional gamblers in Nevada years before computers came on the scene. These guys figured out the strategy by dealing hands to themselves on their kitchen tables. Thousands, tens of thousands, even hundreds of thousands of hands were required for some decisions. These guys, like most professional gamblers ever since, never published their strategies because they were pros. Blackjack was their livelihood, and they'd spent hundreds of hours figuring it out. Why would they tell anyone else what they knew?

One thing that is certain is that the casinos did not know the proper strategy for the game, and neither did the players who had read the most highly regarded books on the subject. Many of the old Hoyle's guides advised players to always stand on totals of 15 or 16, no matter what the dealer's upcard, to split tens and never split nines, and to stand on soft 17. The "smart" players of the time, meaning those who had read one of these books on gambling by one of these reputable authorities, typically made all kinds of plays that we know today to be very costly.

Many people don't get the logic of basic strategy. Let me give an example. When my hand totals 14, and the dealer shows a 10 upcard, basic strategy says to hit. That is the mathematically correct play. Sometimes you will hit that 14 and draw an 8, 9, or 10 and bust. Then the dealer will turn over his hole card, a 6, and you will realize that if you would have stood on your 14, the dealer would have had to hit his total of 16, and he would have busted with that 10. So, by making the "mathematically correct" play, you lost a hand you would have won if you had violated basic strategy.

Some players will argue that there really isn't a basic strategy that is always correct. Blackjack, they insist, is a guessing game.

To understand basic strategy, you have to start thinking like a professional gambler, and that means you have to understand the concept of "the odds."

Let me explain the logic of basic strategy using a different example that illustrates how the mathematics of probability and statistics works. Let's say I have a jar with one hundred marbles in it. Fifty of the marbles are white and fifty are black. You must reach in blindfolded and pull out one marble, but before you do so, you must place a $1 bet on whether that marble you pull out will be white or black. If you pull out the color you guessed, you win $1; if not, you lose $1.

Is this a guessing game?

Absolutely. How could you possibly know which color marble you're going to pull out in advance? If you win, it's just good luck, and if you lose, it's bad luck.

But what if you know that ninety of those marbles are black, and only ten marbles are white? Now, would you bet on black or white before you draw? Any intelligent person would bet on black. It is possible, of course, to pull out a white marble, but you're much less likely to pull out a white marble than a black one. This may be a guessing game, and you could still lose $1 if you do happen to pull out a white marble, but if you bet on black, the odds are in your favor.

A professional gambler makes his living by always thinking in terms of "the odds," and only betting when the odds are in his favor. With this bet, the gambler would bet on black because the odds are 9 to 1 in his favor. If you bet on white, the odds are 9 to 1 against you.

So, getting back to that total of 14 you had when the dealer showed a 10 upcard, you may lose if you take a hit, but the odds are against you if you stand.

If you make your decisions by playing your hunches, you may win some hands, but you will lose more hands in the long run. There is only one correct decision for any given play, and that decision is based strictly on the math. Whether or not you should hit or stand, or double down or split a pair, depends on what the laws of probability show your expectation to be for each of these possibilities. Depending on the rules and the number of decks in use, basic strategy will usually cut the house edge to no more than about 0.5 percent over you. This makes blackjack the least disadvantageous game in the casino, even if you are not a card counter.

Corky Beats the Odds

In October (2004), my buddy Corky, a pro blackjack player who also bets on sports, noticed that a Vegas Strip sports book was giving 50 to 1 against the Boston Red Sox winning the World Series. The Red Sox, in fact, were currently 0-3 against the Yankees in the playoffs, and their chances of winning the American League pennant—let alone the World Series—looked dismal. But, Corky knew that those 50 to 1 odds were way off. Even with Boston down 0-3, he figured it should be 20 to 1 or even 25 to 1 against Boston, but not 50 to 1. Gamblers call this an overlay. The house is "laying" odds way "over" the actual probability of an event. The gambling public, a superstitious lot, had probably pushed the odds against Boston this high due to Boston's legendary "curse."

Corky was not superstitious and he knew an overlay when he saw one. He figured all the wiseguys in town would be jumping on this bet, and the odds would come back down to reality within a few hours. So he went to the betting window and plunked down $1000 on Boston to win the Series. He also bet another $100 for his girlfriend, figuring she'd want a piece of this bet.

As it turned out, his girlfriend wanted no piece of it, so he kept the extra $100 bet for himself. That evening, in a different casino sports book, he saw that this book was also offering 50 to 1 odds on Boston winning the Series. He went and placed another $1000 bet on the Sox, and now had $2100 bet with a 50 to 1 payoff if the Red Sox won the World Series.

The Red Sox came through, and Corky's $2100 bets paid him $105,000.

What is a Half-Percent Advantage in Dollars and Cents?

In dollars and cents, when the house has a 0.5 percent advantage over you, that means the casino will win, on average, fifty cents for every $100 you bet. Let's compare this to some other popular casino games.

GAME	AVG. CASINO WIN PER $100 BET
Blackjack (w/basic strategy)	.50
Baccarat (banker)	1.06
Craps (pass line)	1.41
Dollar Slots (w/97% Payback)	3.00
Three-Card Poker (ante bet w/best strategy)	3.37
Let It Ride (w/best strategy)	3.51
Caribbean Stud Poker (w/best strategy)	5.22
Roulette (double-0 wheel)	5.26
Keno	25.00

This is somewhat of an oversimplification, but you can see that blackjack, with accurate basic strategy, is by far the least costly casino game to play. It also happens to be a game where you can turn the odds to your favor by learning to count cards. But that comes later.

How Basic Strategy Works... The Logic

Let's forget about marbles and get back to cards. Now, I'm not asking you to take out a pencil and paper and start analyzing every hand for yourself based on this logic; you'll end up devising a strategy that will look like the strategies that were being published by the "experts" before those four GIs came along and took the time to do it right. Here's how it works.

In a fifty-two-card deck there are sixteen ten-valued cards: four tens, four jacks, four queens, and four kings. For purposes of simplification, when I refer to a card as a "10" or "X," it should be understood to mean any 10, jack, queen, or king. Every other denomination has only four cards, one of each suit. You are four times more likely to pull a 10 out of the deck than, say, a deuce. Because of this, when the dealer's upcard is high—7, 8, 9, X, or A—he has a greater likelihood of finishing with a strong total than when his upcard is low—2, 3, 4, 5, or 6.

Thus, if the dealer's upcard is a 7, 8, 9, X, or A, and you are holding a stiff—any hand totaling 12 through 16—you would hit. When the dealer's hand indicates strength, you do not want to stand with a weak hand. Even though you are often more likely to bust than to make a pat hand when you hit a stiff, you will lose more money in the long run if you stand on these weak hands when the dealer shows strength. To save money in the long run, you have to hit to give yourself a chance to make a more competitive hand.

Here's how many players think: If I hit this 14, I risk busting my hand right here and now. But maybe the dealer has a 6 in the hole. If I don't take a hit, my hand still has a chance. Maybe the dealer's hand will bust.

Every player is afraid that he will be responsible for his own loss. But that 14 you are holding is already in dire jeopardy when the dealer shows a 10 up. You must fight for the hand's survival by taking the hit, giving it a chance of becoming a stronger hand against that 10. With a 14 against a 10, you must fight to the death.

> ### Tip for Beginners:
> The most common mistake beginners make is to stand too often on their stiff hands (12, 13, 14, 15, and 16). Players are naturally afraid to hit these hands because every one of them could bust (make a total of 22 or more) with a single hit. But when the dealer has a high card (7, 8, 9, 10, or ace) showing, your best odds of winning come from hitting and giving yourself a chance of making a better total.

On the other hand, if the dealer's upcard is 2, 3, 4, 5, or 6, and you are holding a stiff hand, you should stand. Since the dealer must hit his stiff hands, and chance busting even when you are stiff, hitting your weak hands is not advantageous against these weak upcards.

By the same token, if the dealer's upcard indicates he may be stiff, it is also more advantageous for the player to double down or split pairs, thereby getting more money onto the table when the dealer has a high chance of busting. You double down and split pairs less often when the dealer shows a strong upcard.

This is the basic logic of casino blackjack. There are exceptions to these guidelines, as the actual basic strategy decision for any given hand is determined by working out all of the mathematical probabilities. But if you just consider this logic when studying the basic strategy charts, the pattern will become clear to

> ### Tip for Beginners:
> Some beginners think the best way to play is to play the same way the dealer plays: Hit all sixteens and stand on all seventeens. This is not true. The object of the game is not to make a hand as close to 21 as possible, but to beat the dealer. Often the best way to do this is to stand with a low total, sometimes as low as 12

you and it should not be too difficult to memorize.

The False Logic

I'm a great believer in learning from mistakes. These are often the most painful lessons, but they're lessons we remember. If these are mistakes that others have made, then it was their pain, not ours, and we get the lesson for free. If we study what others did wrong, and why they came to their false conclusions, we won't be tempted to think the same way.

Let's look at how some of the early gambling authorities went wrong in their blackjack logic. The bad advice on blackjack strategy in the early gambling books all resulted from the authors' failure to take enough information into account. They had the basic logic, but they didn't carry it far enough. The smartest writers back then were those who admitted that they just didn't know the best strategy. The dumb ones were the ones who said, "I've figured it out. Here's how to play."

Let's take a simple example. The player has a hard 16 versus a dealer's 10 up.

We know today that it is proper basic strategy to hit a total of 16 versus a dealer 10. But the early authorities thought: Any 6, 7, 8, 9, 10, jack, queen, or king will bust the hand, and that's eight out of the thirteen possible hit cards. No brainer. Stand, because you'll bust eight out of thirteen times.

So why is this wrong?

This thinking fails to consider the probability that our 16 is already beaten. We have to take our logic just a bit further and realize that if the dealer has any 7, 8, 9, 10, jack, queen, or king beneath his upcard, our bet on that 16 is already a goner! So, with seven out of the thirteen possible hole cards, we're already dead. Furthermore, if the dealer has a 2, 3, 4, 5, or 6 beneath his 10, he's not dead yet. He has to take a hit and he gets another shot to beat our 16.

And here's where the logic gets really screwy. If the dealer has a 2 beneath his 10 up, then he'll only bust it on the next card drawn if he hits his 12 total with a 10 (four out of thirteen cards). If he hits with a 5, 6, 7, 8, or 9 (five out of the thirteen cards), he beats our 16. With an ace, 2, 3, or 4 hit, he gets yet another chance to beat us.

Now, try going through this process for every possible combination of cards that could be drawn.

Wait a minute! Before you do that, I should mention that there are 145 different ways you can have a total of hard 16 in a single-deck game. These range from the most common ways to hold this hand—like a two-card 9-7 or X-6— to some highly unlikely hands like 3, 3, 2, 2, 2, A, A, A, A. To accurately apply the logic here, you'll have to consider the hit/stand possibilities of every possible hand, assuming with each specific total of 16 that the cards in your hand have already been removed from the deck. Now consider that you must go through this process with all ten different dealer upcards, and with every player hand total, for all of the hit/stand, double down and pair-split decisions.

Are you starting to appreciate how much work the pros went through back in the days before computers just to figure out basic strategy? And how valuable it was in the decades before it was finally published?

And by the way, with that total of 16 versus 10, although the correct overall basic strategy play is to hit, did you know that if your total of 16 is composed of three or more cards, the correct basic

> **Professional Gambler's Rule #3:**
> When you learn something no one else knows, keep it to yourself.

strategy is actually to stand? Do you know why? It's logical when you consider the possibilities. With a two-card 16, your hand is composed of either X-6 or 9-7. Every one of these cards (X, 9, 7, or 6) would bust your hand if you received it for a hit card on your hard 16. So, having two of these cards in your hand means that you have removed two of the possible bust cards from the deck. This makes it less likely for you to bust and more favorable for you to hit. And that's the basic strategy play. But if you have a total of 16 comprised of three or more cards, then your hand is more likely to contain low cards. Not only have you not removed two cards from the deck that could bust your hand, but you have probably removed one or more cards that could have helped your hand. Therefore, with a three-card 16, you should stand.

The basic strategy decision on 16 versus 10 is so close that no one really knew for sure how to play it until computers figured out all of the possibilities. Here's a better rule for perfectionists that will almost always be correct: if you have a two-card 16, hit. If you have a three-or-more-card 16, stand if any one of your cards is a 4 or 5.

It's also pretty easy to see why people believed some of the other common basic strategy errors before computers were around to do the analysis. Why does simple "logic" tell you to split tens against low cards? Because more than half of the deck—any 7, 8, 9, 10, jack, queen, or king—would make each 10 into a pat hand. Why not split nines? Because less than half of the deck will make a 9 into a pat hand. Why stand on all fifteens? Because more than half the deck will bust you, etc., etc. But all of these "logical" conclusions are wrong. In order to find the correct answer, you have to consider every possible way of making the hand, and every possible series of hits for both the player and the dealer.

In any case, here are complete basic strategy charts to save you a lot of math.

> **Tip for Beginners:**
>
> Don't alter your strategy based on prior results. If you keep busting your stiffs when basic strategy tells you to hit, don't start standing on these bad totals. Never try to second-guess the mathematics of the game. Trust that basic strategy is the best strategy in the long run, and stick to it.

BASIC STRATEGY FOR ANY NUMBER OF DECKS

	2	3	4	5	6	7	8	9	X	A
HIT / STAND										
17	S	S	S	S	S	S	S	S	S	S
16	S	S	S	S	S	H	H	H	H	H
15	S	S	S	S	S	H	H	H	H	H
14	S	S	S	S	S	H	H	H	H	H
13	S	S	S	S	S	H	H	H	H	H
12	H	H	S	S	S	H	H	H	H	H
A7	S	S	S	S	S	S	S	H	H	H
DOUBLE DOWN										
11	D	D	D	D	D	D	D	D	D	D
10	D	D	D	D	D	D	D	D		
9		D	D	D	D					
A7		D	D	D	D					
A6		D	D	D	D					
A5			D	D	D					
A4			D	D	D					
A3				D	D					
A2				D	D					

BASIC STRATEGY FOR ANY NUMBER OF DECKS (continued)										
	2	**3**	**4**	**5**	**6**	**7**	**8**	**9**	**X**	**A**
PAIR SPLITS—NO DOUBLE AFTER SPLITs										
AA	$	$	$	$	$	$	$	$	$	$
99	$	$	$	$	$		$	$		
88	$	$	$	$	$	$	$	$	$	$
77	$	$	$	$	$	$				
66		$	$	$	$					
33		$	$	$	$					
22		$	$	$	$					
WITH DOUBLE AFTER SPLITS										
AA	$	$	$	$	$	$	$	$	$	$
99	$	$	$	$	$		$	$		
88	$	$	$	$	$	$	$	$	$	$
77	$	$	$	$	$	$				
66	$	$	$	$	$					
44				$	$					
33	$	$	$	$	$	$				
22	$	$	$	$	$	$				
SURRENDER (late)										
16								¢	¢	¢
15									¢	
INSURANCE: NEVER										

S = Stand   H = Hit   D = Double Down $ = Split   ¢ = Surrender

This generic basic strategy may be used for any game. See the Appendix for comprehensive basic strategy variations according to all rule variations and specific number of decks in play.

Using the Basic Strategy Chart

The charts are straightforward. The player's hands are listed vertically down the left side. The dealer's upcards are listed horizontally along the top. Thus, if you hold a hand totaling 14 versus a dealer 6, you can see the correct basic strategy decision is "S," or stand. With a total of 14 versus a dealer 7, since "S" is not indicated, you would hit. Note: If your total of 14 is made up of a pair of sevens, you must consult the pair splitting chart first. You can see that with a pair of sevens versus either a dealer 6 or 7, you would split your sevens.

Do not attempt to learn all aspects of basic strategy at once. Regardless of the number of decks in play or the rule variations, basic strategy for any game is essentially the same. Since few casinos offer the surrender option, you don't need to learn the surrender strategy unless you intend to play in those casinos.

> **Tip for Beginners:**
>
> The first card you should look at when you get your hand is the dealer's upcard. You can't make a decision on how to play your hand until you know what you're up against.

The basic strategy chart presented here is a "generic" basic strategy, good for any set of rules and any number of decks. Actually, as these conditions change, some of the basic strategy decisions also change. Usually, these changes are for borderline decisions, and do not significantly change the amount of money you will win or lose over time. I know a number of high-stakes pros who know only one basic strategy and ignore the fine changes caused by rule variations and the number of decks in play. In the Appendix, a complete basic strategy, including all the changes according to rule and deck variations, is presented. For now, I advise learning this composite basic strategy, which may be all you will ever need.

Two pair-splitting tables are presented here. I use the symbol "$" to denote a basic strategy pair split decision. The first pair-split table assumes that you are not allowed to double down after splitting a pair. In some casinos, including many Las Vegas Strip casinos and all Atlantic City casinos, players are allowed to double down after pair splits. If you plan to play primarily in these casinos, study the second table. The only differences between these tables are for splitting twos, threes, fours, and sixes. If you'll be playing in games with both rules, just learn the first table, then brush up on the few differences prior to playing in the double-after-split (DAS) casinos.

> **Tip for Beginners:**
>
> The first rules to learn about pair splits are the ALWAYS and the NEVERS. ALWAYS split aces and eights. NEVER split fours, fives, or tens.

The Order of Decisions

Use the basic strategy chart in this order:

1. If surrender is allowed, this takes priority over any other decisions. If basic strategy calls for surrender, throw in the hand.

2. If you have a pair, determine whether or not basic strategy calls for a split.

3. If you have a possible double down hand, this play takes priority over hitting or standing. For example, in Las Vegas and Atlantic City you may double down on any two cards. Thus, with a holding of A-7 (soft 18) versus a dealer 5, your basic strategy play, as per the chart, is to double down. In northern Nevada, where you may usually double down on 10 or 11 only, your correct play would be to stand.

4. After determining that you do not want to surrender, split a pair, or double down, consult the "Stand" chart. Always hit a hard total of 11 or below. Always stand on a hard total of 17 or higher. For all "stiff" hands, hard 12 through 16, consult the basic strategy chart. Always hit soft 17 (A-6) or below. Always stand on soft 19 (A-8) or higher. With a soft 18 (A-7), consult the chart.

How to Practice Basic Strategy

1. **Study the Charts**

   Start with the hard stand decisions. Observe the pattern of the decisions as they appear in the chart, close your eyes and visualize this pattern. Study the chart once more, then get out your pencil and paper. Reproduce the hard stand chart. Do this for each section of the chart separately. Do this until you have mastered the charts.

   Note that the only soft hand in the hit/stand chart is A-7 (soft 18). That's because basic strategy is to always hit soft 17 or less (unless doubling down against a dealer low card), and always stand on soft 19 or more. Soft 18 is the only soft hand where basic strategy differs according to the dealer's upcard.

2. Practice with Cards

Place an ace face up on a table to represent the dealer's upcard. Shuffle the rest of the cards, then deal two cards face up to yourself. Look at your two cards and the dealer's ace and make your basic strategy decision. Check the chart to see if you are correct. After you've double-checked your decision, deal another two cards to yourself. Don't bother to pick up your first hand. Just drop your next and all subsequent cards face up on top of the last cards dealt. Go through the entire deck (twenty-five hands), then change the dealer's upcard to a deuce, then to a 3, 4, 5, etc. You should be able to run through a full deck of player hands for all ten dealer upcards in less than half an hour. Every decision should be instantaneous. Strive for perfection.

> **Tip for Beginners:**
>
> Remember that a soft hand—which is any hand that contains an ace that can count as eleven without going over 21—can never bust with a single hit. Never stand on a hand of soft 17 or less. Always take a shot at improving your total.

To practice your pair-split decisions, which occur less frequently than other decisions, reverse the above exercise. Deal yourself a pair of aces, then run through the deck changing only the dealer's upcard. Then give yourself a pair of deuces, etc. Don't waste time with any exercise you don't need. Your basic strategy for splitting aces, for instance, is to always split them. You don't need to run through a whole deck of dealer upcards every day to practice this decision. Likewise, basic strategy tells you to always split eights, and never to split fours, fives, or tens. You will learn these decisions quickly. Most of your study and practice for pair-splitting decisions should go toward learning when to split twos, threes, sixes, sevens, and nines.

> If you learn to play basic strategy without counting cards, most casinos will have only a 0.5 percent edge over you. This means that in the long run, they will win only about fifty cents for every $100 you bet. The average blackjack player gives up four times this much to the house.

SIMPLIFIED BASIC STRATEGY

You can cut the house edge to about 1 percent by playing an approximate basic strategy that is much easier to learn. We can boil it down to just ten rules. Follow these rules:

1. Never take insurance.
2. If the dealer's upcard is 7, 8, 9, X, or A, hit until you get to hard 17 or more.
3. If the dealer's upcard is 2, 3, 4, 5, or 6, stand on all your stiffs (hard twelves through sixteens).
4. Hit all soft hands of soft 17 (A-6) and below.
5. Stand on soft 18 (A-7) or higher.
6. Double down on 10 and 11 versus any dealer up card from 2 through 9.
7. Always split aces and eights.
8. Never split fours, fives, or tens.
9. Split all other pairs—twos, threes, sixes, sevens, and nines—versus any dealer   upcard of 4, 5, or 6.
10. Surrender 16 versus 9, X, or A.

Note: In multi-action games, your basic strategy does not change. Always play every hand exactly as if it were the only hand on the table. Do not be afraid to hit your stiffs—a common multi-action error.

Even if you learn to count cards, you will play basic strategy on 80 percent or more of your hands. Basic strategy is your single most powerful weapon.

Insurance? Never!
(Well... Maybe Sometimes...)

You may have noticed that the basic strategy decision for insurance is never. Unless you are counting cards, insurance is always a bad bet. Why? The logic on this one is easy. Insurance is essentially a bet that the dealer has a 10 in the hole, and it pays 2 to 1. But the proportion of non-tens (aces, twos, threes, fours, fives, sixes, sevens, eights, and nines) to tens (tens, jacks, queens, and kings) in a deck is 9 to 4, and that's greater than 2 to 1. So, the odds are against you. Unless you've got ESP, in which case you don't need this book, ignore your hunches. Don't take insurance. You will, however, find a contrary argument in the very next chapter regarding taking insurance when you have a blackjack.

The Cost of Errors

Some basic strategy errors are very expensive. Some are not. The "Simplified Basic Strategy" on the previous page, in which the entire playing strategy is whittled down to ten simple rules, was devised by eliminating some of the borderline decisions that would not fit into the easy-to-remember guidelines. But let's look closer at the costs of various common types of strategy mistakes.

COST OF ERRORS		
ERROR	COST (IN $ PER $100 BET)	COST (IN $ PER HOUR)
Stand on 12 v. High Card (7 - A)	17.50	110.00
Stand on 13 v. High Card (7 - A)	14.50	95.00
Stand on 14 v. High Card (7 - A)	10.75	70.00
Stand on 15 v. High Card (7 - A)	7.50	50.00
Stand on 16 v. High Card (7 - A)	4.50	30.00
Stand on A-6 v. High Card (7 - A)	24.00	20.00
Stand on A-7 v. 9, X, or A	4.00	3.50
Hit 12 v. 4, 5, or 6	1.75	5.00
Hit 13 v. Low Card (2 - 6)	6.25	25.00
Hit 14 v. Low Card (2 - 6)	12.25	40.00
Hit 15 v. Low Card (2 - 6)	18.25	60.00
Hit 16 v. Low Card (2 - 6)	23.50	70.00
Not doubling on 11 v. Low Card (2 - 6)	29.00	55.00
Not doubling on 10 v. Low Card (2 - 6)	24.00	40.00
Splitting X-X v. Low Card (2 - 6)	20.25	75.00
Splitting X-X v. High Card (7 - A)	47.25	250.00
Not Splitting 8-8 v. 9, X, or A	5.25	1.50
Take "Even Money" on BJ	4.00	1.25
Insure a Hard 20	4.50	3.25
Insure Any Hand	3.50	28.00

Note: The actual cost of each error will vary according to exactly which high or low card the dealer shows

The cost per hour assumes that you play about one hundred hands per hour, at $100 bet per hand, and takes into account how frequently each type of hand comes up. A good illustration of how these costs can add up can be seen by looking at the three insurance errors at the bottom of the chart.

In the "Cost per $100 Bet" column, they are pretty close in cost, all running from $3.50 to $4.50. But look at the "Cost per Hour" column. If you always take even money on your blackjacks, it only costs you about $1.25 per hour if you are making $100 bets. That's because, even though the error costs you $4.00, you will only have a blackjack versus a dealer ace up about once every two and a half hours. But if you "Insure Any Hand," the hourly cost to you is $28.00. That's because the dealer will have an ace up about once every thirteen hands, and every thirteen hands you'll be paying that $3.50 cost.

The real cost of making errors must take into account both the cost per hand of each error, and the frequency with which each hand occurs.

The Costliest Common Mistake

These days, just about everyone knows that a player should hit 16 versus a dealer 10 upcard. But how bad of a mistake is it if a player stands? Not that bad, actually. If you have a $100 bet on the hand, the cost of standing as opposed to hitting is less than $1.

A much worse error—one you see all the time—is for a player to stand on a soft 17 (A-6) versus a dealer 10 up. Most players would probably see this as a very minor error. Not so. If you fail to hit your A-6, standing costs you more than $20 for every $100 you bet!

Why does this error cost so much more than standing on a hard 16? Because with any soft hand, you have a much better chance of improving. That hard 16 is a loser whether you hit or stand, and most of the time you hit, you will bust. You can't bust a soft hand. Even if you hit it with a 10, it still equals 17. Never stand on a soft 17 versus anything.

THE ODD TRUTH ABOUT "EVEN MONEY"

> Life is brief. It needs to be lived with every advantage.
>
> — *Gerry Spence, How to Argue and Win Every Time*

If you ask most dealers, pit bosses, and casual players, they'll tell you that you should always take "even money" when you have a blackjack and the dealer shows an ace up. The common wisdom is that it's the only bet in blackjack that you cannot lose.

But if you ask most experts on the game, authors of books on blackjack, or just weekend warrior, low-stakes card counters, they'll tell you, "Even money is a sucker bet."

Who is right?

That depends on a lot of factors. The mathematical logic of the game does not support the "experts" as much as they may think it does.

Let's answer the even money question once and for all. In order to find the answer, we have to look at a number of crucial factors in the equation. What is the actual dollar value of a blackjack? What is the value of even money to the casino? And what is the value of even money to the player, both pro and amateur?

THE VALUE OF A BLACKJACK

Let's say I've got a $1000 bet on the table when I'm dealt a blackjack. What is it worth? What is the dollar value? If your answer is $1500, since blackjacks pay 3 to 2, that's pretty close to the right answer, but not quite.

If we specify that the dealer has an upcard of 2, 3, 4, 5, 6, 7, 8, or 9, then you're right. My $1000 blackjack is worth exactly $1500.

But if the dealer has a 10 or an ace showing, then my blackjack is worth less than $1500, because if it turns out that the dealer also has a blackjack, the hand is a push and the value to me goes down to zero.

When the Dealer Has a 10 Up

So, what is my blackjack worth when the dealer shows a 10? As long as he doesn't have an ace beneath his 10, my $1000 blackjack is worth $1500. But when that ace is there, the value to me is zero. I won't lose my $1000, but I also win nothing.

How often will the dealer have an ace beneath his 10? Since one out of thirteen cards in a full deck is an ace, then one-thirteenth of my blackjacks are worth $0, and twelve-thirteenths are worth $1500.

What is one-thirteenth of $1500? According to my calculator, it's about $115.

And how does this affect the overall dollar value of my blackjack when the dealer shows a 10 up? The math is pretty simple:

$$\$1500 - \$115 = \$1385$$

When the dealer has a 10 up, my blackjack is not worth $1500, but $1385. In fact, it will usually pay me the full $1500—but when that ace is in the hole, I get nothing, and that reduces the overall value to $1385. My average return is $1385.

When the Dealer Has an Ace Up

Now, what is my $1000 blackjack worth when the dealer shows an ace? Following the same logic as above, we know that it's not worth $1500. We must account for those times when the dealer has a 10 beneath his ace. How often does this occur?

Since four of every thirteen cards in a deck is a ten-valued card, then on four-thirteenths of the blackjacks I get when the dealer shows an ace, I get paid zero. How does this affect the overall dollar value of the hand?

Since we've already calculated that one-thirteenth of $1500 = $115, then four times this amount is:

$$4 \times \$115 = \$460$$

The dollar value of my blackjack when the dealer shows an ace has been reduced to:

$$\$1500 - \$460 = \$1040$$

Now we have the math we need to answer the even money question.

More than two-thirds of the time (or nine-thirteenths of the time to be exact), I will be paid a full $1500 for the hand. But almost one-third (or four-thirteenths) of the time, the dealer will have a 10 beneath his ace and I'll get zip.

> When I have been dealt a blackjack with a $1000 bet on the table, and the dealer shows an ace upcard, the actual dollar value of my blackjack is $1040.

Now, knowing these facts, let's get back to the even money proposition…

I have been dealt a blackjack, and the dealer has an ace upcard. So, I'm sitting there looking at a hand that I know has a $1040 value, when the dealer says, "I'll give you $1000 for that hand." He is, in essence, trying to "buy" my hand for the house at a $40 discount. Should I sell?

How the Casino Thinks of Even Money

Even money is a good value for the house. They know that on almost one-third of the $1000 blackjacks I get when the dealer shows an ace, they'll be paying me $1000 on a hand for which I should be paid nothing because the dealer's blackjack will push. On the other hand, on more than two-thirds of those blackjacks the dealer doesn't have a 10 in the hole, and they're saving $500 by not giving me the full 3 to 2 payout for my blackjack. In the long run, for every player who takes even money with a $1000 bet, the house makes $40, or 4 percent. Over the course of a day, a casino will make a lot of money from players who are willing to sell their blackjacks at a 4 percent discount.

How the Professional Player Thinks of Even Money

The pro gambler knows that when he has been dealt a $1000 blackjack and the dealer shows an ace up—and I am assuming here that he has no other information about the probability of a dealer having a 10 in the hole—his hand has a dollar value of $1040.

Most of the time, most pros will think, "I have a hand here that has a value of $1040. The dealer is offering me $1000 for it because the house wants to screw me out of $40. I'm not going to take the offer."

But do all pros think this way all the time? No. There are many other practical considerations. By taking even money, a pro knows he can "lock in" a $1000 win. If he holds out for the extra $40, he increases both his risk and his fluctuations. He has to weigh the value of these factors based on the size of his bankroll and what that locked-in $1000 might mean to his overall financial position.

Also, the reason the professional player had a $1000 bet on the table in the first place is often because he was using a card-counting system that indicated to him that there were excess high cards in the decks when he placed the bet. In such a case, there is a higher probability that the dealer has a 10 in the hole, and the value of the player's blackjack might not be $1040, but only $1020, or $1002 when the dealer shows an ace. Even money still may be a "bad bet" mathematically, but pros always weigh the risk against the value. Is it worth risking a locked-in $1000 payout to try for an extra $2? Any professional player would tell you, flat out, No. Not unless you're sitting on a million-dollar bankroll and you can afford huge fluctuations.

> **Professional Gambler's Rule #4:**
> Never take a big risk for a small return.

The only people who will tell you to never take even money on your blackjacks unless your card-counting system tells you it's a "good" bet, are the authors and experts who write books about blackjack, but never play the game professionally.

How Should You Think of Even Money?

Assuming you are not a card counter, just knowing the actual real-dollar value of your hand should help you decide. Since a $1000 blackjack has a $1040 value against an ace, then a $100 blackjack is worth $104, a $50 blackjack is worth $52, and a $10 blackjack is worth $10.40 against an ace.

So, if you've got a $50 even money decision, ask yourself, "Do I want to take the fifty-buck win right now, or should I hold out for the extra two bucks I know I'll get in the long run, even if I don't get paid on this one?"

> **Tip for Beginners:**
> Don't insure your twenties. This is a very common mistake even experienced players make. Insurance is a bad bet if you're not counting cards. And if you have two tens in your hand, then it's an even worse bet. When the dealer shows an ace and you take insurance, you're really just betting that the dealer has a 10 in the hole. Two tens in your own hand lower the odds of that, and cost you money.

In other words, how much do you feel like gambling? Forget what the math guys say. The pros always think in terms of both value and risk. And so should you.

A TRUE STORY

Many years ago, when I was still working at the post office and hitting Reno or Tahoe with my modest bankroll on the weekends, my maximum bet was two hands of $50 each. I was counting cards, mostly in the single-deck games that were abundant then in northern Nevada. Every trip, my goal was to win $1000, or twenty big bets.

On one trip, I had a disastrous start (not unusual), and went about $800 into the negative. I then spent about eighteen hours over the next three days watching my money go up and down, but slowly climbing back to even. It was late Sunday afternoon and I was facing a four-hour drive back to the Bay area. I was happy to be back to even—actually ahead by about $60, almost enough to cover my expenses—and I was lugging my duffel bag through Harold's Club on my way to the parking lot to head home.

As I passed through the blackjack pit, I saw my favorite dealer standing idle at a two-deck game. I decided to give it one last shot, took a seat, and set my duffel bag on the seat beside me. The count immediately skyrocketed. I had an incredible final session with double-downs and pair-split opportunities on almost every round, and I just kept winning. At one point late in the deal, I was up more than $900 for the session, when I was dealt not one, but two blackjacks with $50 bets on the table. And, of course, the dealer showed an ace.

Harold's Club was the only casino in Reno where I would play two-deck games because some dealers would literally deal them to the bottom. And this was probably going to be the last hand before the shuffle.

Insure Blackjacks Only?

Most casinos in the United Kingdom have a strange insurance rule—strange to us Americans, anyway. Players are allowed to insure their blackjacks, but no other hands. With any other two-card hand, if the dealer shows an ace, you are not allowed to take insurance.

Why?

According to the U.K. gaming regulators, insurance is a "bad bet" except when the player has a blackjack, so it is disallowed at all other times for the protection of the player!

Here's a case where gaming regulators actually believed the gambler's myth about even money, and removed from the game one of the most valuable strategy plays a skilled player can make.

Removing an option from the players' strategy arsenal only "protects" unskilled players. As for those of us who understand when and how to take advantage of an option—please, give us the options and let us protect ourselves!

I turned up my blackjacks one at a time, and the dealer asked me if I wanted even money. With the dealer's ace up, and my two blackjacks, the count was no longer high enough to justify taking insurance. In fact, it had literally gone from being a positive count to being a negative count.

With absolutely no hesitation, I said, "Even money."

The dealer, naturally, did not have a blackjack. I could have made an extra $50 on those hands by taking the full 3 to 2 payout. But as I drove home with my $1000+ win for the trip, even knowing I had technically played the hand "wrong," I had no regrets. I knew the two hands weren't really worth the full $50 extra I could have gotten. With the slight negative count, they were probably worth an extra $6 -$8 total. In my mind, I settled on the cost of my misplay as $7. I had given Harold's Club $7 to lock in the $100 win I needed to hit my $1000 trip goal.

A lot of card counters would say I made a mistake. You don't often get a 7 percent edge over the house, and they would say that to forfeit an advantage like that when it comes along is just bad play. But to me, it never was 7 percent; it was just $7. I wanted and needed that $100 win so badly, it was worth $7 for the sheer joy of walking away from the table with a $1000 winning session.

Sometimes, when you take even money, you know it may be a "bad bet," but you're just buying a little happiness.

A Great Mathematician Weighs In

The late Peter Griffin, in his masterwork, *The Theory of Blackjack*, was one of the few blackjack experts who realized that sometimes a card counter should insure a blackjack, even when his counting system did not warrant it. As Griffin put it so eloquently,

"A Kelly bettor should consider insuring at least a portion of his blackjack against a dealer's ace if p, the proportion of unplayed tens in the deck, exceeds $1/3(1 + f)$, where f is the fraction of capital the player has bet. Note that this fraction is somewhat less than 1/3, which is the critical fraction for card counters trying to maximize their expected wealth rather than, as the Kelly criterion decrees, optimizing the average logarithm of their wealth."

So, the next time the dealer asks you, "Even money?"

Just ask yourself, "Is $p > 1/3(1 + f)$?"

And there's your answer!

MEET THE CARDS

Before we get into the nuts and bolts of counting cards, the whole thing will make more sense if we first understand the way each individual card affects our hands, the dealer's hands, and our chances of winning in the game overall. So, allow me to introduce you to the deck.

MEET THE ACE, THE PLAYER'S STRONGEST ALLY

In casino blackjack, the ace is the mother of all cards. This card will make or break your hand more than any other. You will come to love the ace and hate the ace many times throughout a single playing session.

149

First, the bad news: Why do we hate the ace?

When the Dealer Shows an Ace

When the dealer shows that ace as his upcard, you're in trouble. In the long run, if you were to look at the results of all the hands you play against a dealer ace up, you would find that for every $100 you bet, you wind up with only $64 left. When the dealer shows that ace, he almost never busts. He will end up with a pat hand (total between 17 and 21) 83 percent of the time. That means that if you stand with any stiff yourself, you will lose $83 of every $100 you bet.

> Never, ever, stand on a stiff against an ace. You should look at that ace as a big WARNING sign that the dealer is NOT going to bust.

No matter how the cards have been running for you, no matter how much you've been busting, when the dealer shows an ace up, this is no time to play a hunch and stand on a hard 16. This is no time to worry about busting your own hand. You've got to make a pat hand if you want any chance of salvaging any money you've got on the table. If surrender is allowed, just throw in any hard total of 15 or 16—give up half your bet—and be thankful that you got off that cheaply.

About fifteen years ago, one of the first books that described some basic shuffle-tracking techniques suggested that players should look for slugs of cards that contained excess aces and cut these slugs out of play. The specific reason the authors of this book provided for this tactic was that removing aces from the potential cards to be dealt would cause the dealer to bust more often. This sounds logical, and in fact, it's true; the dealer does bust more frequently when fewer aces are available for his hand.

But, this may rank as the single worst piece of advice ever to appear in a widely circulated book on blackjack by a noted authority on the game. Why?

What the Ace Means to the Player's Hand

Let's talk about what the ace means when you get one as one of your cards. We stated above that if you looked at all of the results of all the hands you play against a dealer ace up, you would find that you end up with only $64 remaining for every $100 you bet. But what if you look at all of the results of all the hands you play when you are dealt an ace as your first card? You would find that you wind up with $152 for every $100 you bet!

This is why we love the ace. It may be valuable to the dealer when he gets it, but it's even more valuable to us when we get it. And since the aces will be distributed evenly between our hands and the dealer's hands in the long run, the more aces that are dealt, the more we win. This is why we call the ace our strongest ally. The name of the game is blackjack, and we need that ace to make a blackjack.

For a noted "expert" on the game to instruct players to seek games where they could cut the aces out of play would be viewed by any reputable authority today as insane. That expert was not a professional player, but a writer and system seller. Had he spent any significant amount of time at the tables employing this strategy, he would have seen that something was amiss with his logic. And he could have avoided much embarrassment had he heeded the following rule.

A Brief History of Aces

> **Professional Gambler's Rule #5:**
> Think through every angle. The amateurs miss the obvious.

The very first card counting systems were the ace-counting systems. These systems were used long before Ed Thorp wrote the first book about card counting in 1962. There's a funny story about one of the old-time ace counters in a book by Nevada's first casino magnate, Harold Smith. He founded Harold's Club in Reno back in 1935, and for twenty years it was the biggest casino in the world. This was a time when Las Vegas itself was just a dusty cow town, and Reno was Nevada's big gambling city.

Harold wrote his autobiography, *I Want to Quit Winners*, in 1961, the year before Thorp's book was published, and he tells the story of Joe Bernstein, one of the famous ace counters from the 1950s. Ace counters back then would typically jump their bets from $5 to multiple hands of $500 when the deck was ace-rich. Harold had heard through the grapevine that Joe had just beat the blackjack tables at the Sahara Club in Las Vegas for $75,000, and might be headed to Reno. Joe was known to be a very smart player, but was also very flamboyant and well known in the casinos.

Harold hadn't been in his club in over twenty-four hours, so he went over to warn his bosses to watch out for Joe. Unfortunately, Harold was a bit late. Joe had already been playing at Harold's Club through three shifts, and was currently ahead by $14,000. Remember that, in the 1950s, you could buy a nice house for $14,000.

Harold immediately instructed the dealer not only to shuffle the cards, but to break out a new deck any time Joe raised his bet. Then he informed Joe, "You can't count aces on me!"

Joe just shrugged and said, "You'll have to admit I was doing it pretty good."

Which brings us to:

Professional Gambler's Rule #6:
You're trying to get rich, not famous.

Anyway, like I say, the ace is our strongest ally.

Want to See a Photo of Joe Bernstein?
If you want to see a picture of the legendary 1950s pre-Thorp card counter, Joe Bernstein, go to Binion's Horseshoe Casino in downtown Las Vegas, walk to the back of the pit where the "Poker Wall of Fame" is located, and on that Wall, among the photos of a couple dozen poker legends including Doyle Brunson, Wild Bill Hickock, and Johnny Moss, is old Joe Bernstein.

MEET THE 10, THE MOST IMPORTANT DENOMINATION

Like the ace, the 10 is a valuable card for both the dealer's and the player's hand. But if the dealer shows a 10 up, you're only half as bad off as when the dealer shows an ace. Whereas you'll wind up with only $64 for every $100 you bet when the dealer has an ace up, you'll have about $83 left per $100 bet when the dealer is showing a 10. So, we never like to see a dealer's 10 up. Our hand, overall, is going to be a loser. But that

10 has a value to us that it does not have for the dealer. For one thing, when combined with an ace, the 10 makes a blackjack, and our blackjack gets paid at a higher rate than the dealer's. We get 3 to 2, whereas the dealer only gets even money from us. Also, we have the option of not hitting our stiffs (hard twelves to sixteens) when the dealer looks weak (2 through 6 up), whereas the dealer must always hit his stiffs. That 10 will bust every stiff.

We say the 10 is the most important denomination in the deck because in addition to its blackjack value, there are four times as many ten-valued cards as any other denomination.

The first truly powerful card counting strategy ever published was Ed Thorp's Ten-Count system. And, in fact, all modern card-counting systems today are based on the Ten-Count. If a card counter knows the deck is richer than normal in ten-valued cards, he raises his bet. He will also make more aggressive plays, like splitting pairs and doubling down, more often, especially when the dealer shows a weak upcard, as he knows those extra tens will cause the dealer to bust more often.

So, like the ace, we don't like seeing a 10 as the dealer's upcard, but we like to play when there are excess tens in the deck. Overall, the 10 is our friend. You might note that a few years back when the casinos were trying to invent a blackjack game that would appeal to players but favor the house more strongly than regular blackjack, they came up with "Spanish 21." This is a game where the rules are exceptionally liberal—far more so than regular blackjack—but where four tens are removed from each of the eight decks in play. That is, the game is dealt from an eight-deck shoe that starts out with thirty-two tens removed! Many players, who keep seeing the jacks, queens, and kings, don't even realize that the pip tens are not in the shoe. They think Spanish 21 is a more favorable game than regular blackjack because of all the doubling, splitting, and surrendering options.

Not so. Those tens are much more important to players than a lot of great rules. For a card counter, the tens are the most important denomination in the deck. An individual ace has more value to a player than a 10, but the sheer quantity of tens in the deck makes them more important overall. In fact, the old ace-counting systems, which could handily beat the old deeply dealt single-deck games, can barely get over the house edge in the commonly available six- and eight-deck shoe games today. This is why most card-counting systems today count both the tens and the aces.

DEALER SLANG

Paint: a face card.

Faint: an ace

A Paint and a Faint: a blackjack.

MEET THE 9, 8, AND 7, THE INVISIBLE CARDS

The 9, 8, and 7 are all relatively neutral cards in the game of blackjack. When the dealer shows any one of these cards as his upcard, he'll bust about 25 percent of the time. Because of their neutral value, many card-counting systems do not even count these cards. The counter, instead, ignores them as they come out of the deck. For this reason, some hands are very difficult for a counter to play accurately. If you are dealt a total of 12, for instance, these neutral cards are very important to your hit/stand decision, especially when the dealer shows a strong upcard (7, 8, 9, 10, or ace). The 7, 8, or 9 as a hit card would make your 12 total into a 19, 20, or 21. So, if you had a card-counting system that counted these cards, and you knew that there were very few of these cards left in the deck, you would be correct to stand on some of your twelves against some of these strong dealer upcards.

Unfortunately, the overall value of playing these hands more correctly according to a card-counting system is just not worth the mental effort. Most counting systems simply advise counters to always play basic strategy (which says hit) with totals of 12, 13, or 14 against the strong dealer upcards. But when you first start counting cards, one of the things that will drive you crazy will be hitting these miserable stiffs against a dealer 10 when your count indicates that the deck is rich in high cards, and it seems very likely that you will bust.

There's nothing you can do about this if you are not counting the sevens, eights, and nines. Because that high count also indicates that the dealer is likely to already have a pat hand, you've got to bite the bullet and hit these marginal stiffs.

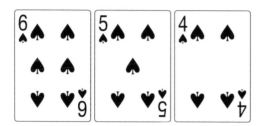

MEET THE 6, 5, AND 4— THE CARDS FROM HELL

These are the cards that we love to see as the dealer's upcard, but hate to see as one of the cards dealt to our hand. Obviously, if we are dealt a 6 and a 5, that's great, since an 11 total is a strong start. Two wrongs do make a right! More frequently, however, these cards mess up our own total and give us a lousy stiff.

When the dealer shows a 6, 5, or 4 as an upcard, he will bust his hand more than 40 percent of the time. For this reason, if he shows one of these upcards, we play our own stiff hands very conservatively. That is, we stand and let the dealer bust.

Contrary to popular belief, most dealers like it when players win. That's because a good portion of a dealer's income comes from tips, or tokes as they're commonly called in the casino industry, and players tend to toke more when they're winning. One dealer might lament to another, "That George had zooks on every hand, but I just kept blowing it."

> **DEALER SLANG**
>
> George: a good tipper.
>
> Zooks: tips or tokes.
>
> Blow it: to deal a player a losing hand when the player has a bet out for the dealer.

The first card-counting system Ed Thorp invented back in 1961, before *Beat the Dealer* was published in 1962, was the Five-Count system.

He simply counted the fives as they were dealt from a single deck, and when all four had come out, he would raise his bet. This, to be sure, is a pretty weak counting system, but the fact is, when you find single-deck games dealt to the bottom, as they were back then, this system will get the money the same as the old ace-counting systems did.

Even though the dealer is in trouble when he shows a 6, 5, or 4 as an upcard, it still works very strongly in his favor to have more of these cards in the deck. The reason for this, again, is the fixed dealing rule that requires the dealer to hit his stiffs. The 6, 5, and 4 are the cards that make most of his stiffs into strong pat hands. These are the cards from hell for a blackjack player. They work strongly in favor of the house, and against us.

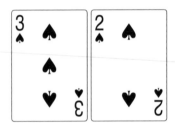

MEET THE 3 AND 2—THE TROUBLE CARDS

The threes and twos are the trouble cards. I call them trouble because of their relationship with the usually ignored sevens, eights, and nines. With no information on the density of the sevens, eights, and nines in the deck, we cannot play our twelves and thirteens with much accuracy, nor can we make informed decisions when the dealer shows a 3 or 2 upcard.

Even so, it's good for us when the dealer shows a 2 or a 3 because overall we're going to win more hands than we'll lose. There's a common saying you'll hear at the blackjack tables that says, "A deuce is the dealer's ace." That saying is a pile of baloney. Let's look at the numbers…

We already said that when the dealer shows an ace, you end up with only $64 for every $100 you bet. When he shows a deuce up, you end up with $110 for every $100 you bet. I'll take a 10 percent edge over the house any day, compared to a house edge of 36 percent over me! No comparison. When the dealer has an ace up, as noted, he only busts 17 percent of the time. With a deuce up, his bust percentage is more than twice as high—35 percent. So, whoever dreamed up that saying about the deuce being "the dealer's ace" was not highly observant.

But we definitely don't like it when there are excess twos and threes in the deck because these little bastards will make the dealer's worst stiffs, 15 and 16, into pat hands. And if we've already stood on a stiff, in hopes of him busting, that 2 or 3 is all he needs to take our money.

Tip for Beginners:

Never blame other players for what happens on your hand. Even the worst blackjack player in the world cannot affect your long run odds of winning or losing. If bad players could affect the odds on your hand, there would be no professional blackjack players at all because even the "good" players play poorly by professional standards. In fact, the player who is making those "bad" plays may even be a professional, who is violating basic strategy for a reason unknown to you (or the casino).

THE PLAYER'S EXPECTATION, BY DEALER'S UPCARD

In most blackjack games, the house edge over the basic strategy player is only about 0.5 percent. But let's look at what the house edge is over us based on each individual dealer upcard, assuming we play perfect basic strategy (and note: When the house edge is negative, that means it's a positive advantage for us).

DEALER SHOWS	HOUSE EDGE
Ace	36%
10	17%
9	4%
8	-5%
7	-14%
6	-24%
5	-24%
4	-18%
3	-14%
2	-10%

In other words, any time the dealer shows a 9, 10, or ace, the house has the edge. Any time the dealer shows a 2 through 8, we have the edge. Our edge is strongest (about 24 percent) when the dealer shows a 5 or 6.

HOW TO COUNT CARDS

> In the gambling hall the crowd was awful. How insolent and greedy they all were!
>
> —*Fyodor Dostoyevsky, The Gambler*

Okay, let's learn a simple and powerful card-counting system. And yes, it is possible for a professional-level system to be both. The Red Seven Count fits the bill.

Many players are frankly amazed when they discover how easy card counting at blackjack really can be. There is an automatic assumption that any professional blackjack player must be counting and memorizing every card as it comes out of the shoe. But, as we have already "met the cards" in the previous chapter, we know that the early counting systems often paid attention to nothing but the aces, or the tens, or just the fives.

One of the reasons many people think card counting must be extremely difficult is because the first really strong system that was published, Ed Thorp's Ten-Count in *Beat the Dealer*, was very cumbersome to use, with a lot of memory work and math required at the tables. With Thorp's original Ten-Count, the player had to keep two running simultaneous counts, beginning one at the number thirty-six, and the other at sixteen. These numbers represented the number of non-tens (thirty-six) and tens (sixteen) in a full deck of fifty-two cards. As cards came out of the deck during the dealing process, the player had to count backwards to maintain the actual number of remaining non-tens and tens in the deck. For example, if the first round of play used five ten-valued cards and seven non-tens, the counts would become twenty-nine and eleven. Then, when the player had to make a strategy decision at any point, he would divide the number of remaining non-tens by the number of remaining tens, to obtain a "ratio." In this case,

$$29 \ / \ 11 \ = \ 2.6$$

The player would then refer to a memorized chart from Thorp's book to determine if he should hit, stand, double down, or split based on this ratio.

But card-counting systems have become a lot easier since then. Here's the thing that's amazing. The Red Seven Count, simple as it is, is more powerful in today's shoe games than Thorp's Ten-Count! (That's assuming you could even use Thorp's Ten-Count in a six-deck shoe. Can you imagine starting your backward running counts at 216 and 96?) Card counting today is a piece of cake!

I first published the Red Seven Count in 1983. It was very controversial when published, as many experts believed it impossible to whittle a system down to the bare basics, require no math whatsoever at the tables aside from the counting itself, and still get any significant edge over the house.

Professional Gambler's Rule #7:

Complexity does not necessarily pay better than simplicity.

Since that time, however, many independent computer simulation studies have shown the Red Seven Count to be exactly as I first described it—a professional-level system that is both easy and powerful. Numerous count system developers since have used the same approach I pioneered, but none have matched both the simplicity and power of the Red Seven. Some authors, like Ken Uston and George C., developed slightly more powerful systems using my unbalanced point count theory, but their systems are also quite a bit more difficult to use than the Red Seven. Others, like rocket scientist Olaf Vancura and Ken Fuchs, developed systems very similar to the Red Seven, but that perform weaker in most game conditions.

I remain of the opinion that the Red Seven Count is the strongest professional-level card-counting system ever devised for its level of simplicity and ease of use.

THE RED SEVEN COUNT

Blackjack players count cards to keep track of the proportions of high cards (tens and aces—the cards that are good for the player) and low cards (the cards that are good for the house) remaining in the decks to be dealt.

We don't need to maintain separate counts of the tens, fives, aces, deuces, or any individual cards. We just need to know if the remaining deck has more high cards than normal or more low cards than normal.

In the Red Seven Count, the high cards (aces and tens) are assigned the value -1, because each time one is dealt the remaining decks are a little poorer in the cards that are good for us.

Low cards (2, 3, 4, 5, and 6) are assigned the value +1, because each time one of these is dealt the remaining decks are a little better for us.

As for eights and nines, they are neutral cards, assigned a value of zero. This means that when we see them we ignore them, and don't count them at all.

We count red sevens as +1, treating them like another low card. But we count black sevens as zero—that is, we ignore them as a neutral card. This is the device that creates the exact imbalance necessary for this count to work as a simple running count system, with no math at the tables. Technically, it does not make any difference whether the red sevens or the black sevens are counted, so long as this precise imbalance is attained.

Start learning to count cards by memorizing these values for each card denomination. Then practice keeping a running count by adding and subtracting these values from a starting count of zero as you deal cards onto a table, one at a time from a deck. If the first card you turn over is a jack, add -1 to your starting count so that your running count is -1. If the next card is a 6, add +1 to your count so that your running count is zero. If the next card is a 4, add +1 again so that your running count is +1.

Example:								
Cards seen:	2	6	A	8	9	X	X	5
Point values:	+1	+1	-1	0	0	-1	-1	+1
Running Count:	+1	+2	+1	+1	+1	0	-1	0

By the time you get to the end of a single full deck of cards, your running count should be +2. If you have miscounted, try again. Then shuffle and go through the deck once more. Build up speed and accuracy. Note that the deck ends at a running count of +2 because of those two extra red sevens we count as +1. They give the full deck twenty-two plus counts, against only twenty minus counts.

How to Practice Counting Cards

Practice, practice, and practice some more at counting down a deck of cards one card at a time. When you are proficient at counting down a deck of cards one card at a time, start turning the cards over two at a time, and count the cards in pairs. This is how you will do it at the casino tables, because it's faster and easier for most people to count cards in pairs. This is because the cards in many pairs cancel each other out, so you don't have to count them at all.

For example, every time you see a 10 or an ace (both -1) paired with a 2, 3, 4, 5, 6, or red 7 (all +1), the pair counts as zero. You will quickly learn to ignore self-canceled pairs, as well as eights, nines and black sevens, since all of these are valued at zero. When you are good at counting cards in pairs, start turning them over three and four at a time. Counting in larger groups really speeds you up. If you turn over a 10, 8 with a 2 and black 7, the change in your running count is zero, because the 8 and black 7 aren't counted at all and the 10 and 2 cancel each other out.

Always strive first to be accurate in your count. Speed without accuracy is worthless. You will do much better in your gambling career if you get in the habit right now of taking the time to learn to do things right.

After you are good at counting cards in pairs and groups of three or four, run through the cards by fanning them from one hand to the other as you count. Allow your eyes to quickly scan the exposed cards for self-canceling pairs, even when these cards are not adjacent to each other. You should be able to count down a deck in this fashion in forty seconds or less before you ever attempt to count cards in a casino. Most pros can easily count down a deck in less than thirty seconds. Most professional teams require players to demonstrate that they can count down a deck in twenty-five seconds or less, with perfect accuracy every time. The legendary card counter Darryl Purpose used to win card-counting contests with his teammates by counting down a deck in eight seconds flat.

HOW TO COUNT CARDS

No matter how fast you get at counting at home, you will probably find it difficult the first time you actually try to count cards at a casino blackjack table. You may find you forget your running count when you're playing your hand or talking to the pit boss. In facedown games, you may miss counting some cards as players throw in their hands and dealers scoop them up quickly. You may forget which cards you have already counted and which cards you have not.

Don't worry about it—every successful card counter has gone through this initial awkward period. You will get better with practice. Before you try counting cards in a casino while actually playing blackjack yourself, spend some time counting while watching others play. Do not sit down to play until you feel comfortable counting while watching the game.

If you expect to play in multiple-deck games, practice counting down multiple decks of cards at home. But be aware that your final running count should go up as you add decks. In a single deck, your final running count should be +2 because of the two red sevens in the decks. But if you are counting down six decks, there will be twelve red sevens in the decks, so your final running count should be +12. Multiply the number of decks you are counting by +2 to get the correct final running count for your practice.

> **Tip for New Counters:**
>
> When in a face-up blackjack game, ignore the first cards dealt by the dealer to each player. Wait until the dealer has dealt the second card to each player, then count the two cards in front of each player.

BLACKJACK QUIZ #2

Here are some practice hands. Imagine that each of these two-card hands has been dealt face up to a player at your table. Hand #1 is your hand, a pair of eights. No problem figuring out the count value of your own hand! Now fill in the total point value of each of the other six two-card hands. The correct answers are on the following page.

Hand # 1:	8♣ + 8♠ = ?
Hand # 2:	10♠ + A♦ = ?
Hand # 3:	7♣ + 5♦ = ?
Hand # 4:	3♣ + 6♥ = ?
Hand # 5:	5♣ + 10♣ = ?
Hand # 6:	7♥ + 10♠ = ?
Hand # 7:	9♠ + 10♦ = ?

ANSWERS TO QUIZ #2

Here are some practice hands. Imagine that each of these two-card hands has been dealt face up to a player at your table. Hand #1 is your hand, a pair of eights. No problem figuring out the count value of your own hand! Now fill in the total point value of each of the other six two-card hands. The correct answers are on the following page.

Hand # 1:	8♣ + 8♠ = 0
Hand # 2:	10♠ + A♦ = -2
Hand # 3:	7♣ + 5♦ = +1
Hand # 4:	3♣ + 6♥ = +2
Hand # 5:	5♣ + 10♣ = 0
Hand # 6:	7♥ + 10♠ = 0
Hand # 7:	9♠ + 10♦ = -1

The World's Fastest Card Counter

According to the late Ken Uston, the fastest card counter he ever met was a player on one of his teams named Darryl Purpose. Uston maintained that Darryl could consistently count down a full deck with 100 percent accuracy in eight seconds! How do you test your accuracy? You must remove one card from the deck, then count through the remaining fifty-one cards. When you finish counting, based on your final running count, you should know if the removed card has a value of +1, -1, or zero.

Years later, I met Al Francesco, the man who taught Uston how to play blackjack, and I asked Al if it was true what Uston had said about Darryl. Al said it was absolutely true. Players on his teams used to bet against each other in speed-counting contests, and Darryl beat them all every time, hands down.

Setting Your Starting Count for Casino Play

To use your running count to make betting and playing decisions at the table, you need to know about the pivot.

What is a pivot? For the Red Seven Count, it's the running count at which you will know your advantage has risen by about 1 percent over the game's starting (dis)advantage. The pivot will be an important indicator in making betting and playing decisions.

If you start with a running count of zero, your pivot will change with the number of decks you are counting, just as your final running count changes with the number of decks.

To keep things simple at the tables, and to make your pivot and other indicators the same for all numbers of decks, the easiest thing to do is adjust your starting count.

To make your pivot equal zero for all numbers of decks, simply multiply the exact number of decks to be dealt by -2 to get your starting running count. With six decks, you should start your running count at -12. With two decks, you start your running count at -4.

Red Seven Starting Counts	
# Decks	Starting Count
1	-2
2	-4
3	-6
4	-8
5	-10
6	-12
7	-14
8	-16

If you always start your running count in this way, your final count—if you count every card in the deck—should always be zero.

Here's a simple chart that shows what your running count should start at with various numbers of decks. And yes, there are a few casinos in this world that deal three-, five-, and even seven-deck games. They're not common, but they exist.

HOW TO COUNT CARDS

> When you practice counting, always start at the appropriate starting count for the number of decks in play. When you come to the end of the deck, you should always have a final running count of zero.

Casino Card Counting "Practice"

I once met a player who had lost more than $2,000 in one weekend just learning to count cards. How could this happen? He was playing with $25 chips and was always betting either $25 or $50 on each hand. He made lots of mistakes and "lost" his count numerous times in the many hours he played that weekend. He told me he felt he had to start practicing in live casino games because it was so much different from practicing on his kitchen table.

I asked him why he didn't "practice" at a $5 game, since there were many available in the casinos where he'd lost his money. He said it had never occurred to him! He had always played at $25 tables before he started to learn to count cards, so he just played at his regular betting level.

It's a great idea to practice counting in live casino games. In fact, it's absolutely necessary to develop your skills. But always practice in the lowest stakes games available to you. Save your bankroll for attacking the tables when you've got the skill.

BLACKJACK QUIZ #3

Below you will find fifty-one cards grouped in twos, threes, fours, and fives. Exactly one card has been removed from the fifty-two-card deck. Using the Red Seven Count point values, determine the missing card's point value (+1, -1, or zero) by keeping a running count from the top of the page to the bottom. Since this is a single deck, your starting count is -2. Since you know that your running count should end at zero after all fifty-two cards have been counted, what is the point value of the missing card? The answer is on the following page.

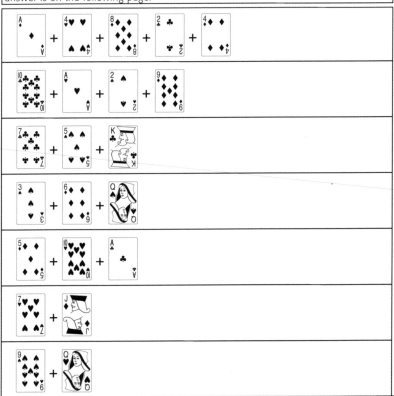

HOW TO COUNT CARDS

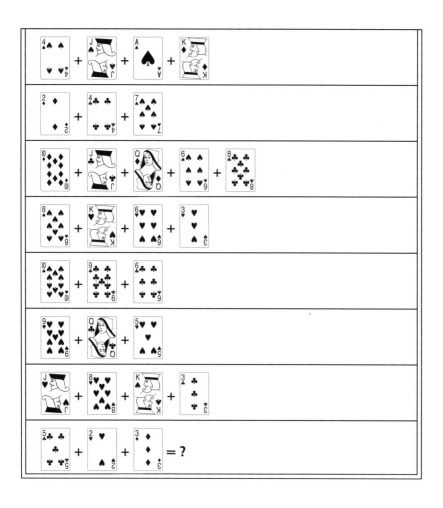

Answer to Quiz #3:

Your final running count should be -1. So, the missing card has a value of +1. The actual missing card is a red 7, the 7 of Diamonds.

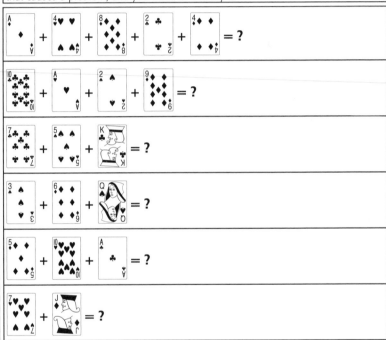

9♠ + Q♥ = ?

4♠ + J♠ + A♠ + K♦ = ?

2♦ + 4♣ + 7♠ = ?

10♦ + J♠ + Q♦ + 9♠ + 8♣ = ?

8♠ + K♥ + 6♥ + 3♥ = ?

10♠ + 9♣ + 6♣ = ?

9♥ + Q♣ + 5♥ = ?

J♥ + 8♥ + K♠ + 3♣ = ?

5♣ + 2♥ + 3♦ = ?

ANSWERS TO QUIZ #4

The cards in Quiz #3 are grouped into fifteen rows (horizontally), each of which contains two, three, four, or five cards. Starting at the top row, add the count values of the cards in each individual row. On a separate sheet of paper, write down the Red Seven Count value of each row, starting at the top. For this test, go for speed. The answers are on the following page. If you find that you have made any errors, study the card grouping(s) that you got wrong. There is often a type of card group that causes a problem, and you need to identify it.

A♦ + 4♥ + 8♦ + 2♣ + 4♦ = +2

10♣ + A♥ + 2♠ + 9♦ = -1

7♣ + 5♠ + K♣ = 0

3♠ + 6♦ + Q♠ = +1

5♦ + 10♥ + A♣ = -1

7♥ + J♦ = 0

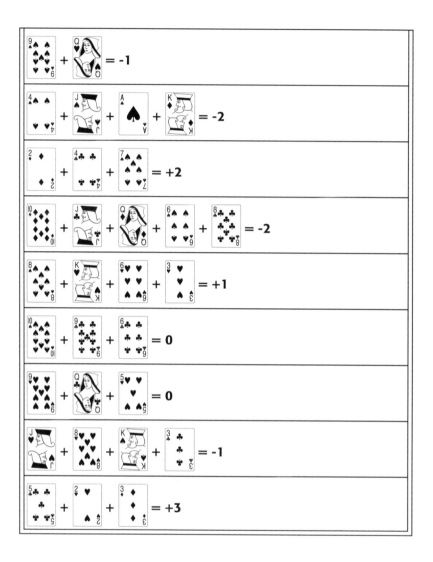

THE RED SEVEN BETTING STRATEGY

Once you are proficient at counting, you can begin to apply the Red Seven betting guidelines at the tables. The idea is to raise your bet when you have an advantage over the house, raise it even more when you have more of an advantage, and keep your bet small when the house has the advantage over you.

Remember, when counting cards in a casino, if you always begin your count at the appropriate starting count for the number of decks in play, your pivot is zero. This means, again, that any time your running count is zero, your advantage will have risen about 1 percent over your starting advantage.

This zero "pivot" is a good indicator of when to first raise your bet for nearly all the traditional blackjack games available in this country. About 80 percent of the traditional games have a starting advantage between -0.4 percent and -0.6 percent. So, your zero pivot usually indicates an advantage for you of approximately 0.5 percent. This is not a huge advantage. It does not guarantee that you will win the hand—far from it. With a 0.5 percent advantage, for every $100 you bet, you will end up in the long run with $100.50, or an extra fifty cents per hundred bucks bet. The important thing is that your count tells you when the edge has shifted from the house to you.

How much should you raise your bet when your running count hits the pivot—or beyond? This depends on many factors, including the rules of the game, the number of decks in play, the penetration (shuffle point), the size of your bankroll, what you can actually get away with in that particular casino, etc. (Casino personnel often view a large betting spread as a sign that a player may be a card counter.) The chart below will provide a guide for the most common games.

UNITS TO BET			
RUNNING COUNT	**1 DECK**	**2 DECKS**	**SHOE**
Negative	1	1	1 (or 0)
0	2	2	2
+2	4	2	2
+4	4	3	2
+6	4	4	3
+8	4	6	4
+12	4	6	6
+16	4	6	8

The general idea is to bet enough when you have the advantage to cover the cost of all the smaller bets you placed when the house had the advantage. Card counters call these small bets waiting bets. Think of the cost of these waiting bets as overhead expenses, or "seat rental." When the edge shifts to your favor, you want to bet a sufficient amount to cover these costs, plus make a nice profit.

Card counters call the difference between your waiting bets and your largest bets, placed when you have your strongest advantage, your betting spread. For example, if you bet $5 at the top of the shoe, but raise your bet to $10 when the advantage shifts to your favor, and bet up to $40 when your count is highest, indicating your strongest advantage, this would be a 5 to 40 betting spread. You may also express this betting spread as 1 to 8, with a betting "unit" of $5.

The guidelines above are not to be taken as strict betting advice. In many one-deck games, for example, a 1 to 4 spread according to the count will get you booted out in short order, especially if your unit size is $25 or more. In most shoe games, a 1 to 8 spread will barely get you over the break-even point. This is why the zero-unit bet is suggested in shoe games at negative counts. It is often impossible to play only at positive counts in shoe games, but it is often wise to leave the table at a negative count.

Note that the suggested bets are in units, not dollars. Your unit size is dependent on the size of your playing bankroll. I'm going to provide some very simple bet-sizing guidelines here that should prove sufficient for most recreational players. If you intend to take your game further, I recommend my book, *Blackbelt in Blackjack: Playing 21 as a Martial Art*, which provides very detailed betting advice for those whose careers depend on casino blackjack winnings as a sole or major source of income. Bet-sizing and bankroll considerations for professional players require a study of standard deviation, normal fluctuations, risk, and the relationship of your advantage to these factors. For now, let's stick with practical advice that will apply to most recreational players.

Beating the Multiple-Deck Games

The best approach for beginners for beating shoe games is table-hopping.

The idea is to play as little as possible when the house has an edge on you. One approach to table-hopping that works in crowded conditions is back-counting.

> **Definition:**
>
> Table-hopping, or wonging, named after the author Stanford Wong who initially wrote about this style of play, is moving from table to table for the purpose of avoiding playing at negative counts. One common method of table-hopping is to start playing a shoe right after a shuffle, and if the count has gone negative after the first round or two, just leave.

> ### Definition:
> Back-counting is counting a round or two and waiting for a situation where the count has already started moving in a positive direction before you sit down to play. It's best to look for a dealer who is just beginning to deal after a fresh shuffle. If the count goes negative, you walk on to another table.

This approach works only in casinos where mid-shoe entry is allowed. Some casinos post signs that disallow new players from entering a game until right after a new shuffle. Back-counting is impractical in any casino where the games are so crowded it's hard to find an open seat, or in any casino where there are only a few tables open. You have to be able to move around without looking like you're back-counting. Game protection personnel are always on the lookout for back-counters.

> ### Casino Surveillance Slang:
> Any player who continually circles a pit, watches the blackjack games at each table for a few rounds, then moves on, is called a buzzard.

If you must sit down to play at a shoe game, and you must play through all hands without jumping in and out as the count swings back and forth from the house edge to a player edge, then you must use a large betting spread or you will be unable to get a significant advantage. Always look for a shoe game where more than 75 percent of the cards are being dealt out between shuffles.

There are three major factors in beating a multiple-deck game:

1. Deep penetration, more than 75 percent of the cards dealt.
2. Playing as little as possible when the count is negative.
3. Using the biggest betting spread you can get away with and that you can afford, based on your bankroll.

> ### Tip for New Counters:
> The single most common reason that card counters fail is negative fluctuations while overbetting their bankrolls. The second most common reason is failure to play with a big enough edge.

If you think that you will win every time you play just because you have an advantage over the house, you are mistaken. Professional players maintain very large playing bankrolls compared to their bet sizes, and they tend to play with much higher edges than amateur players do. You must begin thinking like a pro early if you are to succeed. Start out conservatively in your betting strategy, be selective in your games, and raise your bets only as your bankroll grows.

Let's look at bet-sizing from the perspective of your bankroll size.

The "Trip" Bankroll

It is very important, first of all, for you to define exactly how much money you have available for gambling. Let's say you go to Las Vegas or Atlantic City a few times per year and you always bring somewhere in the neighborhood of $1,500 to gamble with. Sometimes you win, sometimes you lose, but if you lose it all, no big deal. You'll be back again in a few months with another fifteen hundred to take another shot at the casinos because you enjoy playing.

When you go to the casinos, you are always playing with a trip bankroll. This is not your life savings, nor are you depending on this money to make your next mortgage payment. This is expendable income to you, earmarked for entertainment.

As a card counter with a trip bankroll, you can play very aggressively. Divide your total trip bankroll by one hundred-fifty, and use this as your betting unit. With a $1500 bankroll, you divide:

$$\$1500 \ / \ 150 \ = \ \$10 \text{ unit}$$

So, with the betting guidelines above, in the single-deck game you will spread your bets from $10 to $40. In the double-deck games, you'll spread from $10 to $60. And in the shoe games, you'll spread from $10 to $80. Whatever the actual size of your trip bankroll, use this method to obtain your betting unit.

If you think these betting guidelines are not aggressive enough for you, please follow my advice and use them anyway, at least until you learn more. You will soon discover that even when you play blackjack with an edge over the house, the short-term money fluctuations are huge on your way to the long run, and more aggressive betting than this will often get you into trouble. Even with these guidelines, you will sometimes lose your entire trip bankroll before your trip is over! In shoe games, with that high bet of $80, you are starting with fewer than twenty high bets with your initial $1500 trip bankroll. That doesn't give you a lot of wiggle room for bad luck.

If you want to play more aggressively, you should increase your betting spread and your edge over the house by reducing the size of your smallest bet, not by increasing the size of your biggest bet. In a six-deck game, for instance, using a $10 to $80 betting spread, your win rate if you sit through all negative counts is only about 0.5 percent. By spreading from $5 to $80, you would almost double your win rate to close to a full one percent. This betting strategy, which essentially boils down to cutting in half all of the bets you make when the house has the odds in their favor, not only increases your dollar-per-hour expectation, but decreases your negative fluctuations.

The "Total" Bankroll

If the money you intend to go to casinos with represents any significant amount of your total savings, and it is not an easily replenishable amount, then you must size your bets less aggressively. This also means that you must start with a larger bankroll, or play in smaller games, if you want to survive. There are many professional players today who started out with total bankrolls of $5,000 or less, but this is a very tough grind, and often requires a player to (God forbid!) get a job during the toughest times.

As a general rule, if your card-counting bankroll is not replenishable, obtain your unit size by dividing your total bankroll by four hundred. Then use the same betting chart above to size your bets. Serious players will need to use much more precise betting strategies, according to their advantage, table conditions, the necessity for camouflage, etc. Again, those with professional aspirations should see *Blackbelt in Blackjack* for an in-depth treatment of this subject.

THE RED SEVEN PLAYING STRATEGY

Using the Red Seven Count, you can also increase your advantage over the house by changing the way you play some hands according to your running count. Blackjack's basic strategy was developed to play correctly assuming that there are full fifty-two-card decks in play, with all cards present in their correct proportions to each other. But, once we start counting cards, we have collected information that these decks are no longer "normal." Once the decks have gone through some changes as a result of the cards that have been removed from the shoe during the course of playing the hands, some basic strategy decisions also change.

First of all, insurance is the most important strategy change a card counter can make. In single-deck games, assuming you are using a moderate betting spread, insurance is almost as important for a card counter as all other strategy decisions combined.

Conveniently, you have a very nice insurance indicator with the Red Seven Count. In one- and two-deck games, you simply take insurance any time your running count is zero or higher. In all shoe games, take insurance at +2 or higher.

As for other playing decisions, there are only a few to remember. Any time you are at zero or higher with any number of decks, stand on 16 versus 10 and on 12 versus 3. According to basic strategy, you would hit both of these. In single-deck games, the 16 versus 10 decision is the second most important strategy decision for a card counter—insurance being first. After you find these strategy changes easy, there are a couple of others you can add that will increase your advantage a bit more. At running counts of +2 or higher, with any number of decks, stand on 12 versus 2 and on 15 versus 10; and double down on 10 versus X.

THE RED SEVEN PLAYING STRATEGY (ONE OR TWO DECKS)
WHEN THE RUNNING COUNT = ZERO OR HIGHER:
1. Stand on 12 v. 3
2. Stand on 16 v. 10
3. Take Insurance when offered
WHEN THE RUNNING COUNT = +2 OR HIGHER:
4. Stand on 12 v. 2
5. Stand on 15 v. 10
6. Double Down on 10 v. 10

THE RED SEVEN PLAYING STRATEGY (ALL SHOE GAMES)
WHEN THE RUNNING COUNT = ZERO OR HIGHER:
1. Stand on 12 v. 3
2. Stand on 16 v. 10
WHEN THE RUNNING COUNT = +2 OR HIGHER:
3. Stand on 12 v. 2
4. Stand on 15 v. 10
5. Double Down on 10 v. 10
6. Take Insurance when offered

Note that the only difference between the hand-held games and the shoe games is that in the shoe games we wait longer (until a running count of +2) to take insurance. Card counters who play exclusively in shoe games, either table-hopping or using a very large betting spread, can actually replace all of their normal basic strategy decisions with the six Red Seven decisions above, and never change the way they play. Playing like this ensures that you will always be playing correctly when you have your biggest bets on the table, and the "mistakes" you make will all be made when you have a small bet out, and therefore will not be costly. This way, you will have one playing strategy and never change from it. You will not even have to think about whether or not your count requires you to make a strategy change. Playing like this is also excellent "camouflage." You will not look as much like a card counter to casino game protection personnel who are watching your playing decisions if you always play all hands the same way regardless of the count.

TABLE CONDITIONS

The actual advantage that a card counter can get over the house depends primarily on how deeply into the deck the dealer is dealing between shuffles. This is so important, I'll say it again.

> The actual advantage that a card counter can get over the house depends primarily on how deeply into the deck the dealer is dealing between shuffles.

Card counters call the depth of the deal penetration. The deeper the penetration, the more often you'll see counts that indicate you have an advantage and the stronger the advantage will be. Without deep enough penetration, you will find that you simply count down shoe after shoe without seeing any high counts. The worse the penetration, the bigger your betting spread has to be to overcome all those extra waiting bets. If the penetration is 50 percent or less, you're wasting your time counting cards in that game.

Very crowded tables make for slow games. At a full table with six to seven players, you will often play only sixty hands per hour. If you can play one-on-one, or heads-up, with the dealer, on the other hand, you will often be able to play up to two hundred hands per hour. Since your win rate in dollars is a function of your total action, your dollars-per-hour expectation goes up with fewer players at the table. Also, playing more hands per hour means that you will get past the short-term flux and into the long run faster.

For low-stakes card counters, which would include players who never bet as high as $100, single-deck and double-deck games offer more betting opportunities and more profit, assuming the dealer is dealing out more than 60 percent of the cards between shuffles. For players who bet $100 and more, these hand-held games are generally too tough to beat for long plays, as the house will protect these games rigorously if they suspect a card counter is at the table. Big bettors must often stick to shoe games where it is more difficult for the game protection personnel to detect card counters.

A better rule set, which provides less of a house edge off the top, is also important. In the next chapter, we're going to look at the effects of all the different rule variations, and the number of decks in play, that we find in today's games.

Keep It Simple

In multi-deck games, by using this simple running count strategy, you will be taking advantage of about 80 percent of all possible gains from card counting. Using the simple Red Seven Count, you have no strategy tables to memorize. You simply have basic strategy, which you play on more than 90 percent of your hands, and a few changes that you will make according to your running count.

In my opinion, most card counters would be wise to ignore more difficult strategies because of the cost of mistakes if you are not perfect in deploying them. Any system that slows you down, or causes mental fatigue or errors, will put more money into the casinos' coffers than your pockets. Don't be tempted by a system just because it works better on paper. The simple Red Seven Count works at the casino tables and it gets the money. That's the goal.

However, if you find yourself interested in using a more advanced card-counting system to take advantage of every possible gain available from counting, I recommend that you look at the Hi-Lo Lite Count or the Zen Count, both included in *Blackbelt in Blackjack*. There is also an advanced version of the Red Seven Count in that book that is stronger and more versatile than the simple version presented here.

RULES, RULES, RULES, AND MORE RULES

> Blackjack is the only casino game in which the player has reasonably wide latitude to exercise his judgment.
>
> — *Jimmy Snyder, Jimmy the Greek, By Himself*

The rules of blackjack vary from country to country, state to state, city to city, casino to casino, and sometimes even from table to table within a casino. This was not always the case. When Nevada began offering the only legal blackjack games in the U.S. when the state legalized gambling in 1931, for about thirty years there were only two common sets of rules—Las Vegas rules and Reno rules. In both towns, the standard game was dealt from a single deck of cards, from which the dealer typically dealt out fifty of the fifty-two cards. The top card was burned, or turned over, onto the bottom of the deck, and the bottom card itself was never played. If the dealer ran out of cards in the middle of a round, he simply reshuffled the discards and continued play.

In both towns, player blackjacks paid 3 to 2, players could split and resplit any pair, and split aces received only one card each. In Las Vegas, the dealer was required to hit all sixteens and stand on all seventeens. In Reno, the dealer had to hit all sixteens and soft seventeens, but stood on hard 17 and soft 18. In Las Vegas, players had the option of doubling down on any first two cards. In Reno, players could only double down on two-card totals of 10 or 11.

There were a few variations to these rules. Some casinos in Las Vegas allowed players to double down after pair splits. Some casinos in Reno allowed doubling down on 11 only. The insurance rule was invented in the late 1950s, and by the early 1960s, most casinos in both Las Vegas and Reno had adopted it.

SO WHY ALL THE NEW RULES?

Craps is played the same way today that it was played fifty years ago. Roulette? No new rules in the past one hundred years or so. Baccarat? Same old game. Of all the traditional casino table games, blackjack is the one game in which, when you walk into an unfamiliar casino, you have to ask what the rules are. And there are literally dozens of rule variations.

Why?

Because of card counters.

The big changes to the rules and procedures of blackjack started with the 1962 publication of *Beat the Dealer*, and the rules have been getting screwier ever since. Thorp's book put a big scare into the casinos regarding the vulnerability of blackjack to intelligent play. Here's a quick chronological rundown of what happened during that first five-year period of insanity.

1962: E.O. Thorp's *Beat the Dealer* is published containing the Ten-Count system, designed for beating single-deck games. The book becomes a bestseller and players swarm into Nevada's casinos to try their skill at counting.

1963: Nevada's top gaming consultant, John Scarne, states publicly that card counting doesn't work. He calls Thorp a fraud and a phony. Thorp keeps getting press and the card counters keep pouring into Nevada's casinos. The casinos continue to add more and more blackjack tables to accommodate the crowds, but they also keep finding some players who are actually capable of using the Ten-Count. Scarne's public statements that counting doesn't work are having little effect on the general public. Independent analysts are praising Thorp's system, and stories are spreading about some of the counters who are beating the casinos for substantial amounts of money.

1964: The Las Vegas casinos, distraught that some players are capable of legally beating them at a house game, change the standard rules of blackjack. Despite the fact that the casinos are raking in more money than ever from all of the incompetent card counters, the Las Vegas Resort Hotel Association announces that players in Las Vegas casinos will no longer be allowed to split aces, and doubling down will only be permitted on a two-card total of 11. Two weeks later, the casinos go back to their standard rules because their customers refuse to play against the new rules. John Scarne continues to tell players that card counting doesn't work, while advising the casinos to stop dealing single-deck games and start dealing blackjack from four-deck shoes. He also starts telling players that it is dangerous to play in single-deck games, and that they should play in the "safe" shoe games only, which Scarne believes (incorrectly) were impossible to beat with card counting.

1965: Most of the Las Vegas casinos have switched to four-deck shoes. Some downtown casinos have adopted Reno's hit soft 17 rule.

1966: The second edition of *Beat the Dealer* is published; it features the Hi-Lo Count, a system that can handle multiple-deck games more easily than the Ten-Count. The counters keep coming. The public does not believe John Scarne's pronouncements that card counting doesn't work. Too many players are winning. The casinos are making more money from blackjack than ever before in history, but they're looking for a new way to deal with the few competent counters who can beat them. They hate the fact that some players can beat them.

The casinos' search began for some combination of rules, payouts, dealing procedures, and number of decks that players would accept, but that would also leave the card counters with less opportunity for making a profit. Today there are dozens of rule variations for blackjack. Let's look at how all of the dealing procedures and rule variations we find today affect the house edge we're up against as basic strategy players and card counters.

The Number of Decks in Play

Today we find blackjack games being dealt from one to eight decks. The most common games are the one-deck, two-deck, six-deck, and eight-deck games. For a basic strategy player who always bets $100 per hand, and assuming the rules on each game are the same, a traditional single-deck game is roughly break even; a double-deck game costs about thirty cents per hand; and a six- or eight-deck shoe costs about fifty-five cents per hand.

Here's a chart that shows the approximate cost of each number of decks for a $100 bettor:

THE DECK EFFECT	
# DECKS	COST / $100 BET
1	0¢
2	30¢
4	50¢
6 or 8	55¢

The number of decks has an even more severe effect on card counters, however. As we have already noted in our explanation of the Red Seven Count, we need a bigger betting spread in order to beat a game as the number of decks increases, and we'd prefer not to bet at all when the count is negative. Profitable betting opportunities appear more frequently with fewer decks in play. It is much more difficult for a counter to beat an eight-deck game than a two-deck game, all other game factors being equal.

The Soft 17 Rule

We'll start with the rule variations that are most common. First, does the dealer stand on soft 17 or hit soft 17? Both variations of this rule are very common. It is better for the player when the dealer stands on soft 17 because a total of 17 loses more often than it wins. For that $100 basic strategy player, if the dealer hits soft 17, it costs him about twenty cents per hand more than if the dealer stands on soft 17.

Doubling Down

There are a few common doubling variations. The most common rule allows players to double down on any initial two cards. The most common variation on this rule allows doubling down on 10 and 11 only. If a $100 basic strategy player is restricted to doubling down on 10 and 11 only, it will cost him another twenty-six cents per hand in a single-deck game, or about twenty cents per hand in a multiple-deck game.

One other semi-common double down variation allows doubling on 9, 10, and 11. This is only half as costly as the double on 10/11 only rule. The cost is only about thirteen cents per hand in single-deck and ten cents per hand in multiple-deck to that $100 bettor. Back in 1964 when the Las Vegas casinos experimented with allowing doubling down on 11 only for about two weeks, the cost was about seventy-eight cents per hand for a $100 bettor in the single-deck games.

Note: One way to think about the real dollar cost of any specific rule variation is to think in terms of the hourly cost in dollars, and the cost on a weekend trip where you may play for ten hours or so. When I say the cost is seventy-eight cents per hand, and if you are playing at the rate of one hundred hands per hour in moderate crowd conditions, then the cost is $78.00 per hour. And if this is a ten-hour playing trip, then the total cost for that trip is about $780. Don't think these small effects I'm quoting in pennies are meaningless. If you made ten trips per year, this $780/trip cost comes to $7,800!

The Pair-Split Variations

The most common pair-splitting rules are: You may split and resplit any pair, except aces. No doubling down after splits allowed. Split aces get only one card each.

If you are not allowed to resplit pairs, it costs you about two cents per $100 bet in single-deck games, or four cents per hand in multiple-deck games. If you are allowed to double down after splits, you gain about fourteen cents per $100 bet.

Surrender

The surrender (give up half your bet) option is worth about two cents per $100 bet in single-deck games, and about eight cents per hand in shoe games. This assumes that you may not surrender if the dealer has a blackjack. There are a few games outside the U.S. where players may surrender before the dealer checks for a blackjack. This rare "early" surrender rule is worth more than sixty cents per $100 bet when you find it.

Being allowed to double down after splitting is more valuable than not having this option. If your doubling down is limited to 10 and 11 only, this has a cost. Similarly, if you can double down on three or more cards, this

> ### The General Rule on Rules
>
> Any rule that gives you more options has a positive dollar value. Any rule that limits your options costs you money.

is more valuable than being limited to doubling down on your first two cards only.

Casinos offer players more options for two reasons. First, allowing the players more options on how they may play their hands attracts players to the table. Second, and this is very important from the casinos' perspective: Many players make errors using options. For example, the option to surrender half your bet has a small value to a basic strategy player who knows when to take this option. Many amateurs, however, surrender much too frequently. Casinos make much more money from players who use options incorrectly than they lose to the few smart players who understand the correct strategies. Also, as we'll see, casinos can often offer more options to players without giving up their house edge if they remove some other player benefit, such as the standard payout on blackjacks. Be careful of any game with rules that look too good to be true.

Let's look at the approximate values and costs of the rules we might encounter in blackjack games today. Again, we'll look at these effects assuming a $100 bet for a player using basic strategy. Let's start with the favorable rules.

VALUE (+ OR -) PER $100 BET			
	1-DECK	**2-DECK**	**MULTI-DECK**
THE GOOD RULES			
Double After Splits:	+0.14	+0.14	+0.14
Resplit Aces:	+0.03	+0.05	+0.07
Draw to Split Aces:	+0.14	+0.14	+0.14
Late Surrender:	+0.02	+0.05	+0.08
Late Surrender (w/ Hsoft17):	+0.03	+0.06	+0.09
Double After Ace Splits:	+0.10	+0.10	+0.10
Double on 3+ cards:	+0.24	+0.23	+0.23
Early Surrender v. 10 Only	+0.19	+0.21	+0.24
21 Pushes Dlr. 10-up BJ:	+0.20	+0.20	+0.20
5-card 21 Pays 2 to 1:	+0.20	+0.20	+0.20
6-card 21 Pays 2 to 1:	+0.10	+0.10	+0.10
Suited 6-7-8 Pays 2 to 1:	+0.01	+0.01	+0.01
7-7-7 Pays 3 to 2:	+0.01	+0.01	+0.01
6 Cards Unbusted Wins:	+0.10	+0.10	+0.10
THE GREAT RULES			
Early Surrender:	+0.62	+0.62	+0.63
Early Surrender (w/ Hsoft17):	+0.70	+0.71	+0.72
BJ Pays 2 to 1:	+2.32	+2.28	+2.26
Suited BJ Pays 2 to 1:	+0.58	+0.57	+0.56

The surrender option is always valuable, but notice the huge difference in the value of late surrender versus early surrender. Remember, early surrender means that the dealer will allow you to give up half your bet when he has a 10 or ace showing before he checks to see if he has a blackjack. This is a rare rule today, but international travelers occasionally find the option available at casinos in Asia, Eastern Europe, South America, and elsewhere.

Double After Splits
One favorable rule that exists in every Atlantic City casino is the player's option to double down after splitting a pair. Do you know which pairs to split when you are allowed to double after splits? Card counters who play in Nevada have to know these changes because the casinos in Nevada are pretty much split fifty/fifty on whether or not players are allowed to double after splits. As it turns out there are some pretty simple rules to remember the differences—you don't even have to memorize a complete chart.

Here's what to remember:

1. The only changes to make are for splitting twos, threes, and fours.
2. With no DAS, we never split fours, and we split twos and threes versus 4-7.
3. With DAS allowed, we split fours against 5 and 6, and we split twos and threes versus 2-7. All other pair splits stay the same.

Note that those special bonus payouts—on six cards, three sevens, suited 6-7-8, etc.—aren't worth much. Any of the rules that provide player options, such as surrender, are worth more to card counters than they are to basic strategy players.

I don't know of any casino that has the "BJ Pays 2 to 1" rule as a standard house rule. But this rule regularly shows up in casinos for limited promotions. A recent 2 to 1 promo took place last year in a Mississippi casino. I know one pro who flew in a team of fifty players and won $600,000 in one day. Here's another true story about a casino that tried this promotion some years back.

The Alton Belle Massacre

In April of 1994, the Casino Windsor opened in Canada, just across the bridge from Detroit. It was immediately packed with gamblers day and night. The huge Detroit/Flint/Toledo gambling market now had a more convenient gambling option than driving to Illinois, where the riverboats had been in operation for a few years, or visiting Michigan's out-in-the-woods Indian casinos. Casinos had not yet been approved in Indiana at this time.

The Illinois casinos felt the pinch. The Canadians had stolen three states from their market. The 1994 midwestern winter made things even tougher for the Illinois riverboats. No Michigan, Indiana, or Ohio gamblers would drive hundreds of miles to play in Illinois when they could zip across the Ambassador Bridge to Windsor to play in Canada. The Illinois riverboats felt they needed to do something to get some gamblers onto their tables.

In November of 1994, with their crowds at an all-time low, the Alton Belle riverboat in Alton, Illinois decided to give midwesterners a reason to drive. They decided to run a promotion called "Two-Fer Tuesdays," in which blackjacks would pay 2 to 1 on Tuesdays throughout the entire month of December. They started announcing the promotion around Thanksgiving weekend in area newspapers, including the St. Louis Post Dispatcher. St. Louis, Missouri was the biggest population center close to Alton, Illinois, just a quick drive across the Mississippi River.

On that first Tuesday in December, the crowds that showed up boggled the minds of the casino staff. Their marketing directors were slapping each other on their collective backs and talking pay raises and Christmas bonuses. They hadn't seen such lines waiting to board their boat since the first week they opened four years earlier. And this was December, traditionally the slowest month of the year. Every seat at every blackjack table was soon filled and the aisles were jammed with players who couldn't find a seat. Some of the players who couldn't get a seat were actually paying seated players to give up their places. And most astonishing of all, just about every betting spot on every table had a $500 maximum bet!

What a promotion!

Unfortunately, there was one factor the Alton Belle hadn't considered.

Stanford Wong.

Stanford Wong, the well-known author of *Professional Blackjack*, had heard about the promotion from one of the midwestern subscribers to his monthly newsletter, *Current Blackjack News*. Wong sent a fax to his subscribers telling them about the value of the promotion. If the casino paid 2 to 1 on blackjacks and allowed $500 maximum bets, then a player who simply played basic strategy and bet $500 per hand would have an expected win of about $500 per hour. And that was assuming only sixty hands per hour, with no card counting!

The Alton Belle was not swarming with midwestern gamblers, but with professional gamblers who had flown in from all over the country. The players made a killing. By mid-day on the first Tuesday in December, the casino cut the blackjack table maximum from $500 to $200, and still lost an estimated $300,000 on that day. By the end of the month, many pros had been evicted from the tables, and the table maximums on Two-Fer Tuesdays had been cut to $50. The casino's total Two-Fer Tuesday losses for the month were estimated to be between $500,000 and $1 million.

In any case, some promos can be quite lucrative for smart players.

> Better odds aren't everything to some gamblers. Some people crave atmosphere over value. These are the folks who keep the light bills paid and the faux volcano spewing.
> — *Michael Konik, The Man with the $100,000 Breasts*

The Double Down Dilemma

Doubling down has two basic effects on your overall results:

1. You'll win more money.

2. You'll win fewer hands.

How is this possible?

When you forfeit your right to continue hitting after only one card is delivered to your hand, just so you can have a larger wager, you often put yourself in the position of having to violate basic strategy after that double-down card is delivered. For example, if I double down on an 11 against a dealer 7 up, and my double-down card is an ace, 2, 3, 4, or 5, I'm up a creek without a paddle. Had I just hit my 11, I could continue to follow basic strategy and hit again.

On the other hand, if I'm dealt a 7, 8, 9, or 10 as my double-down card, I'm a very strong favorite against that dealer 7, so strong that the double-bet win on these occasions will more than make up for the extra losses that occur from relinquishing the right to hit my stiffs.

Some years ago, I almost discovered a way to exploit this knowledge. I found a casino in Atlantic City that offered a weird "Streak Bet." It was a side-bet that paid bonuses depending on whether the player had a winning streak of two, three, four, or five hands.

I quickly analyzed the value of the rule based on the player's normal expected wins and losses, and discovered a high house edge. I had my laptop with me and tested the rule when I eliminated all of the player double downs that would win more often if the player had just hit instead of doubling. The player win steak probabilities increased, but the rule still had a house edge.

So, I analyzed the option once more, by testing the win/loss results at progressively higher counts, and discovered that when the count got high enough, I could beat the house if I bet the streak bet and stopped doubling down whenever just hitting would win more hands. Unfortunately, in that six-deck shoe game with poor penetration, I would almost never find an opportunity to bet the streak. I'm just waiting for some casino somewhere to offer the streak bet in a one- or two-deck game.

In any case, the fact is, when you double down, you'll win fewer hands, but more money.

Let's look at the effects of some rules we'd rather not see.

RULES, RULES, RULES, AND MORE RULES

	1-DECK	2-DECK	MULTI-DECK
THE BAD RULES			
Double on 10-11 only:	-0.26	-0.21	-0.18
Double on 9-10-11 only:	-0.13	-0.11	-0.09
Double on 8-9-10-11 only:	-0.13	-0.11	-0.09
Dealer Hits Soft 17:	-0.19	-0.20	-0.21
No Resplits:	-0.02	-0.03	-0.04
No Ace Splits:	-0.16	-0.17	-0.18
No Hole Card (European):	-0.10	-0.11	-0.11
THE MISERABLE RULES			
Double on 11 only:	-0.78	-0.69	-0.64
BJ Pays 6 to 5:	-1.40	-1.39	-1.38
BJ Pays 1 to 1:	-2.32	-2.28	-2.26

That European No Hole Card rule is standard in most European casinos. Here's how it works. The dealer takes no hole card. He deals his second card only after the players have completed their hands. If the dealer's upcard is a 10 or ace, and he makes a blackjack, any players who doubled down or split pairs will lose all bets on the table. In the few U.S. casinos where the dealers take no hole cards, if players double or split, they lose only their initial bet on the hand. That European version of the No Hole Card rule has a cost.

Of the "Miserable Rules," Blackjack Pays 1 to 1 (even money) is the worst of the miserable lot. This is a standard rule on "Super Fun 21" games, but that variation of blackjack has lots of other unusual compensating rules that are not in these charts. Super Fun 21 is described in more detail later.

The BJ Pays 6 to 5 rule has just about become the "standard" single-deck rule in Las Vegas. When the Las Vegas casinos tried to change their rules in 1964 by allowing doubling down on 11 only and no splitting aces, the cost of those two rules combined was about ninety-four cents per hand to a $100 bettor. Players back then would not accept the rule changes. They refused to play, and the casinos were forced to go back to the old rules. Note how much greater the cost of BJ Pays 6 to 5 is to players ($1.40 per hand to a $100 bettor), yet the Las Vegas casinos can't add single-deck tables fast enough to accommodate the players who want into these games today!

Have players gotten stupider in the past forty years? No, but the casinos have gotten smarter. When they tried changing the rules in 1964, they did it by removing options for the players. The BJ Pays 6 to 5 games remove none of the normal options; they simply change a payout. Players hardly notice. Too bad. If you play in a casino that offers these single-deck 6 to 5 games, avoid them. If the same casino offers shoe games with the traditional 3 to 2 blackjack payout, those shoe games give you much better odds, whether you are a basic strategy player, a card counter, or just a gambler playing your hunches.

Only One Resplit?

In Nevada, most casinos allow players to resplit pairs twice, to a total of four hands. In Atlantic City, players can resplit only once to a total of three hands.

What does this resplit restriction in Atlantic City cost the player?

Almost nothing.

Although the Atlantic City casinos have removed a player option that most Nevada players consider standard, it makes little difference because of the infrequency of occurrence. It wouldn't be unusual for you to play for a week and never have a single opportunity to resplit to a fourth hand.

It's always best to have as many options as possible, but the option to split to four or more hands is about as exciting and valuable as your boss giving you a five-cent pay raise that only applies every other Tuesday.

You may note that, depending on the number of decks, the cost of "No Resplits" runs from -0.02 percent to -0.04 percent. This is two to four cents per $100 bet. But the cost of only one resplit is so low, we have to estimate it in thousandths of a percent. Any rule that costs only a fraction of a penny per $100 bet, in my opinion, isn't worth listing in a chart.

THE NON-BASIC RULES	1-DECK	2-DECK	MULTI-DECK
No Insurance:	00.00	00.00	00.00
Multi-Action:	00.00	00.00	00.00
Over/Under:	00.00	00.00	00.00
Royal Match:	00.00	00.00	00.00
Super Sevens:	00.00	00.00	00.00
Lucky Ladies:	00.00	00.00	00.00

The cost of all of these rules is zilch because the correct basic strategy is to ignore them. Card counters, however, would find the No Insurance rule expensive, because there is a lot of money to be made on this option for counters.

Multi-Action

Multi-action games have no effect on basic strategy players, provided you continue to play basic strategy. There's the rub. The rule is actually designed to get amateurs to violate basic strategy.

Here's how multi-action works. Some casinos use special table layouts that allow players to place up to three simultaneous bets. In these multi-action games, the player will place three separate bets, which must all be for the same amount, but he will be dealt only one hand (two cards) as in any normal game. The player will also play his hand only once. The dealer, however, will play out his hand three times. He will use the same upcard but will draw a new hole card, and new hit cards if necessary, against each successive player bet. This means that the player may have up to three different results on the same hand.

> **Tip for All Players:**
>
> If a game has a special rule or option that you are unfamiliar with, don't take guesses about how to play it. Most new rules or options are gimmicks that the casinos invent to squeeze a bit more money out of uninformed players. Stick with what you know.

For example, let's say the player is dealt a hard 14 against a dealer 10 up. The player has three $10 bets on the table. The player hits and is dealt a 3, for a total of 17, and stands. Then:

1. The dealer deals himself his first hole card, which is an ace, and his blackjack beats the player's first bet.
2. The dealer takes that first bet, discards the ace, then deals himself a second hole card, which this time is a 7. His 17 pushes the player's second bet.
3. The dealer leaves that second bet on the table and throws away the 7, then deals himself a third hole card, this time a 5. He hits his 15, busts it with a 10, and the player wins the third bet. So, in this scenario, the player lost one hand, pushed one hand, and won one hand. Overall, the player broke even on his three bets.

In multi-action games, all other blackjack rules and options remain the same, and you do not have to bet more than one spot. The problem is that even knowledgeable players are often tempted to stand on their stiffs versus dealer high cards when they play multiple hands. Their logic is: If I bust this 16, I will lose all three of my bets. If I stand, the dealer will have to play his 10 against my hand three separate times. He will probably not beat me on all three hands, so I should just stand on my 16.

This certainly sounds like a logical argument for not hitting your stiffs in multi-action games. But it is faulty logic. Computer simulation tests have shown that you should use the exact same basic strategy in multi-action games that you use in regular blackjack. If basic strategy works on one hand against a specific dealer upcard, it works identically on all of your bets, no matter how many times the dealer changes his hole card and plays out his hand. Although you chance busting when you hit a stiff, and losing three bets, a single hit might also make your hand into 20 or 21, giving you a much better shot of coming up with a win versus that dealer 10 than you had with that miserable 16.

One thing that most professional gamblers learn early, and it is one of the things that separate them from the masses, is that a player mustn't be wimpy. Instead of trembling at the thought of losing three bets by

---

Professional Gambler's Rule #8:

The difference between the professional gambler and the wannabe often comes down to guts.

---

hitting your hard 16 against a 10 in a multi-action game, you should be bravely attempting to improve that lousy total precisely because that hand is going to play out three times, and you refuse to sit there and watch the dealer hammer you. If you bust the hand, so be it. At least you took the shot you had to take to give yourself the best chance at winning. This brings us to…

All four of the "side bet" rules—Over/Under, Royal Match, Super Sevens, and Lucky Ladies—can be beaten with card-counting systems. Over/Under is the most valuable if you use a special counting system designed for it. Royal Match and Lucky Ladies both offer decent opportunities for low-stakes counters, but for Royal Match you would need a suit-counting system. Super Sevens can be beaten, but the value is negligible. I'll cover each of these options in short chapters to follow.

THE I-CAN'T-BELIEVE-IT'S-NOT-BLACKJACK GAMES

These are the games that look sort of like blackjack, play sort of like blackjack, have rules very similar to blackjack, but—don't kid yourself—aren't blackjack. These games include Spanish 21, Super Fun 21, Double Exposure 21, Blackjack Switch, "Player-Banked" and "Player-Pool" Blackjack, and California No-Bust Blackjack. These games are so weird; I will cover each of them in separate chapters.

For now, let's move on to the "side bets," mentioned above under the Non-Basic Rules. One short chapter on each…

HOW TO BEAT "OVER/UNDER 13"

The "Over/Under 13," often just called "Over/Under," is an optional side bet (actually two separate bets) that your first two cards will total either over 13 or under 13. There is a special area on the table layout for you to make these bets. Aces always count as one for this bet. A total of 13 always loses. If you win on an over or under bet, you are paid 2 to 1.

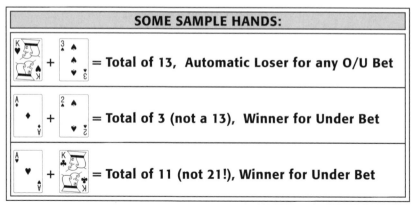

SOME SAMPLE HANDS:

K♥ + 3♠ = Total of 13, Automatic Loser for any O/U Bet

A♦ + 2♠ = Total of 3 (not a 13), Winner for Under Bet

A♥ + K♣ = Total of 11 (not 21!), Winner for Under Bet

Note that if you place an over bet and you are dealt a blackjack, you will lose the over bet—because the ace always counts as one. But you will still win your regular blackjack hand and be paid 3 to 2. Over/under bets have no effect whatsoever on the results of your regular blackjack hand. Once the over/under bets are settled, you revert to the normal house rules for the play of the hands.

Do not place over/under bets without using a card-counting system. The house advantage is 6.5 percent on the over bet, and more than 10 percent on the under bet if you're just guessing.

This rule is most often offered on six- and eight-deck games.

Most casinos that offer the over/under bet limit the amount that the player may bet on this option. In many cases, this bet limitation, in conjunction with generally poor penetration, makes the over/under bet pretty worthless.

But the over/under option can be so valuable to card counters that if it is available on a game with decent penetration, say 75 percent or more on a six-deck shoe game, or 80+ percent on an eight-deck game, over/ under bets will often offer higher returns than all other card-counting gains—from bet variation, playing strategy changes, and insurance— combined. If the betting limit on the over/under bet is restricted to a maximum well below the maximum allowed on the regular blackjack hand, and if you regularly place blackjack bets at those higher levels, then this would not be true.

Let me clarify this. If a game has a table limit of $2000, with over/ under bets allowed up to $100, and you regularly bet up to $1000 on your high bets, then you will likely find more card-counting gains from betting and playing your blackjack hand correctly than you can get solely from the over/under option with that $100 limit. But if you generally spread your bets from $10 to $100, then for your purposes that over/under option is being offered at your personal table maximum bet, and you have a greater win potential from over/under betting than you can expect from all of your other regular card-counting gains combined.

The reason I want you to understand this is that in order to take full advantage of the gains available from the over/under option, you must use a special counting system designed for this purpose. The Red Seven Count can get some of the available over/under profit, but not all. If you have an O/U game available to you for some length of time, then it may be worth your efforts to learn a special counting system for it. Over/Under games are most often found in casinos in Asia and Eastern Europe, as well as on various cruise ships. If you have O/U games available to you for a decent period of time, then learning an over/ under counting system may pay dividends.

If you use the Red Seven Count, and you unexpectedly find yourself in a game where over/under bets are allowed, then you can add about one-tenth of a percent to your edge over the house by placing over bets at very high running counts.

The strategy: In a six- or eight-deck game, never place an over bet until you are in the last three decks of the shoe. That is, in a six-deck game, you would never place an over bet as the first three decks are being dealt. In an eight-deck game, you would never place an over bet as the first five decks are being dealt. In the last three decks of the deal, place an over bet any time your Red Seven running count is +10 or higher. (Never place an under bet.)

There is much more potential gain from using a special counting system. As you are unlikely to ever find this option available in single- or double-deck games, there is no point in learning a balanced card-counting system that would allow you to take advantage of both the over and the under bets. Virtually all of the gain available from shoe games comes from making optimal over bets, and we can get most of this gain with an unbalanced counting system that provides a simple running count index. Here is an excellent counting system I call the "Over Count," as it is designed to beat the over bet only.

The Over Count Values
Ace, 2, 3, 4, 5 = +1
10 = -1

Notice that the ace is counted as a low card with a +1 value, instead of as a high card with a minus value as in traditional card-counting systems. Like the Red Seven Count, the Over Count's +/- values are not balanced. The Over Count has twenty plus counts but only sixteen negative counts in a full deck.

To use this system, we begin our running count at -24 in a six-deck shoe game, or -32 with eight decks. Our starting count is always four times the number of decks in play, so with four decks, we would start counting at -16, etc.

Using the system is very simple because all betting and strategy changes are made at a running count of zero. Any time your running count is negative, play basic strategy. If your count is zero or positive, here's how you play:

- Raise your blackjack bet to your maximum.
- Place the over bet at the maximum allowed.
- Take insurance if the dealer has an ace up.
- Surrender hard 15 or 16 versus 9, 10, or ace, if allowed.
- Surrender 14 versus 10.

- Stand on 16 versus 9, 10, or ace.
- Stand on 15 versus 10.
- Stand on 12 versus 2 or 3.
- Double down on 10 or 11 versus all upcards.

With 75 percent penetration in a six-deck game, or 80 percent penetration in an eight-deck game, you can beat these games easily with a 1 to 4 betting spread. A bigger betting spread, or deeper penetration, will increase your win rate substantially.

Quite a few people highly placed in casino management that I know recognize that card counting itself cannot really bankrupt a casino... For any card-counter who's competent, there are ten who aren't really competent, and there are thousands of people who are pouring money over the tables at a rate that not even the best card counters could compensate for on a one to one basis.

— *Peter Griffin, Extra Stuff: Gambling Ramblings*

A Brief History of Over/Under

This rule was invented in 1988 by Ken Perrie, a pit boss at Caesars Tahoe. It was first offered to players in that casino, and later spread to many other Nevada casinos. Because of the high house advantages on both the over bet and the under bet off the top, the casinos did not believe that counters could take advantage of the option. In fact, both Stanford Wong and I—as well as other experts—initially advised card counters to ignore it as a worthless sucker bet.

I was alerted to its possible value for counters by Jake Smallwood, a semi-pro player, who urged me to analyze the effect of card counting. I did, and was amazed to discover that despite the high house edge, the option had enormous value for counters. In 1989, I published the first system for beating Over/Under games.

At that time, some casinos were offering Over/Under in single- and double-deck games with no betting restrictions. These games were so lucrative that some counters with modest bankrolls actually launched their careers as high-stakes pros solely on the basis of their over/under profits.

It was two years before Over/Under disappeared from the hand-held games, to be offered only in shoe games with lots of betting restrictions. More than one pro player has told me that publishing that *Over/Under Report* in 1989, and offering it for sale for $29, was probably the dumbest mistake I ever made. At that point, I guess I hadn't yet learned Professional Gambler's Rule #3: When you learn something no one else knows, keep it to yourself. But this does bring us to:

Of course, this pro gambler's rule does not mean you should ever violate the tip provided in the rules chapter that emphasized that you should never guess at how to

> **Professional Gambler's Rule #9:**
> When a casino offers any new option, look for its big mistake.

take advantage of a new rule or option you are unfamiliar with. Most pros thought the over/under rule was a waste of time until mathematical analysis showed otherwise. If you are capable with math, and especially if you have a pretty good grasp of probability and statistics, then you may be able to discover value in some new casino game before anyone else does. Then you follow Professional Gambler's Rule #3 (as I neglected to do back in 1989).

Incidentally, the inventor of Over/Under, Ken Perrie, later invented another side-bet option called "Super Sevens." You'll find a separate chapter on that option coming up.

HOW TO BEAT "ROYAL MATCH"

> Let's say the odds are 200 to 1 in your favor. Then a dark, desperate idea crosses your mind. You find yourself envisioning a way to lose. The minute the idea strikes you, you're only a 5 to 1 favorite. That's because there's a good chance the God of Irony will have intercepted your idea and decided to use it.
>
> — *Mike Caro, Caro on Gambling*

"Royal Match" is a side bet. It is especially popular in Nevada, where single-deck games are still available in abundance. You'll recognize its presence on a table when you see a small betting circle beside each of the main betting spots, usually with the words "Royal Match" or the initials "RM" inside of it. There is also often a placard on the table announcing that Royal Match bets are allowed.

There are two versions of Royal Match offered, the single-deck version and the multi-deck version. We are only interested in the single-deck version. This version pays 3 to 1 if the player's initial two cards are suited, and 10 to 1 if the initial two cards are a suited king and queen.

The multi-deck version has different payouts and cannot be beaten with card counting. The multi-deck payouts are 2.5 to 1 for any two suited cards, and 25 to 1 for a suited king and queen. This may sound like better payouts but they are actually much worse. You will make most of your money from the Royal Match option by getting any two suited cards. A suited king and queen occurs less than once every three hundred hands. The higher king/queen payout doesn't begin to make up for the lower payout on any two suited cards.

And, incidentally, if you ever find a six- or eight-deck game with the single-deck payouts, you don't need a system to beat Royal Match. You will have the edge over the house on every hand, so just keep placing the bet! On the other hand, if you ever find the multi-deck payouts on a single-deck game, forget it. That's as bad as Royal Match can be.

The house edge on this rule at single-deck, with the standard 3 to 1/10 to 1 payouts, is about 3.8 percent. That means if you placed a $10 bet on Royal Match every hand and played one hundred hands per hour, you would lose $38 per hour, on average, just from this bet. What this rule has in its favor, however, is what mathematicians call high volatility. This edge has extreme ups and downs based on the balance and imbalance of the suits of the cards that have been dealt. This fluctuation of advantage is far more extreme than we find in normal blackjack games. Royal Match bets occasionally have player advantages of 10 percent or more, a situation that virtually never occurs in regular blackjack using a card-counting system.

> ### Royal Match Tip:
>
> Before you bet this option, be absolutely sure the payouts are 3 to 1 for two suited cards, and 10 to 1 for a suited king/queen. If these payouts are 2.5 to 1 and 25 to 1, you can't beat it!

Despite this, professional blackjack players have little interest in Royal Match. The reason is that Royal Match typically allows a maximum bet of only $10 to $25 (and occasionally up to $50). The long run dollar return from placing advantageous Royal Match bets is also limited because you will have an advantage on only a fraction of the total number of blackjack hands you play.

Royal Match opportunities are ideal for low-stakes card counters who are trying to crank up their hourly win rate to build a bank, or basic strategy players who do not want to count cards but still want to get an edge over the house.

A BIT OF HISTORY

Royal Match first appeared in Nevada about fifteen years ago. Card counters totally ignored it. In 1993, an anonymous author published a $100 report titled "The Davies System: A 'Suit-Counting' Method for Beating the House at Royal Match." The system, as the title of the report suggests, requires a player to keep four separate counts indicating the number of cards dealt in each of the four suits. A reputable mathematician and blackjack researcher of that time, John Leib, ran some computer simulations of the Davies system and discovered that it did, in fact, beat the house at Royal Match. Leib's study was published in *Blackjack Forum*. The report sold for a few months, then disappeared.

To my knowledge, the only other authority to recognize the potential value of Royal Match, and publish a counting system for beating it, is James Grosjean in his book, *Beyond Counting*. Grosjean starts with the assumption that counting four separate suits would prove too difficult for most players, so he analyzes a simple system of his invention whereby the player keeps a simple +1/-1 count, balancing the red cards against the black cards. Grosjean acknowledges that this counting method is far inferior in win potential to an exact count on each of the four suits, but the practicality of actually being able to use it at the tables is in its favor.

BUT YOU DON'T NEED TO COUNT THE FOUR SUITS

My take on this rule, however, is that many players could find advantageous betting situations without resorting to the mentally strenuous task of counting down all four suits separately. I also think the Grosjean approach of simply balancing the red suits versus the black suits is too weak. The most advantageous betting situations that occur result from imbalances between individual suits. Red/black counting, though easy, would miss many of these imbalances. Any imbalance between the spades and clubs, for instance, would not be identified. An imbalance between the hearts and spades could be missed by a red/black counting system if the clubs and diamonds were even slightly imbalanced in reverse.

Let's look at a weird example to illustrate the type of problem that exists with a red/black counting system. Let's take a deck in which twenty-two cards have been dealt that included eleven hearts and eleven spades. The remaining deck consists of thirty cards that include two hearts, two spades, thirteen clubs, and thirteen diamonds. The player advantage on the Royal Match bet in such a deck is slightly greater than 50 percent if all of the king/queen pairs are still available to be dealt, but even if the king/queen pairs in the hearts and spades suits are no longer available (which would be likely), the player advantage on the Royal Match bet would still be better than 48 percent. This is a monstrous edge, yet red/black counting would not recognize any advantage, since the reds and blacks are completely balanced in the remaining deck.

I don't mean to say that you will often (or ever!) see such an unlikely imbalance as in the above example. I only mean to illustrate the deficiency of red/black counting in identifying the actual Royal Match advantages that might occur in a real-world game.

I suggest that you take advantage of the Royal Match betting opportunities that occur with the following simple system:

THE SIMPLE ROYAL MATCH SYSTEM

1. You will rarely have an advantage on Royal Match until at least seven cards from one suit have been dealt from a single deck. You do not need to keep separate counts on each suit; just watch for any suit that has come out excessively off the top, and count until you see at least seven of that suit.

2. If seven cards have been dealt from one suit, then to make the Royal Match bet advantageous, you would need to have at least one suit where no cards have been dealt. If at least one card from each of the other three suits has been dealt, don't bet on Royal Match. Again, you do not need to keep a separate count on all four suits. If you see seven clubs on the table on the first round, just take notice of whether any of the other suits have not yet had a single card dealt. If, say, not a single diamond has been dealt, bet the Royal Match.

3. For expert players: Technically, if all of the king/queen pairs are still available, that is, not a single king or queen has yet been dealt, then you would have an advantage if seven cards of one suit have been dealt, even if one or two cards from every other suit has already been dealt as well. Again, I'm not suggesting that you have to "count" kings or queens

to take advantage of this. If you scan the table and see a single king or queen, the "count" is over. You will need that stronger suit imbalance to get an edge on a Royal Match bet.

4. f nine or more cards have been dealt from a single suit, then you would usually have an advantage even if every other suit had at least two cards dealt. So, if your count on the dominant suit you're watching reaches nine, and at least one other suit has had less than three cards come out, bet on Royal Match.

That is the whole system, and that's all you have to know to make money on this option. The easy way to play Royal Match is to play at a table where four or five other players are playing, so that you will see eighteen to twenty cards or so on the first round, and there will be a second round before the shuffle. You simply look for a dominant suit that has seven or more cards dealt on the first round, and if any one of the other suits meets the criteria described above, you place a Royal Match bet for the second round. After that first round, there is no need to keep a count for the second round because you won't have an opportunity to bet again before the next shuffle. It's simple, quick, and easy. There's no memory work and no math to speak of, other than the ability to count to seven.

What's It Worth?

Like so many other opportunities in blackjack, the value of this option goes up with deeper penetration. If you can play Royal Match at one of the old seven-spot tables, with players on each betting spot and two rounds between shuffles, the advantageous betting situations will come up much more frequently than if there are four spots in action with only two rounds between shuffles. If you are playing heads up, or with few other players at the table, and you can find a single-deck dealer who will deal another round after 50 percent of the cards have already been dealt, then it would definitely be to your benefit to continue counting a dominant suit, and looking for a Royal Match betting opportunity through all of the rounds until the last one.

As a basic guideline, if you have a situation with seven cards dealt from one suit and zero cards dealt from at least one other suit, your advantage on the Royal Match bet will usually range from 1 percent to 3 percent, depending on how many king/queen pairs are remaining, and exactly what the distribution of the other suits consists of. If eight of a suit have been dealt with zero cards dealt from at least one other suit, your advantage will usually range from about 3 percent to 10 percent. With nine cards dealt from one suit and zero cards dealt from at least one other suit, your advantage will usually range from about 6 percent to 20 percent.

APPROXIMATE ROYAL MATCH ADVANTAGES		
ANY SUIT	**ANY OTHER SUIT**	**PLAYER ADVANTAGE**
7 Dealt	0 Dealt	1% to 3%
8 Dealt	0 Dealt	3% to 10%
9 Dealt	0 Dealt	6% to 20%

If you are a card counter and you have a playing partner—a wife, girlfriend, or buddy—you could train your partner to watch for Royal Match betting opportunities while you just keep your regular count. You will often go through many decks without a Royal Match bet, but occasionally you will find a very strong advantage that will warrant a maximum bet, even with a modest bankroll. Royal Match bets are not usually restricted to the size of your blackjack bet.

One nice feature of the Royal Match bet is that casinos consider it a true sucker bet. Placing the bet never makes you look like a card counter. In fact, this bet will peg you as a gambling fool in the eyes of most bosses and surveillance personnel. If you are a card counter on a limited bankroll, and you play single-deck games with a small betting spread, placing regular Royal Match bets, especially if they are for more than the minimum allowed, will not only increase your edge over the house, but will probably buy you a lot of table time and possibly deeper penetration. If you can learn to do a quick scan of the cards just to watch for one dominant suit and one missing suit, you'll get real value from this bet.

NEVADA CASINOS WITH ONE-DECK ROYAL MATCH GAMES (SUBJECT TO CHANGE WITHOUT NOTICE):	
CITY	**CASINO**
Carson City	Nugget
Gardnerville	Topaz Lounge
Jackpot	Barton's Club
	Cactus Pete's
	Horseshu
Las Vegas	El Cortez
	Four Queens
	Golden Gate
	Gold Spike
	Lady Luck
	Las Vegas Club
	Plaza
	Western
Laughlin	Edgewater
Sparks (Reno)	Rail City
Verdi	Boomtown
Wendover	Peppermill
	Rainbow
	Silversmith

HOW TO BEAT "SUPER SEVENS"

Hindsight is easy, but it is foresight that pays off.
— *Burton F. Fabricand, The Science of Winning*

Super Sevens is an optional $1 side bet that has no effect on your regular blackjack hand. When you place a Super Sevens bet, you are wagering that the first one, two, or three cards dealt to your hand will be one, two, or three sevens. Here are the payoffs:

SUPER SEVENS PAYOUT SCHEDULE	
First card any 7	Pays 3 to 1
First two cards unsuited 7s	Pays 50 to 1
First two cards suited 7s	Pays 100 to 1
First three cards unsuited 7s	Pays 500 to 1
First three cards suited 7s	Pays 5000 to 1

You can see here that the real reason players place this bet is that there is a remote possibility of actually winning $5000 for a $1 bet! Just as a matter of record, you should know that the odds against your being dealt three suited sevens in a six-deck game are about 63,000 to 1, so that 5,000 to 1 payoff is a bit short. But, the fact is that all of those other payouts for various combinations of sevens make up most of the wins you can expect if you place this bet.

The overall house edge is about 11.4 percent, so if you're just playing a guessing-and-hoping game, over the long run it'll cost you about eleven cents every time you place a Super Sevens bet.

But, believe it or not, despite that high house edge, there is a very simple card-counting system for beating the Super Sevens bet. Unfortunately, because this betting option is always limited to a $1 maximum bet, the potential gain from using the counting system is about fourteen cents per hour, depending on how deep the penetration is on the game. With really deep penetration, you might even be able to win about twenty-five cents an hour! Yow! Let's form a Super Sevens card-counting team!

In the interest of completeness, since I doubt any other blackjack expert has yet published a Super Sevens card-counting system to go for that fourteen cents, here are the count values:

All 7s = -11
2, 3, 4, 5, 6, 8, 9, 10, ace = +1

This is an unbalanced count, making it very easy for you to earn that fourteen cents an hour. Here's how you win: In a six-deck shoe, start your running count at -24. In an eight-deck shoe, start your running count at -32. No, those are not typos. This is a very unbalanced counting system. We're trying to beat a house edge of 11 percent! As the cards are dealt, as per the above chart, you simply add one to your running count for every non-7 you see, and you subtract eleven from your running count for every 7 that is dealt. Any time your running count is zero or higher, place that Super Sevens bet!

Now, if you're actually crazy enough to learn and use this card-counting system, in an effort to beat a casino for fourteen cents an hour, you should bear in mind that this counting system will be of absolutely no value to your regular blackjack hand, where the house edge will assuredly be grinding your bankroll down at a much greater rate than fourteen cents an hour.

On the other hand, if you use Snyder's Snazzy Super Sevens System, I guarantee you that you will not be kicked out of any casino for card counting! And that's a personal guarantee, backed by my promise to send you fourteen cents—a full hour of Super Sevens pay—if you are ever thrown out for being a Super Sevens counter.

On the other hand, consider this: If you are using a card-counting system to play your regular blackjack hand, you can use the Super Sevens bet as pretty cheap camouflage to look like just another gambler at the table. Since the cost is only about eleven cents per hand, you can place five Super Sevens bets per hour for an average cost of about fifty-five cents.

HOW TO BEAT "LUCKY LADIES"

> In the highly fashionable but slightly disreputable atmosphere of the gambling rooms... Lady Luck was born.
> — *Warren Weaver, Lady Luck: The Theory of Probability*

Like Over/Under and Super Sevens, Lucky Ladies is a side bet that has no effect on your regular blackjack hand. Like Over/Under, most casinos restrict the bet to a $25 maximum. This is another one of those weird bets where the house edge off the top is huge—about 25 percent, the same as playing keno—but it can actually be beaten with card counting.

The option is never offered in single-deck games (at least, not that I've seen). It is usually offered in six-deck shoe games, and is occasionally offered in two-deck games. The payout schedules are different, based on the number of decks. You win if your first two cards total 20 (two tens or A-9), and you win more with specific two-card twenties.

Here are the standard payoff schedules:

LUCKY LADIES TWO-DECK PAY TABLE	
Any 20:	Pays 4 to 1
Suited 20:	Pays 10 to 1
Matched 20 (such as two jacks):	Pays 25 to 1
Queen of Hearts Pair:	Pays 200 to 1
Queen of Hearts Pair w/dealer BJ:	Pays 1000 to 1

LUCKY LADIES SIX-DECK PAY TABLE	
Any 20:	Pays 4 to 1
Suited 20:	Pays 9 to 1
Matched 20 (such as two jacks):	Pays 19 to 1
Queen of Hearts Pair:	Pays 125 to 1
Queen of Hearts Pair w/dealer BJ:	Pays 1000 to 1

That $25 maximum bet is not there because the casinos fear card counters are going to beat them at their Lucky Ladies games; it's because the casinos do not want to have to make a payout bigger than $25,000 if some lucky player actually gets dealt a Queen of Hearts pair when the dealer has a blackjack. That 1000 to 1 payoff is the reason a lot of players are attracted to this option. Just as a matter of interest, you should probably know that the odds against your being dealt a queen of hearts pair when the dealer has a blackjack, in the six-deck game, are almost 70,000 to 1 against it happening. And in the two-deck game, the odds against it are about 115,000 to 1 against it. So, that 1,000 to 1 payoff isn't really something to write home about.

Where the card counter can make his money on this option is on all of those other twenties that occur. One nice thing about Lucky Ladies is that you don't really need a "special" card-counting system to take advantage of it. The Red Seven Count works just fine.

But, that is also the problem with trying to win money at Lucky Ladies that we don't find at, say, Royal Match. The times when you will want to place this bet are precisely when you have a big bet on the table because your count is high and you also have a big bet on your regular blackjack hand. Betting the Lucky Ladies bet makes you look more like a card counter. Royal Match bets, or Super Sevens bets, make you look like a regular gambler—and not a threat—because these bets have no correlation with any blackjack card-counting system.

But, if you're willing to chance it, you can make money placing Lucky Ladies bets with the Red Seven Count if you follow these guidelines:

Six decks: Never place a Lucky Ladies bet in the first four decks of the deal, no matter how high your count. Place the bet in the last two decks if your running count is +10 or greater.

> Two decks: Never place a Lucky Ladies bet in the first deck of the deal, no matter how high your count. Place the bet in the second deck if your running count is +6 or greater.

WHAT'S IT WORTH?

At the two-deck game, with $25 Lucky Ladies bets, you'll probably add about $6 per hour to your win rate. The small value is due to the fact that you just won't see the counts you need to place the bet that often.

At the six-deck game, with $25 Lucky Ladies bets, you'll probably add about $2 per hour to your win rate. You'll place the bet even less often.

Is it worth it? Quite frankly, in the six-deck shoe game, I think it's a bad bet, primarily because the fluctuations can be high compared to the win potential. In the two-deck game, it's a judgment call. In my judgment, I'd be afraid I'd look too much like a card counter, in addition to the big fluctuations.

A WORD ABOUT THOSE DAMNABLE FLUX

I'll be using the term fluctuation (or flux) throughout this book, so perhaps I ought to explain what I mean by it a little more clearly. For simplicity, let's use a coin-flip example. If you were to flip an honest coin four times, you would expect your results to be exactly two heads and two tails. But, if you were to ask a statistician to calculate the odds of your coming up with exactly two heads and two tails, he'd tell you that the odds against that result are almost 2 to 1. In fact, you will come up with exactly two heads and two tails only about 37 percent of the time. On 63 percent of your four-flip series, you'll get either three or four heads or tails.

That's fluctuation, and it's the same in blackjack.

It doesn't seem fair that this happens, but as gamblers, there's nothing we can do but learn to live with flux.

Let's take another coin-flip example to explain how it works when we bet with an edge. If I told you that you could flip an honest coin, and you'd lose $100 every time it came up tails, but you'd win $102 every time it came up heads, you would have a clear mathematical advantage in this game. On average, every other flip, you'd come ahead $2.

But, what if all the money you had to gamble with was $1000? Would this be a good game for you?

No. Because even though you're flipping an honest coin, the likelihood of losing your $1000 just because of normal fluctuation is very high. In fact, despite your mathematical advantage in this game, you are more likely to run into a bad run of tails that will break you than you are to come out ahead if you just keep betting $100 per flip. You just can't bet 10 percent of your bankroll with a 1 percent edge. You're headed for the poorhouse.

Now, if you had $100,000 in the same game, you would still experience both negative and positive fluctuations in your results, but your bankroll would slowly but surely climb at the rate of $100 for every one hundred coin flips, and I'd never break you. For all intents and purposes, you would be like a casino with a small house edge. Sometimes I'd beat you when a bunch of tails just happened to land, but in the long run, you'd just keep winning my money.

If you want to make a living from gambling, you have to think like a casino. There is no way to eliminate flux. Somebody will hit a royal flush on your video poker machine, and you have to pay out the four thousand coins. There's no way to avoid it. You have to have both the mathematical advantage as well as the money behind you to ride out the flux if you want to make a living from gambling. There is no casino on the planet that loses money on their gambling tables in the long run. And there's no pro gambler who doesn't win year after year if he's doing it right, and has the bankroll to back up his play.

Beware of the Big-Flux Bankroll Eaters!

Believe it or not, blackjack is actually a game with relatively mild fluctuations compared to many other casino games. This is because blackjack has mostly even-money payouts. You bet $100 to win $100. The problem with many side-bets and gimmick bonuses we find added to blackjack games, however, is that the probability of winning is a longshot. When we are able to get an advantage on these bets, our advantage is based on getting a payout much bigger than even money.

Any time you have an opportunity to make money on a betting option that pays more than even money, you can expect your bankroll fluctuations to be much greater than on an even-money payout game. You will only win the Lucky Ladies bet about one out of every ten times that you place it. This means that if you are betting $25, you can expect to have many runs of Lucky Ladies bets where you lose hundreds of dollars before you hit a win. Sometimes you may win the bet a few times in succession, but there is no way to control the high fluctuations other than cutting back on your bet size.

If your bankroll is very limited, then be careful of betting on any of the side-bets that feature big payouts for small bets. Just because you can get an edge in a game does not mean you should place the bet.

HOW TO BEAT "SPANISH 21"

There is a kind of fatal fascination in gambling which some persons appear to be wholly unable to resist. It is therefore quite as well that those who will indulge in such an expensive propensity should do so, at least, with their eyes open.

— *John Neville Maskelyne, Sharps and Flats*

Now we're getting into the I-can't-believe-it's-not-blackjack games. For convenience, let's just call these games "pseudo-blackjack." They look like blackjack. They feel like blackjack. They play like blackjack.

They're not blackjack.

THE BIG TRICK

Every pseudo-blackjack game has a big trick to it—something the house did to fundamentally change the game that is not immediately apparent to the players, but that is very apparent to the house in their bottom-line profits. With Spanish 21, the big trick is the removal of all the pip tens. All of the jacks, queens, and kings are there, but the actual tens, the ones with ten pips (diamonds, hearts, clubs, or spades) on them, are nowhere to be found.

You may recall from our "Meet the Cards" chapter that we labeled the tens "the most important denomination." You may also recall from that same chapter that we emphasized that "all modern card-counting systems today are based on Ed Thorp's Ten-Count." For blackjack players who are attempting to beat the house, card-counting strategies are based primarily on the tens. It is the presence of excess tens in the deck that provide us with our strongest advantages.

So, in the Spanish 21 game, what those devious casino game inventors did was remove all of the pip tens from an eight-deck shoe, which is to say, they took out thirty-two of our beloved tens! That's a hell of a lot of tens!

Years ago, some of the casinos in Puerto Rico had a reputation for removing tens from their shoe games. This was not a good reputation as far as players were concerned. In fact, it was considered to be cheating. There is a book that was published in 1999, written by a former Nevada Gaming Control agent, Bill Zender, *How to Detect Casino Cheating at Blackjack*, in which Bill describes a cheating technique called the "short deck," in which the dealer (or boss) secretly removes tens from the deck in order to give the house an unnaturally high advantage over the players.

Well, with Spanish 21, it's no secret! They just up and stole thirty-two of those tens out of the shoe, and said, "Card counters welcome!"

They put all kinds of bonuses and extra good rules into the game that you don't get with regular blackjack. But, unfortunately, all those great rules just won't make up for all those missing tens.

You actually can get a small advantage on Spanish 21 with card counting, but you need a relatively huge betting spread, which requires a relatively huge bankroll, and the strategy is much more difficult. In fact, the Spanish 21 basic strategy is much more difficult than regular blackjack because of all those weird bonuses and options. But, for the sake of completeness, I'm going to provide a "short" version of Spanish 21, just in case you find yourself on a desert island where it's the only game available, and you're feeling like a glutton for punishment.

I presented a "simplified" basic strategy for regular blackjack games in chapter two, which consisted of ten simple rules to remember. For Spanish 21, I can't get it down to fewer than fifteen rules, and even then, this is far from ideal. You can cut the house edge to about 1 percent by playing this approximate basic strategy that is much easier to learn than the full chart.

SIMPLIFIED SPANISH 21 BASIC STRATEGY

1. Never take insurance.
2. Always double down on 11.
3. Double down on 10 versus 2 through 8.
4. Always hit hard 12 and 13.
5. Stand on 14 through 16 versus 2 to 6, and hit 14 through 16 versus 7 to ace.
6. Always stand on hard 17 and soft 18 up.
7. Always split aces and eights.
8. Never split fours, fives, or tens.
9. Split all other pairs—twos, threes, sixes, sevens, and nines—versus 2 to 6.
10. Surrender hard 16 and 17 versus ace.
11. Double down on A-5, A-6, and A-7 versus 4, 5, and 6.
12. Hit all other soft totals.
13. Surrender after doubling with 12 to 16 versus 8 to ace.
14. Always hit hard 14 and 15 comprised of five or more cards.
15. Always hit soft 17 and 18 comprised of five or more cards.

The Full Strategy

Depending on the exact set of rules and the number of decks (six or eight), the house edge at Spanish 21 is not that dissimilar from traditional blackjack for a basic strategy player. It ranges from about 0.4 percent to 0.8 percent. In Atlantic City, where dealers stand on soft 17, it's only about 0.4 percent. In Nevada, where dealers usually hit soft 17, it's more like 0.8 percent. If the redoubling option is allowed, then even the hit soft 17 game has an edge of only about 0.4 percent. But these house edges are assuming that you learn perfect basic strategy for the game, not the fifteen rules above. And that basic strategy is so much more difficult than the basic strategy for regular blackjack.

It's the bonus payouts that make it difficult. For example, the Spanish 21 basic strategy with a soft 17 is to double down against a dealer 4, 5, or 6. But if it's a three-card soft 17, then you hit versus 4, and double versus 5 and 6 only. If it's a four-card soft 17, you hit versus 4 or 5, and double versus 6. But if it's a five-card soft 17, then you don't double against 4, 5, or 6; you just hit. Virtually all of the hard and soft double down decisions, and many of the hard and soft hit/stand decisions, change depending on the number of cards that make up your hand.

It's hard for me to imagine that any player would actually devote the memory work necessary to learning this complete strategy when regular blackjack basic strategy is so much easier, plus you can actually beat regular blackjack by counting cards. For all practical purposes, you can't beat Spanish 21 with card counting. The absence of all those tens really does hurt. The dealer busts much less frequently. Your double downs fail more often. That house edge hardly ever goes away.

So How Do You Beat Spanish 21?

The title of this chapter is "How to Beat Spanish 21." So, how do we beat it? If you've got a fairly substantial bankroll, and you're willing to chance getting thrown out of the casino for card counting, you can beat this game. First, learn the complete Spanish 21 basic strategy in the Appendix. You will also need to use the Red Seven Count. In an eight-deck (minus the thirty-two tens) Spanish 21 game, start your running count at -48. In a six-deck (minus the twenty-four tens) Spanish 21 game, start your running count at -36.

In the eight-deck game, bet one unit until you have reached the last three decks of the deal. Then, if your running count goes over zero, bet at least thirty units. That is, raise your bet from $5 to $150. In the six-deck game, again bet one unit until you have reached the last three decks of the deal. Then, if your running count goes over zero, bet at least twenty-five units. That is, raise your bet from $5 to $125.

That's all there is to it.

Of course, I think the absolute best way for players to beat this game is to avoid playing it. If no one plays, the game will die, and perhaps a real blackjack table will take its place.

HOW TO BEAT "SUPER FUN 21"

In accordance with the traditional wisdom spouted by Nick Tosches above, in the traditional blackjack game, basic strategy tells us that we should not double down on a total of 10 when the dealer shows a face card. It is precisely this traditional wisdom that makes Super Fun 21 a beatable game for card counters. In Super Fun 21, the basic strategy is to always double down on a total of 10, even against dealers' tens and aces. Many players, dealers, and even pit bosses will think you are stupid when you make these plays, and that's why smart players can beat Super Fun 21 games. It's a more difficult game to beat than the traditional blackjack game, but you will often have wider latitude to apply your count strategy without the casino feeling threatened.

I'm calling Super Fun 21 a "pseudo-blackjack" variation because it is different enough from the traditional game that if you approach it with standard basic strategy and card counting—with no adjustments for the rule variations or bigger house edge off the top—you will not beat the game. The fact is, however, Super Fun 21 is much closer to traditional blackjack than Spanish 21 is, and you can beat this game with the Red Seven Count and a big betting spread.

THE BIG TRICK

Whereas in Spanish 21, the casinos' big trick was the removal of all of the pip tens, the big trick in Super Fun 21 is that player blackjacks pay even money instead of 3 to 2. If you look at the chart of rule effects in chapter six, this rule is the single most costly rule for players listed in the chart, earning for the house an extra $2.32 for every $100 you bet.

And, as with Spanish 21, the house attracts players to this game by offering a whole slew of liberal rules that—once more—do not really make up for the huge cost of the big trick. In fact, Super Fun 21 is quite a bit worse for a basic strategy player than Spanish 21. In a Super Fun game, the house edge against you even with perfect Super Fun basic strategy is almost a full 1 percent. That's about twice as costly for a basic strategy player as the cost of the traditional game.

But this extra cost can be more than made up for with card counting, and the Super Fun strategy is not nearly so difficult as the Spanish 21 strategy. Super Fun 21 is always dealt from a single deck, and in addition to blackjacks paying only even money, the other bad rule is that dealers hit soft 17. Here are the good rules:

SUPER FUN 21 RULES

- Players may double down on any number of cards.
- Players may double down after pair splits.
- Resplits to four hands are allowed, including resplits of aces.
- Players may also hit and double down on split aces.
- Players may surrender on any number of cards.
- Players may surrender after doubling down.
- Player blackjack beats dealer blackjack.
- Player blackjack in diamonds pays 2 to 1.
- Player hand totaling 21 with five or more cards pays 2 to 1 (except after doubling).
- Player hand totaling 20 or less with six or more cards is an automatic winner (except after doubling).

The Super Fun basic strategy is very close to the basic strategy for the traditional game—so close that if you know the traditional game strategy, you can easily learn the few differences in the Super Fun strategy. Rather than provide a list of simple rules for approximating the Super Fun 21 basic strategy, I'm going to describe the Super Fun strategy in comparison to the traditional strategy. This should make it easier for you to learn and remember. If you don't know basic strategy for the traditional game, but you want to learn the perfect Super Fun strategy, there is a comprehensive Super Fun 21 strategy in the Appendix.

SUPER FUN 21 BASIC STRATEGY (COMPARED TO THE TRADITIONAL GAME)

1. Exactly as in the traditional game, you stand on all stiffs (12 to 16) against dealer upcards of 2-6, except hit 12 against 2 or 3 (again, just as in the traditional game).

2. As in the traditional game, you hit all stiffs (12 to 16) against dealer 7, 8, 9, 10, or ace.
    Exception: Surrender 16 versus 10 or ace, and 15 versus ace.

3. Always double down on hard 10 or 11.
    Double down on 9 versus 2-6.

4. Soft double on A-2 versus 5 and 6.
    Soft double on A-3, A-4, and A-5 versus 4, 5, and 6.
    Soft double on A-6 versus 2-6.
    Soft double on A-7 versus 3-6.
    Soft double on A-8 versus 6.

5. Always split aces and eights.
    Never split fives or tens.

6. Split twos, threes, and sixes versus 2-7.
    Split sevens versus 2-8.

7. Split fours versus 5 and 6.

8. Always split nines except versus 7 or 10. (And, yes, you split nines versus ace!)

9. With four or more cards: Never double down or surrender, just hit.

10. With five or more cards: Hit every stiff (12 to 16) and hit every soft hand (except soft 21).

The above Super Fun basic strategy is close to perfect. The multiple-card strategies for four- or five-card hands are close to perfect and easy to remember. You can find the exact multi-card-hand strategy in the Appendix. Those seemingly weird plays with four- or five-card hands are actually pretty logical if you think about the bonus payouts you get with five- or six-card totals. For instance, you would always hit a five-card soft hand (other than soft 21) because you can't bust a soft hand with one hit and any six-card hand is an automatic winner.

Likewise, in Super Fun 21, we hit all of our five-card stiffs, even against dealer low cards. Consider the fact that if you hit a hard 14 with an ace or deuce—technically a terrible hit card in the traditional game—you have an automatic winner in Super Fun 21. So, with five cards in our hand, we play very aggressively.

In any case, the Super Fun basic strategy is fairly easy to learn if you already have the traditional basic strategy memorized. Now, how do we beat the game with card counting? That is also pretty easily accomplished. The Red Seven Count is an excellent counting system for this game.

BEATING SUPER FUN 21 WITH THE RED SEVEN COUNT

Use the Red Seven counting system exactly as you would in the traditional game. As in any single-deck game, our starting count is -2. Here's how you bet, according to the running count:

RED SEVEN SUPER FUN 21 BETTING STRATEGY	
COUNT	BET (IN UNITS)
0 or less	1
+1	2
+2	4
+3	8
+4 or more	the farm

That's it. With this betting strategy, you will beat the game. That "farm" bet you place at a running count of +4 or more, means that you bet whatever you can get away with. This will depend on both your bankroll and what you believe the casino's tolerance for bet spreads is at this game. One nice feature of Super Fun 21 is that casinos have considered it a sucker game that card counters are not much interested in, so some casinos have been more tolerant of big bet spreads.

As with any card-counting game, you want to play with the deepest shuffle point you can find. If the dealer is only dealing out half a deck between shuffles, you will not get many good betting opportunities. One nice feature of Super Fun 21 is that it is generally offered at low stakes. This means your low bets can be very low compared to your high bets. And, because some casinos consider this to be a game of little interest to counters, these low-stakes Super Fun 21 tables are often not monitored by game protection personnel the same way traditional blackjack games are. When you sit down at a Super Fun table, the immediate assumption of casino personnel is that you are a recreational player, not savvy about the odds of the games.

You can also increase your win rate slightly by deviating from the Super Fun basic strategy according to your running count on a few hands. Here's how to play:

RED SEVEN SUPER FUN 21 PLAYING STRATEGY	
RUNNING COUNT	**STRATEGY CHANGE**
0 and above	15 v. 10, Surrender instead of Hit
-3 and below	16 v. 10, Hit instead of Surrender
-3 and below	13 v. 2, Hit instead of Stand
-3 and below	12 v. 4, Hit instead of Stand
-3 and below	10 v. 10, Hit instead of Double

Depending on how deep the dealer is dealing the game, and how much of a betting spread you can use, the Red Seven betting and playing strategy should get you an edge over the house of somewhere between 0.5 percent to a full 1 percent. Again, remember, penetration is the name of the game. And you need that big betting spread in order to beat this game. If all your bankroll can afford is a $5 to $20 spread, Super Fun 21 is not for you. If you can spread $5 to $50, or better yet, $5 to $100, you'll get them.

Some casinos, especially in Las Vegas, know that card counting can beat these games, so you may find yourself being asked to leave if you use a big spread. Or, conversely, the dealer may be instructed to shuffle the cards earlier if you raise your bet. So, quit the game and find a better opportunity. We're here to make money, right? It's only super fun when we win! If they won't let us win, we leave.

Who Invented Super Fun 21?

In 1981, the Vegas World Casino in Las Vegas introduced a game called "Experto Blackjack." It was a single-deck game with good rules—dealer stood on soft 17, and the player could double down on any two cards—but blackjacks paid even money. The gimmick was that fifty of the fifty-two cards were dealt out, making the game really tempting to "experts," hence the game's name. This game was the brainchild of Vegas World owner, Bob Stupak, and his poker whiz buddy, David Sklansky.

Experto Blackjack was, in fact, beatable with card counting, provided the player truly was an expert counter who could take full advantage of many of the unusual plays that would come up when only a few cards were left in the deck, and—most importantly—could use a big betting spread in those same late-deck opportunities. Unfortunately, Stupak was a very sharp guy who really understood card counting, and whenever a counter showed up who appeared to have the ability to beat the Experto game, he would limit the player's betting spread.

I knew a few card counters back then who told me they could and did beat the Experto game, even with the bet restrictions. Stupak was a gambler himself, and he respected real experts. One counter told me that after Stupak restricted him to a 1 to 3 spread, he continued playing and continued to beat the game. Stupak came down to the table just to watch him, as he admired the player's skill. The player did finally quit playing because his edge was extremely small and he knew he could get better blackjack games around town. I suspect Experto Blackjack was the forerunner, and initial inspiration, for Super Fun 21.

Flash forward to 2001. The Vegas World Casino is long gone, replaced by the Stratosphere, and Experto has not been seen for fifteen years. A former card counter, Howard Grossman, who once played on Ken Uston's teams, rekindles the Experto idea with a new twist. He creates a single-deck game with blackjacks again paying even money, but instead of dealing the cards to the bottom, he inserts a slew of player options.

Super Fun 21 takes off big time. Grossman is a smart guy who knows what the public wants. Only real blackjack experts understood the value of dealing out fifty cards in the deck. But everyone understands there is value in doubling down on three or more cards, hitting after doubling, surrendering after hitting, etc.

In any case, sad to say, Super Fun 21 was invented by a card counter.

HOW TO BEAT "DOUBLE EXPOSURE"

> "It's a funny thing—gamblin'. It's like running a grocery store. You buy and you sell. You pay the going rate for cards and you try and sell 'em for more than you paid. A gambler's ace is his ability to think clearly under stress. That's very important, because, you see, fear is the basis of all mankind."
>
> —*Pug Pearson, as quoted by Jon Bradshaw in Fast Company*

Double Exposure is a game that attracts players because of a big gimmick: The dealer exposes both of his first two cards before the player plays his hand! Wow! No hole card! How can we possibly lose at this game?

THE BIG TRICK(S)

The dealer wins ties, and player blackjacks pay even money.

That's all.

The killer here is the dealer wins ties rule. That one costs you about 9 percent. Think about it. The most common tie hand in blackjack is a dealer 20 versus a player 20. This is the most common tie because there are four times as many ten-valued cards as any other denomination.

> If you play double exposure, you will continually find yourself with a hand totaling 20 facing a dealer 20, and you have to hit, praying for an ace. Let's just say you bust an awful lot in double exposure.

So, although we would have a killer advantage over the house if we could see both of the dealer's cards in the traditional game, the big trick in Double Exposure more than negates that edge.

Double Exposure games are usually dealt from six- or eight-deck shoes. There are a few rule variations that differ from casino to casino. Some casinos rule that a tied natural is a win for the player. Some rule that a tied natural is a push. Some rule that dealers stand on soft 17, while some rule that dealers hit soft 17. Some rule that players may double down after splits, while in others there are no doubles after splits. Most casinos allow players to double down on any two cards, while in others, doubling is restricted to 10-11 or 9-10-11 only. Insurance is generally allowed at Double Exposure games. If the dealer's first card is an ace, insurance will be offered before exposing the second card.

If we look at the worst game, where tied naturals push, the dealers hit soft 17, doubling down is allowed on 10-11 only, and the player may not double down after splits, the house edge is about 1.75 percent. That is not good at all. However, more than one percent of that edge comes from the double down restriction. As soon as the player is allowed to double down on any two cards, the house edge is not much worse than a normal shoe game. With favorable rules, some Double Exposure games are even better than most shoe games.

So, my first rule for anyone who wants to beat Double Exposure is: Do not play if you are not allowed to double down on any first two cards. The game will not be beatable. Most casinos with double exposure games allow players to double down on any first two cards. Based on the other rules, the house edge off the top will generally range from about 0.2 percent to 0.7 percent.

The second most important rule is the soft 17 rule. The house gets an extra 0.4 percent if the dealer hits soft 17. If you have a choice between two double exposure games with different soft 17 rules, definitely take the stand on soft 17 game.

THE BASIC THEORY

You can beat Double Exposure games with the Red Seven Count. The basic approach to beating these games is similar to beating regular blackjack games. You will play more aggressively, doubling and splitting to get more money on the table, when the dealer is weak, and you will play more conservatively, not doubling or splitting, when the dealer has a strong hand.

Double Exposure strategy charts look very complicated because there are so many more dealer hands to play against than in a regular blackjack game. In the normal game, the dealer has only ten different possible upcards. In Double Exposure, we have to consider twenty-six different dealer totals—all hard hands between 4 and 20, plus all soft hands from A-A to A-9.

Looking at the basic strategy, one thing you'll quickly notice is that there is a very distinct difference between a real dealer stiff (say a hard 14) and a dealer total that is simply weak, like a hard 4 (two deuces), but is not yet really a stiff hand.

As an example, our proper Double Exposure basic strategy when the dealer has a hard 14 is to double down on all soft totals from A-2 to A-9, and all hard totals from 5 to 11. Yes, we double down on a total of 5 against a hard 14! Against a dealer total of 4, however, we only double down with hard 10 or 11, or soft 18. Big difference.

THE SIMPLIFIED BASIC STRATEGY

Even with all of those twenty-six different dealer totals, we can describe a very close approximation of Double Exposure basic strategy with a dozen simple rules. Here's how to play:

1. If the dealer has a pat hand (17 to 21), you must hit any hard or soft hand that does not beat his hand, and (obviously) always stand if you have his pat hand beaten. Example: you have a hard 19, and the dealer has a soft 19. You must hit.

2. Stand on any hard total of 16 to 21 that is not already beaten by a dealer pat hand. Example: you have a hard 16, and the dealer has a total of 11. You stand. I'm using this example because your intuition may tell you that the dealer's hard 11 is a strong starting hand, and your 16 is weak. You would think you would hit. Wrong. Follow the rule and stand.

3. Stand on all hard totals of 12 to 15 versus dealer hard totals of 4, 5, 6, and 12 to 16.

4. Hit 12 to 15 against dealer totals of 7 to 11.

5. Never double down or split a pair against a dealer pat hand (17 to 21).

6. Double down on totals of 10 and 11 versus all dealer stiffs (hard 12 to 16) as well as against dealer hard totals of 4 to 8 and soft totals of 14, 15, and 16.

7. Double down on totals of 8 and 9 versus all dealer stiffs (hard 12 to 16).

8. Double down on totals of 5, 6, and 7 versus hard 14, 15, and 16.

9. Double down on all soft hands (except soft 21) versus all dealer stiffs (hard 12 to 16).

10. Double down on soft 17, 18, and 19 versus dealer hard totals of 4, 5, and 6.

11. Other than the soft doubles above, hit all soft totals of A-2 to A-7, and stand on A-8 and A-9.

11. Split aces against any hard or soft total of 2 to 6 and 12 to 16.

12. Split all other pairs (except fours and fives) against dealer hard totals of 4, 5, and 6 and all dealer stiffs (hard 12 to 16).

If you learn these twelve rules, you will be playing a fairly accurate Double Exposure basic strategy. A more comprehensive basic strategy for Double Exposure is contained in the Appendix.

THE RED SEVEN BETTING STRATEGY

Use the same betting strategy for Double Exposure that you use for regular blackjack games. Start your running count at -12 in the six-deck game and at -16 in the eight-deck game. Bet one unit at all negative counts, and raise your bet when your running count gets to zero. Follow the same betting schedule for other bet raises at Double Exposure as described in chapter five for regular blackjack.

As with any blackjack game, you want to find a game with the deepest penetration, and you want to use the biggest betting spread you can get away with. Because Double Exposure is dealt from a shoe, you would prefer to table-hop and avoid playing at negative counts. Unfortunately, because these games are few and far between—of the relatively few casinos that offer Double Exposure, many have only one table—you may not have a choice of these tables to back-count and table-hop. So, to beat the game, you want to get a betting spread of at least one to eight units, and more if possible.

THE RED SEVEN PLAYING STRATEGY

Mercifully—because the Double Exposure basic strategy is so complex—there are few playing strategy adjustments to make based on your count. Knowing both of the dealer's cards really does play most of your hands for you.

Here are the playing strategy adjustments to make based on your Red Seven running count:

AT A RUNNING COUNT OF ZERO:
Stand on hard 13 v. 11 (instead of hit)
Stand on hard 14 v. 10 (instead of hit)
Stand on hard 15 v. 9 (instead of hit)
Stand on hard 16 v. 7 (instead of hit)
AT A RUNNING COUNT OF +2, IN THE SECOND HALF OF THE SHOE ONLY:
Take insurance.

Other strategy variations at Double Exposure are not worth much. If you have a good Double Exposure game available to you, then I would advise you to learn the comprehensive basic strategy in the Appendix. Most blackjack card counters are not attracted to Double Exposure because the game strategy is so complex and the tables that offer this variation of blackjack are so rare. For this reason, casinos are much more tolerant of players who spread their bets at Double Exposure, and rarely are these games closely watched by surveillance. Also, most pit bosses, dealers, and game protection personnel are clueless about the basic strategy. They cannot even tell when you are playing correctly, so you do not need camouflage plays.

Some Basic Strategy Practice Hands

After studying the twelve basic strategy rules above, see if you can play each of these ten hands correctly. For each player hand, determine whether you should hit, stand, double down, or split based on the dealer's exposed total. The answers are on the following page.

Or, if you're feeling brave, try answering the decision question without studying the twelve basic strategy rules. Then turn the page and see how well your intuitive feel for the game compares to reality.

DOUBLE EXPOSURE QUIZ

PLAYER HAND	DEALER HAND	DECISION?
= hard 11	= hard 17	_____
= hard 20	= hard 13	_____
= hard 8	= hard 14	_____
= hard 12	= hard 5	_____
= soft 12	= hard 17	_____
= soft 20	= hard 15	_____
= hard 18	= soft 18	_____
= hard 13	= hard 10	_____
= soft 18	= soft 16	_____
= hard 16	= soft 13	_____

HOW TO BEAT "DOUBLE EXPOSURE"

DOUBLE EXPOSURE QUIZ ANSWERS		
PLAYER HAND	DEALER HAND	DECISION?
= hard 11	= hard 17	Hit
= hard 20	= hard 13	Split
= hard 8	= hard 14	Double
= hard 12	= hard 5	Stand
= soft 12	= hard 17	Hit
= soft 20	= hard 15	Double
= hard 18	= soft 18	Hit
= hard 13	= hard 10	Stand
= soft 18	= soft 16	Hit
= hard 16	= soft 13	Stand

If you didn't study the twelve rules first, then I'll bet you got less than 70 percent correct. Unfortunately, a passing grade is 100 percent. If you actually want to make money at this game, there is no room for errors. You must play the basic strategy at the very least in accordance with the twelve rules I provided.

Professional Gambler's Rule #10:

There is no room for guesswork when your money's on the table.

Who invented Double Exposure?

The first version of this game was invented by a mathematician named Richard Epstein, and was described in his book, The *Theory of Gambling and Statistical Logic* (1967). In Epstein's version of the game, the dealer won ties, but blackjacks paid 3 to 2, giving the player better than a 2 percent advantage over the house. (Gee, I wonder why no casino ever offered this version?) Epstein called the game Zweikartenspiel, a German word that loosely translates as "two-card gamble."

The first live casino Double Exposure game appeared at—you guessed it!—Bob Stupak's Vegas World in 1979. There were a number of minor differences between Stupak's and Epstein's versions of the game, the main differences being that Vegas World offered the game dealt from a five-deck shoe, while Epstein's version of the game proposed it as a single-deck game; and, unfortunately, in the real-world casino game, blackjacks paid even money.

Blackjack Hall of Famer Julian Braun developed the first Zweikartenspiel basic strategy, which was published in Epstein's book. But when the live casino game appeared with different rules, two other Blackjack Hall of Famers—Stanford Wong and Peter Griffin—worked out the first strategy for card counters.

HOW TO BEAT "BLACKJACK SWITCH"

> Two immediate things happen when you drink. One, your senses are dulled, and two, you lose your inhibitions. Both are deadly sins at a gambling table.
>
> — *Edwin Silberstang, How to Gamble and Win*

If you want to commit a mortal sin at a blackjack table, have a few drinks while you're playing "Blackjack Switch." This is a truly fun but crazy variation on the game, created by a British player named Geoff Hall, no doubt to drive players nuts. If you are a player who likes to play two hands per round, you'll probably like this game automatically, and you will definitely be tempted to give it a try. Did you ever look at your two hands and wish you could switch the 10 from one hand with the 5 or 6 from the other one and give yourself a blackjack? Did you ever sit there muttering to yourself, "If only these same cards had been in a different order." If so, you will love this game.

What makes this game even more fun, for me, is knowing what to do and how to play when the dealers, pit bosses, and game protection personnel are all clueless as to the proper strategy, so I look like just another nutty (but lucky) gambler when I'm sitting there kicking their butts. Yes, you can beat this game with the Red Seven Count!

If you ever gamble in Internet casinos, you've probably seen "Blackjack Switch" listed among the game options. The Internet version uses different rules than the live casino games I've found in Las Vegas. The strategy provided here is for the live games, since the Internet games are reshuffled after every round and you can't beat them with card counting. There are at least three downtown Las Vegas casinos that have begun offering Blackjack Switch games in recent years. So, keep your eyes open. If this game is not available at any casino where you play right now, it may turn up soon at a casino near you.

THE GIMMICK

The big draw of this game is that you play two simultaneous hands and you are allowed to switch the second cards dealt to each hand if you so desire. That is, if one of your hands has a 6 and a 10, and the other hand has an ace and a 5, you may switch the 10 from the first hand with the 5 from the second hand to have two hands of 11 and blackjack!

How can we possibly lose at this game?

THE BIG TRICK

Well, there are a couple of big tricks to this game. First, player blackjacks only pay even money. Second, a dealer total of 22 is an automatic push on any hand except a player blackjack. In other words, if you double down on that 11 and catch a 10 for a total of 21, then the dealer hits his hand to 22, your 21 hand just pushes, and—if you are holding a blackjack against the dealer's 22—your blackjack wins, but only even money.

THE RULES OF THE GAME

In other respects, Blackjack Switch is similar to any standard shoe game. The game is dealt face up from either six or eight decks. All players must play two hands, and both hands must have equal bets. Only the second card (or top card) dealt to each hand can be switched. You cannot switch a first card from one hand with a second card from the other. This is important.

HOW TO BEAT "BLACKJACK SWITCH"

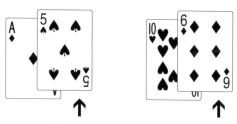

Only these two cards may be switched.

In the two hands shown above, much as we'd like to, we cannot switch cards to make a blackjack.

Other rules: The dealer hits soft 17. You may double down on any two cards and double down after pair splits. Resplits up to four hands are allowed. Insurance is allowed but the dealer checks for blackjack before the player switches. So the player does not have a chance to switch one hand to a blackjack if the dealer has a blackjack. A player blackjack pays even money, and is the only hand that will beat a dealer total of 22. Otherwise, a dealer total of 22 will push all player hands, including 21. A dealer blackjack will push a player blackjack.

The difficulty for most players in this game is knowing when to switch. Some hands, such as the first hand described above where a player could switch to make a blackjack and an 11 out of a hard 16 and a soft 16 are obvious switches. Anyone with the most basic understanding of the game would know that the switch is creating two strong hands out of two weak hands. But it's not always so obvious whether to switch or not. For instance, what do you do with that A-5 and 10-6 above?

The switch strategy provided below will get the house edge against the basic strategy player down to about 0.25 percent, a smaller house edge than a traditional blackjack shoe game. This is yet another blackjack variation beatable with card counting, but only if you take the time to learn the correct strategy.

After you have made your switch decision, the basic strategy for Blackjack Switch is very similar to basic strategy for a regular blackjack game, and the card-counting strategy with the Red Seven Count is also very similar. The hard part is the switch, and it's not really that hard—just different from any decision you're accustomed to making in a blackjack game. It's not just a question of which hand is better, this one or that one, against a specified dealer upcard, but which two-hand set, these two hands or those two hands, are jointly better against a specified dealer upcard. So, let's learn to switch!

The Switch

The first strategic play you must decide on in this game is the switch. Before you can play your hands, you must decide if you would be better with the two different hands you can get by switching your top cards. Switching strategy is not really difficult once you define the dealer's upcard and the two hands you've been dealt against that dealer upcard.

Defining the Dealer's Upcard

We have three types of dealer's upcard:

- Strong: any upcard from 7 to ace.
- Weak: any upcard from 3 to 6.
- Deuce: any 2. We have separated this upcard from the weak upcards because the deuce is less likely to bust in BJ Switch. That's because a dealer total of 22 is an automatic push against all player hands except blackjack.

Defining the Player's Hands with the WLPC System

There are four different types of player hands—Winner, Loser, Push, and Chance. For shorthand, I call this the WLPC classification. In defining the player hands, we make an assumption that the dealer has a 10 in the hole. Obviously, this is not always the case, but we make this assumption anyway in order to define the potential strength of our hands with the WLPC classification system. Here are the WLPC player hand definitions:

- Winner: Any blackjack and any hard or soft total from 18 to 20 that beats the dealer's total (assuming 10 in the hole) is a winner. Or, any player total of 8 to 11 that beats the dealer upcard. Examples: Player 18 versus dealer 7 is a winner. Player 9 versus dealer 8 is a winner.

  A pair that we would split is a winner only if each of the split cards would qualify as winners versus the dealer upcard. Examples: 8-8 versus 7 is a winner. 7-7 versus 6 is not, because although we would split 7-7 versus 6, a player 7 is not in the group of player hands (8 to 11 and 18 to 21) that can qualify a hand as a winner. Note that we do count the 7 as a strong dealer upcard, but it does not ever qualify a player hand as a winner.

Finally, the only player hands that qualify as winners versus a 2 are: 10, 11, 19, 20, and 21.

- Loser: Any player hand, pat or stiff, that is beaten by a dealer's strong upcard (7 to ace) is a loser. Examples: A-5 versus 7 is a loser. 19 versus 10 is a loser. 8-8 versus 9 is a loser.
- Push: Any hand from 18 to 20, or 8 to 11, that would push the dealer's strong upcard. Examples: 19 versus 9 is a push; 20 versus 10 is a push; 8-8 versus 8 is a push. A-7 versus 8 is a push. Note that 16 versus 6 is not a push because it fails to meet the definition in two ways. One, 16 is not a total from 18 to 20 or 8 to 11; and two, 6 is not a strong upcard for the dealer.
- Chance: Any soft or hard hand totaling 3 to 7 or 12 to 17 against any dealer upcard from 2 to 6 is a chance hand. 2-2, 3-3, and 6-6 that you would split versus dealer weak cards are chance hands. All hard and soft totals other than 10, 11, 19, 20, and 21 versus a dealer deuce are chance hands. A player 7 or 17 versus a dealer 7 is also a chance hand. In other words, a chance hand is a hand where your cards are weak, but so is the dealer's total. 17 versus 6 is a chance hand.

The WLPC classification system simply allows you to quickly make a judgment as to whether your hand is more likely to win, lose, or push—or if both your hand and the dealer's upcard look weak, then you simply have a chance.

Some Sample Hands

After studying the hand definitions above, look at these sample hands versus various dealer upcards and be sure you understand why each one is categorized as winner, loser, push, or chance.

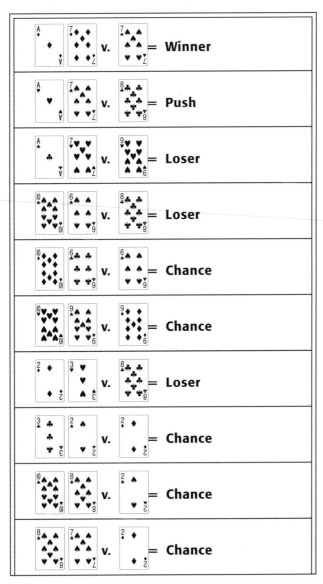

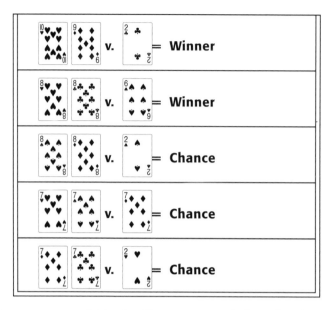

Once you can quickly classify any two-card player hand versus any dealer upcard as a winner, loser, push, or chance, you are almost ready to make your switch decisions. Before you can make these decisions correctly, you must know how the different types of hands should be ranked according to your win potential. These rankings are pretty logical. From best to worst, the hands we'd like to hold are:

1. Winner
2. Push
3. Chance
4. Loser

The winner and loser classifications as first and last choice are obvious. Do note that a push is better than a chance.

The Two-Hand Set Ratings

Now the game starts to get interesting. Since you will always have two hands in play, you must be able to quickly classify both of your hands versus the dealer upcard. Then you must be able to mentally switch the top cards of each hand, and classify the other two potential hands you can hold if you choose to switch. Here's an example:

Player Hands:  and Dealer Upcard:

We quickly see that both hands (17 and 15 versus 8) are losers. So, we mentally make the switch and we see in our mind's eye:

Player Hands:  and Dealer Upcard:

Note that we switched the top cards, the 7 and 9. We immediately see that our hands have changed from loser/loser to winner/loser. Logic immediately tells us that it is better to have one winner and one loser than it is to have two losers, so we make the switch. That one was easy.

There are only nine possible two-hand combinations that we can be dealt. Based on our overall win potential, this is how we rank our two-hand totals, from best to worst:

Two-Hand Set Power Ratings

1. Winner/Winner
2. Winner/Push
3. Winner/Chance
4. Winner/Loser
5. Push/Push
6. Push/Loser
7. Chance/Chance
8. Chance/Loser
9. Loser/Loser

You will have to spend some time learning the two-hand power ratings. It may not be obvious to you that a winner/loser is better than a push/push, but a single winner in your hand is always better than no winner. Before you can make your switch decision, you must know what you are switching from and to, and which two-hand set is stronger. You might also note that I make no distinction between winner/loser and loser/winner. For our purposes, these sets are identical.

Also note that there is no listing for a push/chance set. Based on our hand definitions, this combination is impossible. A push hand requires a dealer upcard from 8-A, while a chance hand requires a dealer 2-7.

Here's how to practice the switch decisions you'll need to make in a casino game:

1. Deal a dealer upcard.
2. Deal yourself two face-up hands.
3. Classify both hands as dealt, for example, winner/push
4. Mentally switch and classify both hands again
5. Make your switch decision based on the power ratings

Some Sample Hands:

Player Hands:  Dealer Upcard:

You have a blackjack and a 19 versus a dealer 9: winner/push

If we switch, we have 10-10 (20) and 9-ace (20) versus dealer 9: winner/winner

I chose this example to show you that contrary to what your intuition might tell you, you will sometimes be better off switching from a blackjack if it means turning a hand that is not a winner into a winner. In fact, if blackjack paid 3 to 2, we would not switch. But with blackjacks paying even money, a blackjack is just another winner.

Player Hands:  Dealer Upcard:

Same two hands, blackjack and 19, this time versus a dealer 10: winner/loser

If you switch, you have 10-10 (20) and 9-ace (20) versus dealer 10: push/push

So, because winner/loser beats push/push in our power ratings, here you do not switch.

Player Hands: and Dealer Upcard:

You have a blackjack and a 17 versus a dealer 7: winner/chance

If you switch, you have 10-10 (20) and 7-ace (18) versus dealer 7: winner/winner

Again, we find that it is better to switch from the blackjack to turn a chance into a winner.

Player Hands: and Dealer Upcard:

You have a 15 and a 15 versus a dealer 10: loser/loser

If you switch, you have 10-6 (16) and 9-5 (14) versus dealer 10: loser/loser

Same power rating. Abysmal situation. It doesn't make any difference what you do. Pray!

When Switching Does Not Change the Power Rating

The above hand brings up a good question. If our two hands have the same power rating whether we switch or not, is it always just a coin flip? Does it ever make a difference? The answer is that it does make a difference in certain specific situations. For example, if you have two losers, say two fifteens versus a dealer 10, turning them into a 16 and 14 versus a dealer 10 is a waste of time. Both sets are equally bad. But let's look at some hand combos where we would switch despite the fact that the power ratings of both two-hand sets are identical.

When to Switch a Chance/Chance for Another Chance/Chance:

Let's say you had two thirteens versus a dealer 3 (chance/chance), and you could turn them into a 12 and 14 versus a dealer 3 (still chance/chance). In this case, you would be better off to switch. Why? Because your basic strategy with the two thirteens is to stand on both hands. With a 12 and 14, your BJ Switch basic strategy is to stand on the 14 but hit the 12. Because you are turning a stiff that you would stand on (13) into a hand that you can take action on (12), this 12 still has a chance of turning into a strong hand. So, the rule is: A stiff that you will hit is better than a stiff that you will stand on, all other factors being equal. This is an important concept because when we study the basic strategy for BJ Switch, we will see that unlike traditional blackjack, there are a number of stiffs that we hit versus dealer low cards.

When to Switch a Loser/Loser for Another Loser/Loser:

The rule: If you have two stiff losers (hands totaling 12 to 16 or 2 to six), but you can make one stiff loser a pat or possible pat hand (17 to 20 or 7 to 11) by switching, even though it would still be classified as a loser, switch. Here's an example:

Player Hands: and   Dealer Upcard:

With a 15 and a 16 versus a dealer 10, we have two losers. By switching, we'll get a 17 and a 14, still two losers but with one hand now a pat 17. Switch! It's not really that a pat loser is better than a stiff loser, but that by switching, the hand that remains a loser has a better chance of improving with a hit.

When to Switch a Winner/Winner for Another Winner/Winner:

There are also occasions when we would switch from one winner/winner set to another winner/winner set. Here's the rule: If you have two winners of different value versus a strong dealer upcard (say 20 and 18 versus 7), always switch if you can improve the weak winner, even if the stronger winner gets weaker (which it will). Example:

Player Hands: and   Dealer Upcard:

With a 20 and an 18 versus a dealer 7, you have two winners. With a switch, you'd have 19 and 19 versus 7, still two winners. Do the switch because you are improving the weaker winner versus a strong dealer upcard, even though you are making the stronger winner weaker.

When to Switch a Winner/Chance for Another Winner/Chance:

Let's say you have an 18 and a 14 versus a dealer 6. This set is classified as winner/chance. By switching, you can make yourself a 19 and 13 versus that dealer 6, still a winner/chance set. Do the switch in order to make that winner a stronger winner. Remember that a chance hand only wins if the dealer busts, so a 13 and 14 versus a 6 are virtually identical hands. Totals of 18 and 19, on the other hand, are not identical. Your 18 will beat a dealer 17. Your 19 will beat a dealer 17 or 18.

The Rules on switching Blackjack

Finally, after you know all of the above switching rules, there are a few exceptions to the rules on switching that only apply when you have, or can make a blackjack. First, never switch from a blackjack unless it raises the power rating of a hand. Specifically, ignore the rule about making a weaker winner into a stronger winner if you must give up a blackjack to do so. Also, always keep (or make, if possible) a blackjack versus any dealer upcard from 2 to 6. When you can switch from a blackjack to raise a power rating, do so only versus the strong dealer upcards (7-ace).

The WLPC strategy may strike you as confusing at first, but you will be surprised at how fast you get at making your switch decisions. The logic will sink in pretty quickly if you're an experienced blackjack player. If you're not an experienced blackjack player, then I would not recommend that you start out by learning Blackjack Switch.

There will be many hands where switching does not raise the two-hand set power rating, nor do you see any logic, despite the fact that you will have different hand totals. Example: you have a 20 and an 18 versus a dealer ace—loser/loser. You can make two nineteens if you switch, still loser/loser. Or, you have a 14 and a 16 versus a dealer 5, chance/chance. If you switch, you can make two fifteens, still chance/chance. Don't fret over hands like these. They really make no difference to your overall result.

You will make most of your money by following the WLPC strategy to raise the power ratings of hands where this is possible. You'll gain a small amount more by switching when the power ratings do not change, but the logic of the game would advise a switch—for instance, really paying attention to such factors as stiff hands you can take action on versus stiff hands you cannot, etc.

HOW TO BEAT "BLACKJACK SWITCH"

The best way to learn the WLPC switch strategy is to simply deal two-hand sets to yourself, make your decisions, then check the switching rules above to see if you've acted correctly. The most confusing two-hand sets will be those that have identical power ratings or contain pairs and soft totals. Don't worry too much about your judgment calls on these hands when the switched hands have identical power ratings. Just check the rules to see if any of the identical power rating switch factors apply.

Now, perhaps you realize why the casinos are not too worried about players beating them at Blackjack Switch. The switch decisions are not intuitive to most players, and there are no books (until this one!) explaining how to rank the hand sets and when to make the switches. One thing you will discover as you practice with cards or on your computer, however, is that this switching strategy quickly becomes very automatic. Most hand sets play themselves as you will primarily be seeing opportunities for turning losers and pushes into winners. Also, take your time when you practice, as well as at the live casino tables. The dealer will give you time and other players will also be taking time to make these decisions. You might want to sit at third base, if possible, so that you have the longest time to study and evaluate your hand sets.

It won't take you very long to notice that you are one of very few players making correct switch decisions. The house edge against most players on this game is high, and the nice thing is that the dealers and bosses do not even know the correct switch decisions! You will not look like a smart player to the house.

BLACKJACK SWITCH QUIZ

Note: In all player hands, the second card is the top card that can be switched. That is, in the first two-hand set, 5 / 6 and 10 / 2, the 6 and the 2 are the switchable cards.

	PLAYER HANDS	DEALER UPCARD	SWITCH (Y/N)?
1.	5/6 and Q/2	9	_____
2.	10/J and 9/8	7	_____
3.	3/5 and J/10	7	_____
4.	7/5 and 8/A	2	_____
5.	A/7 and K/9	J	_____
6.	A/9 and 8/8	7	_____
7.	7/Q and 10/A	7	_____
8.	4/10 and 4/3	7	_____
9.	7/8 and 8/10	7	_____
10.	6/6 and 5/4	9	_____

HOW TO BEAT "BLACKJACK SWITCH"

BLACKJACK SWITCH QUIZ ANSWERS

Note: In all player hands, the second card is the top card that can be switched. That is, in the first two-hand set, 5 / 6 and 10 / 2, the 6 and the 2 are the switchable cards.

	PLAYER HANDS	DEALER UPCARD	SWITCH (Y/N)?
1.	5/6 and Q/2	9	N
2.	10/J and 9/8	7	Y
3.	3/5 and J/10	7	N
4.	7/5 and 8/A	2	N
5.	A/7 and K/9	J	Y
6.	A/9 and 8/8	7	N
7.	7/Q and 10/A	7	Y
8.	4/10 and 4/3	7	???
9.	7/8 and 8/10	7	Y
10.	6/6 and 5/4	9	Y

I'm going to go through these decisions one at a time. Note that there are ten questions on the test, numbered from 1 to 10. Here are the answers, with explanations, in order.

1. Totals of 11 and 12 are a winner/loser versus 9. If we switch, we get 7 and 16 versus 9: loser/loser. No switch. That one was easy.

2. A total of 20 and 17 versus 7 is a winner/push set. If we switch, we get 18 and 19, a winner/winner set. So, we switch.

3. Totals of 8 and 17 versus 7 is a winner/chance. If you switch, 10 and 15 is a winner/loser. No switch.

4. Totals of 12 and 19 versus 2 is a chance/winner set. If we switch, we get 18 and 13, a winner/chance set. However, the decision on this one is clearly N, no switch, because both the winner and the chance hands are stronger hands without the switch. Obviously, 19 is stronger than 18. But 12 is also a stronger chance than 13 because fewer hit cards will bust it. This is blackjack logic you should be familiar with. The worst stiff hand is 16. A total of 12 is actually a much better starting hand.

5. A-7 and 19 versus 10 is a loser/loser. If we switch, we get 20 and 17, a push/loser. So, we switch.

6. A total of 20 and 8-8 versus 7 = winner/winner. If we switch, we get 19 and 17 versus 7 = winner/chance. No brainer. Don't switch.

7. Totals of 17 and 21 (blackjack. versus 7 = chance/winner. If we switch, we get 18 and 20 versus 7, a winner/winner. Here is a case where we relinquish our blackjack to turn our push into a winner. (And note that the dealer 7 is a strong upcard, so switching from a blackjack to raise the power rating is correct..

8. Totals of 14 and 7 versus a dealer 7 = loser/push. If we switch... Hey, nothing happens! We can only switch the top cards, remember? Any time your bottom cards are identical, switching will just give you the same hands. Likewise, any time your top cards are identical, switching will just give you the same hands. That was just a trick question. Sorry.

9. Totals of 15 and 18 versus 7 = loser/winner. If we switch, we get 17 and 8-8 versus 7 = chance/winner. So, we switch.

10. 6-6 and 5-4 versus 9 = loser/push. If we switch, we get 10 and 11 versus 9 = winner/winner. Obviously, a good switch.

It will definitely take you some time to get up to speed with smooth and accurate switch decisions, but once you get it, you'll find it easy. In fact, it will amaze you that other players at the table in a casino can take so long to make decisions (often the wrong decisions) that you see instantly.

THE BLACKJACK SWITCH BASIC STRATEGY

The basic strategy for Blackjack Switch is the strategy you follow to play your hands after you make your switch decision. I've boiled it down to sixteen rules. If you want to learn the "perfect" basic strategy for Blackjack Switch, you'll find it in the Appendix. Other than for a few of the minor pair-split decisions, it is identical to the strategy below.

The Insurance Rule
1. Never take insurance.

The Hard Hit/Stand Rules
2. Stand on all hard totals of 17 or higher.
3. Hit hard 12 to 16 versus 7 through ace.
4. Hit hard 12 versus 2, 3, and 4; and hit hard 13 and 14 versus 2.
5. Stand on all other stiffs (12 through 16) versus 2 through 6.

The Soft Hit/Stand Rules
6. Always stand on soft 19 and 20.
7. Stand on soft 18 versus 2 to 8, but hit versus 9, 10, or ace.
8. Always hit soft 17 and below versus 7 through ace. (See doubling strategy versus 2 through 6.)

The Hard Doubling Rules
9. Double down on 10 and 11 versus 2 through 8.
10. Double down on 9 versus 6

The Soft Doubling Rules
> **11.** Double down on A-6 and A-7 versus 5 and 6.
>
> **12.** Double down on A-5 versus 6 only.

The Pair-Split Rules
> **13.** Always split aces and eights.
>
> **14.** Never split fours, fives, or tens.
>
> **15.** Split all other pairs—twos, threes, sixes, sevens, and nines—versus 4, 5, or 6.
>
> **16.** Also split nines versus 8 and 9.

BEATING BLACKJACK SWITCH WITH THE RED SEVEN COUNT

Use the Red Seven Count exactly as you would in a normal blackjack game. In order to do this you must get the count of all hands on the table before you look at your hand to evaluate your switch decision. This is not a game for a slow card counter. If you are not very proficient at counting cards, don't even dream about trying to count cards at Blackjack Switch yet. If you are a good, fast, and accurate counter with the Red Seven counting system, then you should have no problem keeping the count.

THE RED SEVEN BETTING STRATEGY

In an eight-deck BJ Switch game, start your running count at -16. In the six-deck BJ Switch game, start your running count at -12. Whenever your count is negative, bet one unit. Raise your bet at zero and on positive running counts exactly as you would with the Red Seven Count in normal blackjack games, and use the same bankroll guidelines for bet-sizing. (See chapter five.) I would also advise being aggressive in your betting strategy if you feel you can get away with it. Blackjack Switch tables are not heavily monitored by game protection personnel for card counters. Most counters do not play this game, or even know how to play this game. I would advise a spread of at least one to twelve units in the six-deck game, and one to sixteen units in the eight-deck game.

THE RED SEVEN PLAYING STRATEGY

The Red Seven playing strategy is similar to the Red Seven playing strategy for the regular game, but there are a few differences.

WHEN THE RUNNING COUNT = ZERO OR HIGHER:
1. Stand on 12 v. 4
2. Stand on 16 v. 10
3. Couble Down on 10 and 11 v. 9
4. Double Down on 9 v. 5
WHEN THE RUNNING COUNT = +2 OR HIGHER:
5. Stand on 12 v. 3
6. Stand on 15 v. 10
7. Take Insurance when offered

That's it! You are now a proficient Blackjack Switch player. Have fun and beat them for whatever you can get away with.

HOW TO BEAT
THOSE WEIRD
CALIFORNIA GAMES

> When the California gold discoveries set in motion a tremendous flow of traffic across the region's arid plains, professional gamblers established themselves at the settlements that sprang up along the main traveled routes and lay in wait to fleece the unwary...
>
> — *Oscar Lewis, Sagebrush Casinos*

California has more bizarre variations of casino blackjack than any other state in the U.S. Incredibly, this is due to a state law that was passed a century ago. In an attempt to shut down the wild gambling saloons that had flourished in San Francisco's lawless Barbary Coast district since the Gold Rush, the state legislature made many games, including twenty-one and all house-banked casino-style games, illegal.

Flash forward a hundred years and you have all kinds of unusual card games being offered in California's poker rooms and Indian reservation casinos where the target total is 22 instead of 21, where other traditional features of blackjack have been altered so as to skirt the law, where games are being banked by players, by syndicates of players, by player "pools," where jokers are added to the shoes, etc., etc.

Thanks to a state referendum that passed a few years ago, the Indian reservation casinos in California are now legally permitted to offer standard, house-banked, casino blackjack games. In this chapter, we are not concerned with these traditional casino-style games that are now abundantly available in the Indian casinos. Many of the bizarre blackjack variations that were invented during the years when traditional twenty-one was illegal in the state have remained, and these are the games we will look at in this chapter. The state's poker rooms, for example, are still forbidden to offer traditional blackjack games, so any of the games you find that are not in Indian reservation casinos are non-traditional variations on the game. And some of the games being offered in the Indian reservation casinos are still the pseudo-blackjack variations simply because the games became popular with the casino's customers when the traditional games were forbidden.

So, when you're in any California casino or poker room, if you see a blackjack table, be careful. It may not be the game you think it is. These games usually have names like "California Blackjack," or "California 22," or "Newjack 21," or "No-Bust Blackjack," etc. You should also know that there is no one strategy for the California games. There are at least a dozen variations of pseudo-blackjack in the state, and each variation has its own quirks, rules, and optimum strategies. I am going to run down the various features you commonly find in the California games, and I will explain how the professional players deal with these variations.

NO HOUSE BANK

In traditional casino blackjack, we play against the house. If the house is not banking the game, then players must pay a commission to the house in order to play. This commission is usually collected as a per-hand fee, based on the size of each player's bet. For instance, bets up to $25 might require a fifty-cent fee per hand. Bets from $26 up to $100 might require a $1 fee per hand, etc. We can easily evaluate the fee as a percentage of the amount we bet. For instance, a $1 fee for a $100 bet is a cost of 1 percent to play the hand. If we must pay fifty cents to play a $25 hand, then this is a 2 percent commission. If the minimum commission is fifty cents, and we play a $5 hand, then we are paying a 10 percent commission. Most card counters in traditional blackjack games try to get an edge over the house of about 1 percent. This means that if we must pay a fee to play each hand, we would need a much larger advantage over the house in order to get a positive expectation from playing the game.

Most professional players find that there is a greater advantage to dealing and banking the California games than there is in attempting to beat the games as players. In games where the deal passes from player to player, there is usually a limit on the dealer/banker's commission. For instance, the person banking the game may have to pay a maximum commission of $2 per round. If there are five players at the table, each betting a couple hundred bucks per round, then this commission is only a fraction of a percent of the banker's action.

You must realize, however, that it takes quite a bit larger bankroll to bank a game than it does to play it as a player. Many players never bank the game when it is their turn, as they cannot

afford to do so. Some casinos require a banker to have a minimum bank in order to act as a banker to ensure that the banker will have sufficient funds to pay off winning bets.

In some of these California games, players never bank the games. The games are banked by syndicates of professional players who have large enough bankrolls to withstand the flux. Often, when the game is banked by a syndicate, the banker does not play. He simply watches the house dealer to make sure the payouts are correct.

In other casinos, games are banked by a player pool. This is a weird banking concept that was invented by the California casinos to eliminate the necessity of having either players or syndicates bank the games. The casino sets up a "pool" for all of the house winnings collected by the dealers, and then distributes these funds later to the players in the form of bonuses or prizes. In these games, players are not allowed to bank the game even if they want to.

These player-pool games also attract professional players, but only on those occasions when the pool of funds is distributed via bonus payments to players. For instance, some casinos may declare certain nights "BJ Pays 2 to 1 Night," and distribute the house winnings back to the players in this way. If the game is an otherwise traditional game, where the 2 to 1 blackjack bonus is worth more than 2 percent, then provided you play with a commission of less than 2 percent, you will be playing with an advantage.

HOW MUCH DOES THAT COMMISSION COST?

Let's say you are playing in a casino where there is a $1 minimum fee per hand, and the fee goes to $2 when your bet goes over $100. If you never intend to place a bet over $100, then the cost of the hourly fee will be $1 (per hand) times the number of hands you will play per hour. If the table where you play is not crowded, say two to three players, then you may expect to play about one hundred hands per hour, and your fee for playing these hands will be about $100 per hour. If this was a typical Nevada-style blackjack game, not some pseudo-variation of the game, then a basic strategy player betting $10 per hand, without any fee, would expect to lose about $5 per hour assuming the house had a typical 0.5 percent advantage. If this player played for four hours, he would expect to lose, on average, about $20.

Now, consider the effect of that $1 fee per hand in the same game. Instead of losing $5 per hour, this basic strategy player would expect to lose $105 per hour, and in a four-hour play, would expect to be behind by $420, instead of $20. So, those $1 fees, or even fifty-cent fees, can get very expensive to small bettors.

If you ever play in a California casino, or any casino, where a fee is collected for each hand played, you should figure out the hourly cost of the fee as above, by multiplying the fee by the number of hands per hour you would expect to play. You can also figure out the cost of the fee in the game as a percentage of your bet by dividing the amount of the fee by each bet size. Let's take an example.

The Hollywood Park Casino in Los Angeles has a fee schedule that requires a minimum fee of $1, and a fee of $1 per $100 of the player's bet, with the fee always rounded up. This means that as soon as your bet goes to $101, you would have to pay a $2 fee. Here is a schedule that shows various player bets from $10 to $500, the fee required for each bet size, and the percentage of the player's bet that the player is paying to play his hand at each betting level.

FEE SCHEDULE, $1 PER $100, ROUNDED UP		
BET	**FEE**	**PERCENTAGE (%)**
$10	$1	10%
$20	$1	5%
$25	$1	4%
$40	$1	2.5%
$50	$1	2%
$60	$1	1.7%
$75	$1	1.3%
$100	$1	1%
$125	$2	1.6%
$150	$2	1.3%
$175	$2	1.1%
$200	$2	1%
$250	$3	1.2%
$300	$3	1%
$350	$4	1.1%
$400	$4	1%
$450	$5	1.1%
$500	$5	1%

Note in the schedule above that the fee—as a percentage of your bet—is very high at the lower betting levels. In every case, the percentage is lowest (always exactly 1 percent) when you are betting in exact increments of $100. This Hollywood Park game, incidentally, is not a traditional blackjack game, but a "no-bust" variation of blackjack that includes jokers as "wild cards." We'll discuss these variations below.

Target = 22

Many California games have a target total of 22 instead of 21. This is very different from traditional blackjack for two reasons. First, the values of all hands are different. A hard 17 is no longer an automatic standing hand. Nor is a starting total of 12 a poor start. More importantly, we cannot make an automatic winner with an ace and a 10. We need a pair of aces to make a two-card 22, a much rarer hand.

No Bust

Another frequent feature in California games is that any hand that exceeds the target total, whether 21 or 22, does not automatically lose.

The hand closest to the target is the winner. For example, with a target of 22, a player total of 24 would beat a dealer's total of 19. If both hands are equidistant from the target, say totals of 20 and 24 in a game with a target of 22, then the hand which is under the target total wins. In some casinos, if both the player and dealer exceed the target, then the dealer's hand will win on a tie. In other casinos, if either the player or dealer exceeds the target total, while the other one does not, then the hand that does not exceed the target is the winner, even if the hand that exceeds the target is closer to the target. Example: With a target of 21, if the player hand equals 22, and the dealer hand equals 18, the dealer hand would win since it did not go over the target.

These no-bust variations are, again, very fundamental changes to the game, and the way we think of hand values in the traditional game no longer apply. And all of these variations on how the no-bust rule is applied further complicate the strategies.

Wild Cards

In addition to these fundamental changes to the structure of the traditional game, many California casinos add "wild" cards to the decks in play. Typically, it is jokers that are added, anywhere from one per shoe to one for each number of decks in play. On top of that, there are different ways of valuing the joker. In some casinos, a joker in any hand makes that hand an automatic winner. In other casinos where 22 is the target, jokers are valued the way the ace is valued in traditional blackjack, with the difference being that the joker counts as either two or twelve points. In some casinos where a single joker is used, a hand with a joker not only wins but pays a bonus. All of these wild-card variations further change the character of the game.

Dealer's Options

There are also some casinos where the dealer has options on how to play his hand. In one variation of the game, dealers may either hit or stand on 17, at their option. This is a hugely favorable rule for the dealer/banker. If the dealer sees that a player has stood with a total of 16, he may stand on his 17. If he sees a player already has his 17 beat, he can take a hit.

HOW CAN THE AVERAGE PLAYER BEAT THE CALIFORNIA GAMES?

Any and all of the above blackjack variations could be analyzed, and a precise basic strategy could be developed. The problem is that each game would have its own unique set of basic strategy charts that could be used in no other variation of the game. Most of the people that I know who have done these analyses are the big banking syndicates. Some of these syndicates are multi-million-dollar operations and it is in their interest to know what their edge is over the players at their tables, and to know the proper way to play if not banking. In addition, a few very smart professional players have analyzed a particular variation as part of planning a specific advantageous play.

Some of these California games may present profit opportunities for professional players who: 1) devise accurate basic strategies; and 2) develop card-counting strategies for betting and playing based on the weird rules. But because there are a dozen-plus variations on these games, and they are all located in the same state, with a particular variation often available at only one casino, no blackjack expert has ever taken it upon himself to do this tedious work, at least not for publication. This is one of those instances where if you discover a valuable way to exploit a game, there will be much more value to you in exploiting it than in writing a book about it.

What can the average player, who is not a mathematician or computer programmer, do to beat these games?

First, you can look for traditional games where the only unusual rule is that the players must pay a commission to play. These games will only be found in certain Indian reservation casinos, not in the poker rooms. Unless you can afford to bank these games, and you have the option to do so, then you must wait for whatever nights the casino returns the house winnings to the players in the form of bonuses. In most cases, to get an edge on these special nights, you will have to play with a bet sized to keep the cost of the per-hand commission to as small a percentage of your bet as possible. Using the simple method I described above, you should be able to do this analysis.

If you can afford to bank a game, then in almost every case that I know of there is an advantage to banking. This is true even in the weird no-bust, joker, and "Twenty-two" variations of the game. There is a reason why the professionals and syndicates go after these banking opportunities, and that's because the edge is with the banker. I can guarantee you that these pros have analyzed these games and know exactly what their percentage edge is, based on the rules and the way most players play. If you have sufficient funds to bank one of these games, then you probably have the funds to hire a computer programmer to analyze a game for you. If you have more brains than money, there is a free blackjack simulation program called SimSimp available on my Web site, www.blackjackforumonline.com, that is designed for easy reprogramming for analyzing special games and rules. Despite the fact that bankers in these games are likely to have an edge, I would not advise anyone to bank an unusual game without first getting an analysis of what that edge is. I know of one California no-bust game where the bankers do not have an edge if the players play the correct basic strategy. Fortunately for the bankers, most players do not know the correct basic strategy. Unfortunately for the players, the commission they must pay to play is greater than the edge they can get!

For blackjack players in California, who neither have the funds to bank games nor the desire to develop an accurate strategy using the SimSimp software, my advice would be to just play in the traditional games that are now available in the Indian reservation casinos. And play at the tables where no commission is required.

It used to be that the best way to beat the California games was to drive to Nevada. Now, you don't have to drive so far.

SECTION THREE:

HAVING FUN IN A COMBAT ZONE

LIKE IT OR NOT, YOU ARE THE ENEMY

> Card counting isn't illegal, but who wants to argue legalities with a burly goon who politely (for the time being) asks you to leave the premises?
>
> — *Mike Orkin, Can You Win?*

What really makes blackjack fun, even if you're not a professional player, is knowing that the casino is so worried that you might be. And if they're not worried about you, then you can watch them worry about other players. Some guy at your table raises his bet and the pit boss runs to the phone. He's probably ordering the eye in the sky to do a "skills check." You might see guys in suits having a conference in the pit, or suspicious characters hanging around behind a player, trying to watch him without being seen. It is, of course, much more fun when you think it's you they're worried about. But once you understand how seriously the pit personnel take this game, the fun factor skyrockets. You really are sitting in the middle of a war zone.

PLAY VERSUS WORK, US VERSUS THEM

If you play blackjack, you will find an entirely different attitude in the pit personnel than if you play any of the other games. There is an "us versus them" atmosphere that pervades the blackjack pit. It's the pit personnel versus the players, and it's a dead-serious battle. There is a reason why this antagonism exists in the blackjack pit and is nonexistent at the other casino games.

We live in a society where the only people who make money playing games, in general, are athletes, and only a relative handful of the very top athletes at that. Most of us don't even dream of making money in any way other than, dare I say… working. And playing a game just isn't working. When we play a game, we're not providing a service to anyone. We're not producing anything of value. We're not selling anything. So, it's not just the money that appeals to us, but money for nothing. Getting money from gambling is like getting paid for fooling around. Just the thought that there is a casino game where professional players make their living attracts us to the blackjack tables.

Making money by gambling is not really that easy. The casino itself is a business. The dealers are not playing games. They're doing a job. They punch a time clock and follow the boss's orders. The pit bosses aren't playing games, nor are any of the managers, surveillance personnel, or security guards. Only the customers are playing games. So, when you show up in a casino to play blackjack against the house dealer, it's not like you're showing up at your buddy's house to shoot some hoops one-on-one with him. You and your buddy are both playing the same game. Those casino dealers are not playing a game. The house isn't fooling around.

So, for everyone who works in the casino, this is a very serious business. They are in the business of taking your money. They fully expect you to pay to play. They know you're there to play. They want you to have fun so you'll come back as often as you can afford to. But you are a customer, and you are supposed to lose. Your losses pay their salaries. They have rigged the games against you to ensure your loss. They know that you will, in fact, win on some visits. That's part of the lure of gambling. But they also know that, in the long run, you don't really stand a chance. They have set the odds against you, and casinos thrive on the odds.

It is this situation that sets up the "us versus them" relationship between a casino and its customers that does not exist in any other business. Grocery stores compete with other grocery stores; hair salons compete with other hair salons; gas stations compete with other gas stations. None of these businesses competes with their customers. Their customers support them. Whether the product is gas, groceries, or a haircut, the customer pays for a desired product or service, and the business makes a profit.

But the "product" the casinos are offering is money. That changes everything. They can't just advertise that they'll sell you $98 if you give them $100, which is technically what they do. So, they offer a chance at $200 for $100, and that gets people to buy the product, which actually has a value of only $98. Or at least, in theory, it's supposed to have a value of only $98. That's how the casino's accountants figured it. The

> ### Know Your Enemy
>
> **The Floorperson:** The floor supervisor usually wears a suit and watches the games. It is his job to record buy-ins and cash-outs, check player IDs, and watch payouts on large wins. If he is suspicious of a player, he will often stop and watch how hands are being played, and he may notify the pit boss. Most floorpersons are hoping to rise up in management. In the big casinos, because of tips, dealers often make more money than floorpersons. Many of those who work the floor are also dealers, and they go back and forth as needed. These employees are called dual rates in the industry. Many of those who work the floor have very bad attitudes. They are the lowest paid employees in the pit, and if there is a problem, they will get the blame. Getting blamed for problems will keep them from advancing. Always be friendly to the floorperson. If possible, compliment him or her, and ask for advice on a restaurant or show.

problem is that some players can consistently get $102, $105, or more for their $100, and this makes the casino's accountants very upset. The player who keeps getting $105 for his $100 is hurting business. The casino's stockholders take this very seriously. They start looking for new accountants, new managers. Somebody has to take the blame. Meanwhile, throw out the customer!

Know Your Enemy

The Pit Boss: The Pit Supervisor also wears a suit, and will either be watching table games himself or standing at the podium in the center of the pit trying to look busy. If a dealer or floorperson alerts him to any suspicious play, he will use the telephone at the podium to call the eye in the sky. If you see a boss pick up the phone, he is often asking surveillance to perform a "skills check" on a big player. The pit boss may watch any player whose play is unusual, or who is winning. If a player raises his bet, the boss may look through the discards to see if the bet raise might have been due to the count going up. If he strongly suspects that a player is using an intelligent strategy to play his hands and raise and lower his bets, he may "camp out" at the corner of the table and stare at the player in question in an attempt to intimidate any player capable of really winning. If he feels a situation may be serious, he will call his supervisor, the shift boss.

DEALER SLANG

Bleeder: a pit boss or floorman who is worried about a winning player.

THE FIELD OF BATTLE

Casinos have always been battlefields. There is a legal way to beat just about every game in the house, and the casinos know this. They take incredible measures to eliminate the possibility of players getting an edge on them, but they can never totally eliminate that possibility.

Virtually every card game is vulnerable. In the process of play, cards sometimes get nicked, bent, or scratched, giving perceptive players information they're not supposed to have. Sloppy dealers often flash cards during the process of dealing that are supposed to be hidden from the players. Hand shuffles are often inadequate and "trackable" by players who have trained themselves to follow shuffles.

And any game based on math and/or memory may be leaving alert players with valuable information the house was not figuring into the game. There are professional players who do nothing but hunt for mathematical advantages in new games and ill-considered casino promotions.

Roulette teams have been known to spend weeks looking for wheels with "biases" for certain numbers. Some casinos have lost millions to players who have discovered such wheels.

Slot players have formed teams to beat "progressive jackpot" machines, especially at video poker. In the old days, there were players who knew how to "pop the handle" on the mechanical reel slots in order to line up the cherries for a jackpot.

New games are especially vulnerable to professional attack. I have three different books, all recently published and by different authors, that describe the relatively new game of Three-Card Poker. Every book states that players should look for dealers who flash the bottom card when removing the cards from the shuffle machine. Why? Because sloppy dealers tend to do this. With the correct strategy, a Three-Card Poker player who sees just one of the dealer's cards will have better than a 3 percent edge over the house. There are players today who make a living from playing Three-Card Poker.

In the old days, there were crap players who taught themselves to slide one of the dice in order to get an edge on certain numbers. Casinos in Nevada made regulations against dice sliding, and many casinos now require shooters to hit the backboard when they throw the dice.

Know Your Enemy

The Shift Boss: The shift boss is in charge of the entire casino during his eight-hour shift. He will almost always be somewhere on the floor when the casino is busy, but at slower times may be in his office. He has complete jurisdiction to handle problems, irregularities, or make decisions on suspicious players during his watch. He has access to all of the records the casino has on a player's history. If a player is barred from playing in a casino, it is usually the shift boss's decision. If the casino suffers any inexplicable big loss during his shift, he will have to answer to the casino manager.

DEALER SLANG

Grave: the graveyard shift, generally begins between 2 and 4 a.m.

Swing: the swing shift, generally starts between 6 and 8 p.m.

Day: the day shift, generally starts between 10 a.m. and noon.

There was a keno player who won hundreds of thousands of dollars at the Casino de Montreal some years back when he discovered that the computer program that was used to pick the numbers had a flaw that made the numbers predictable.

Any player who makes his living beating casino games does so by finding a weakness in a game that the casino does not know about. There are slot players who look for machines that overpay. There are players who live on cash back bonuses from players clubs. There are sports bettors who find odds that favor the players.

So, the situation with blackjack being a game that professional players can beat is not unique. The only unique thing about blackjack is that it is so easy for so many players to beat it. There are dozens of books on card-counting systems for beating blackjack. There is really no reason for any smart player to play blackjack in a casino without having an advantage over the house. But, in fact, fewer than one out of one hundred blackjack players ever apply themselves to beating the house. Blackjack remains the casinos' number one money-making table game.

Know Your Enemy

The Casino Manager: There is only one casino manager so he is often not on the premises. He generally works a forty-hour week. Casino managers are usually on the premises during any big events when the casino has large crowds. He rarely socializes with players, though he will often get to know the top VIP players who play at reserved tables in the private rooms.

Even so, the casinos hate the fact that there are some blackjack players who can beat them, and they spend enormous amounts of money on blackjack game protection. In fact, there is more money spent on protecting blackjack games than on all other casino games combined. Casinos are wary of new players at their blackjack tables, and especially players who place big bets. You may be a customer, and the dealer may be smiling and acting friendly, but if you've got a big bet on the table, you are being watched and your play is being scrutinized and analyzed by people who are being paid to be suspicious of you.

THE CUSTOMER IS ALWAYS SUSPECT

For a lot of casino managers who must answer to casino owners and stockholders, blackjack is a never-ending headache. In no casino game is the house money more vulnerable than at blackjack. And what's worse, it's not cheaters or thieves who are threatening the casino profits; it's smart players who are following all the rules. They are breaking no laws, but just happen to be a bit smarter than the casino's "game protection" staff.

And to those casino surveillance agents, the "eyes in the sky," blackjack is a nightmare. Imagine going to work each day to face the job these poor souls must endure for their meager paychecks. They sit for eight hours in a small dark room, surrounded by walls of video monitors, trying to pick out from the hundreds of blackjack players in action the few who might be raising their bets suspiciously, or winning too consistently, or playing their hands in any unusual way. The problem the surveillance agent faces is that there are many blackjack players raising and lowering their bets on hunches, sometimes scoring nice wins due to lucky cards, and playing their hands in unusual ways just because they are unskilled players.

But "bad" players can look a lot like "good" players, and vice versa. The last thing any casino manager wants to do is kick out a bad player, especially one who's betting big money, just because he's having a lucky run of cards. It happens all the time. Any bad player will ultimately give it all back to the house and then some, assuming he's allowed to keep playing. You don't want to throw this guy out with the house's money in his pockets. This is the kind of customer a casino wants to cultivate. You've got to schmooze him, give him the steak house, a Jacuzzi suite, whatever he wants!

> ### Know Your Enemy
>
> The Surveillance Agent: Generally, you will not see any of the surveillance personnel while playing. They watch the games from the surveillance room, where they are surrounded by video monitors. They will come onto the floor, however, if a pit boss or shift boss requests them to do so, usually to get a closer look at a player. They dress casually and do not wear badges or anything else that would indicate that they work for the casino. They may watch games from behind a table, or even sit down at a table to watch. If any "customer" ever sits down at your table just to "watch"—unless he is an obvious spouse or friend of another player at the table—and the dealer doesn't ask him to leave, it is probably a surveillance operative who was called to the table by someone on the pit crew. Surveillance is a very low-paying job with a high turnover rate. Many surveillance employees are poorly trained and can only recognize the most amateur of card counters. More and more, they tend to rely on software to analyze players and blacklists provided by outside surveillance services to identify undesirable customers.

On the other hand, you can't let a pro, who simply looks like a bad player on a lucky streak, keep playing and winning, and playing and winning, and playing and... The owners and stockholders just don't understand that good players can look like bad players. A surveillance agent can lose his job if some team of blackjack pros hits the casino for $50,000 (or $500,000!) during his shift, and nobody in surveillance figures out what happened until they watch the videos the next day (and they watch a lot of videos the day after any big hit).

The guys up in surveillance live lives of quiet desperation, talking a language that only they understand. They're watching the buzzards, studying the squirrels, sweating the scorpions, and worrying that the headstones might actually be peek freaks. They discuss the suspected rat-holers, the sluggers, the heat-seekers, and the nursers.

Meanwhile, to most of the players down in the pits, blackjack is just a game. They know nothing of the buzzards and peek freaks in their midst. Let's see who can get closer to twenty-one! Hey, cool, the dealer busted! I just won ten bucks! They have no consciousness whatsoever that they are sitting smack dab in the middle of a battlefield, where devious plots are being hatched and attacks are being launched, while both sides smile for the cameras, nervously eyeing each other.

Know Your Enemy

The Security Guard: Most security guards wear uniforms, including a badge, a pair of handcuffs on the belt, and a holstered gun. A few wear suits and wander the floor like plainclothes cops. They are not trained in game protection. They do not recognize cheating or advantage play. They are not part of the surveillance department. They are basically on the premises as cops. They will escort drunks off the property and remove other unwanted persons from the casino floor as directed by a boss.

A couple years ago, one of those surveillance guys who went just a little batty sitting up in that dark room got fed up with the gig. The long hours. The low pay. No respect. So, using the pseudonym "Cellini," he wrote a book called *The Card Counter's Guide to Casino Surveillance*, charged $100 per copy (and no, you won't find it on the shelves at Barnes and Noble!), that has since turned into an underground classic among professional blackjack players. Cellini, now deceased, spilled the beans, everything, the way the whole surveillance/game-protection system works. Needless to say, the casinos are not happy about this book. But I'm happy, because—as a writer—I'm always looking for ways to increase my vocabulary. Let's just look at a few of the terms those surveillance guys throw around while they're discussing what they see on those video monitors around them.

A GLOSSARY OF SURVEILLANCE TERMS (WITH THANKS TO CELLINI)

Buzzard: This is any player who is circling a blackjack pit—watching the tables, but not sitting down to play. If you've ever done this, then you've probably been called a buzzard by the guys upstairs. They suspect that you may actually be a professional player, and that you have card-counting "spotters" at the tables, and you're waiting for a signal from one of them to enter a game.

Squirrel:

This is a player who jumps in and out of games at different tables, playing a few hands at each, but never settling in. Have you ever done that? Then you've probably been labeled a squirrel by those guys watching you on the surveillance monitors. They suspect you may be jumping in and out of games because your card-counting spotters keep finding hot shoes to signal you into.

Scorpion:

This is any player who has enough of a bankroll to "sting" the house for a big score. Any squirrel who's jumping in and out of games with $500 bets or more is a scorpion who is causing some serious migraines upstairs.

Headstone:

This is any player who sits in the same seat at the same table for a long time. Have you ever done this? You're a headstone. Players like this can be worrisome because—even if they're betting small—they may be card-counting spotters for a team of pros, using signals to call big players (BPs) into the game. So, even if you're sitting there betting $5 a hand, if you scratch your head and suddenly some guy shows up at your table who puts down a $300 bet, you are under suspicion. Headstones are also often suspected of being "peek freaks."

Peek Freak:

This is a professional player who has found a poorly trained dealer who has a habit of inadvertently flashing his hole card as he's placing it under his upcard. Peek freaks spend a lot of time looking for these sloppy dealers, whose hole cards can only be glimpsed from a very specific viewing angle. This is why headstones are often suspected of being peek freaks. Why does that guy like that seat so much? He's

279

been there for hours! And, incidentally, underhanded as it may seem, this type of play has been found in the courts to be 100 percent legal. The casinos don't like it, but the law says it's the dealer's job to hide his hole card, not the player's job to ignore it if he's seen it.

Rat-Holer:

This is a player who takes chips off the table while continuing to play, and puts them in his pockets. Have you ever done this? You're a rat-holer. You're under suspicion. Professional players sometimes do this to try to hide their winnings.

Slugger:

This is a player who, when cutting the cards, makes a number of attempts to get the cut-card into the deck. Have you ever done this, perhaps because the dealer was holding the deck so tightly that the card simply would not slide in? Those guys upstairs may suspect you of being a shuffle-tracker, a professional player who has visually followed a slug of high cards (tens and aces) through the entire shuffle, and is now attempting to cut that slug right to the top.

Heat-Seeker:

This is any player who is jumping his bet size up and down erratically, or making highly unusual plays (let's hit this hard 18!), that most "normal" players would find bizarre. This could be a player who is attempting to attract the attention of the pit boss and surveillance, so that another player, or team of players, can get away with some very lucrative play at a different table without being watched. Then again, that guy who just hit his hard 18 may have already hit the hard liquor a bit too much!

Nurser:

This is a player who has an alcoholic beverage in front of him, but he sips it so lightly it hardly goes down. Those guys in surveillance know that gamblers drink, and pros don't. This could be a pro who's just trying to look like a gambler.

The interesting thing in this chart, if you haven't noticed, is the incredibly low salary of the surveillance monitor. $20,000 per year is not much of a salary, especially since these guys get no tips. This is one of the reasons why there is such a high turnover rate in this job category. Most of those who enter the casino job market as surveillance monitors are actually hoping to get a pit or other management level job within a short time. These are the game protection personnel who are responsible for catching card counters and other advantage players. Most have very little training or experience, which is why they are easy to fool.

But, whether you like it or not, if you are on the players' side of the tables, you are the enemy. It doesn't matter how you play or how much you're betting, you are under suspicion. And there's one thing you can do at a blackjack table that will really drive them nuts.

Win.

And that's the subject of the next chapter.

Average Annual Salaries for Las Vegas Strip Casino Management Personnel

Casino Manager: $120,000
Shift Manager: $90,000
Pit Boss: $60,000
Floor Person: $40,000
Surveillance Supervisor: $40,000
Security Guard: $35,000
Surveillance Monitor: $20,000

WINNING IS DANGEROUS

Las Vegas teaches us the very startling lesson that Hell and Heaven may be the same place...

— *David Thomson, In Nevada*

I'm going to start this chapter by telling you a couple of true stories that illustrate the title. The first story takes place in a Nevada casino, and the second one takes place in a midwestern riverboat casino. Both incidents are true experiences that happened to me.

STORY #1

Some years back I went into a small casino in northern Nevada and found a double-deck game that literally had me drooling. I watched the game briefly and realized I could beat it without using any betting spread whatsoever. The casino had only half a dozen blackjack tables, with betting limits from $3 to $200. I took a seat and bought in for $200 in red and green chips. No blackjack player in the casino that I saw was betting more than $20, and I didn't want to freak out the pit with $100 bets. The dealer's chip tray, in fact, contained no black chips, just red, green, and silver.

I came off the top with two hands of $30 each, and as I won, I moved my bets up to $40, $50, and finally topped out at two hands of $80 each. Because I was the "big player" in this casino, I didn't think it wise to make any $100 bets. The game was wonderful, and I had sat there for almost two and a half hours, when I looked down to see that I had a virtual mountain of red and green chips in front of me. At the same time that I realized that I had probably taken about everything from this game that I could take without the pit boss having a heart attack, it struck me that I couldn't actually carry all of these chips to the cashier without either coloring up a lot of the red chips, or getting a chip rack.

So, I stood up and started pushing stacks of red chips to the dealer. As it turned out, I had more than $300 in nickels, and even the quarters were going to be unwieldy to carry. As I was stuffing quarters into my pockets so that I would not have to request a chip rack, I got the tap on the shoulder. The shift manager very politely told me that my play was just "too strong" and that I would no longer be allowed to play blackjack.

Of course, I acted dumbfounded, like I could not fathom why they would not allow me to play, and I asked what was wrong with the way I played, other than the fact that I'd had a "lucky run" of cards. All he would say was that my play was "too strong" and that their decision was final. In cashing out, I found that I had slightly more than $1800 in chips, and I had never bought in again after that first $200 buy-in. So, I had won more than $1600 with bets ranging from $30 to $80.

I also knew that they had no clue as to what I was doing to get an advantage. They could easily have ascertained that I was not using a card-counting system, and I'm sure they knew this. But the mere fact that I had won so much so fast, relative to my buy-in and bet sizes, scared them. They didn't want to take any chances.

Basic Strategy Pop Quiz

Player Hand: A♥   6♠♠

Dealer Upcard: 6♦

How do you play it??
(Answer on next page.)

STORY #2

My wife and I were traveling in the Midwest a couple years ago. We stopped at a riverboat casino and went in to look at the games. They had an easily trackable shuffle on their six-deck shoes, so we decided to play. The blackjack table limit sign said the max bet was $1000, but we did not see any action that big on the tables. There were a few players betting black chips on a $25 minimum table, so we sat down to play. My feeling was that this casino could take pretty big action, provided they were comfortable with the player. So, to set them at ease, I decided to come right off the top with two hands of $500 each, and then play two hands of $300 to $600 throughout the rest of the first shoe, without making any bets or plays according to the count. I would simply endure the flux, whatever happened, with no advantage over the house. I simply wanted them to see me as a player so I could beat them later when they wouldn't be watching so closely.

For the next half-hour, my wife and I played like regular gamblers, raising and lowering our bets at whim, based on hunches, and using no intelligent strategy. But right off the bat, I started winning. I was just getting great cards, and the dealer kept busting. The count, in fact, was going down, and since I didn't want to look like a card counter, I didn't lower my bets. In fact, I started pushing my bets up to $600, $700, and $800. But the count kept going down and I kept winning. And, due strictly to luck, I started winning on the second shoe as well. By the halfway point of the second shoe, a whole congregation of suits was convened in the pit, watching and discussing my play. It was amusing the hell out of me, since I wasn't actually doing anything but getting lucky hands.

At the end of the second shoe, I was up $19,000. Within seconds, a boss approached me with a security guard and informed me that I would not be allowed to play any more blackjack.

"We don't like your style," he said.

"My style? You mean just because I was winning?"

"We just don't like your style," he repeated. "You may play any of the other games on the boat, sir, but not blackjack."

What killed me about this barring was that I had never even done anything to get an edge. I was just playing with no edge at all in order to look safe to the casino. There was nothing about my "style" of play that would actually have looked unusual to anyone, and I am not listed in any of the casino blacklist services. I was just being dealt lucky hands. Yet, purely on the basis of winning, I was disallowed from continuing to play.

The Moral

Winning at blackjack is dangerous. Had either of these two wins occurred at a crap table, or on a roulette wheel, I would not have been barred from further play. I would have been viewed as just a lucky gambler. But casinos are very afraid of "lucky" blackjack players. They do not have to recognize you as a card counter, or any other type of advantage player, in order to tell you to take a hike. Remember, if you play blackjack, you are the enemy.

Basic Strategy Pop Quiz Answer

Player Hand:

Dealer Upcard:

How do you play it??

Answer: This hand is one of the most commonly misplayed hands among amateur players. Most players think you should stand. Not so. If doubling down is allowed, then double down on your soft 17 versus the dealer 6. If doubling down is not allowed, then hit your soft 17. Never stand on this hand.

Many players have told me through the years that they initially decided to learn about card counting only after they had been backed off from a casino blackjack table following a lucky win. These players had never really put much faith in card counting until they saw how scared the casinos were of card counters.

SURVIVAL TIPS

Here is a list of tips to keep in mind if you want to keep the welcome mat out when you play blackjack. It is important for all blackjack players to keep these things in mind, not just card counters. Many non-counters, just playing blackjack for fun, have been kicked out of casinos just for winning. You can win all you want at craps, roulette, baccarat, or any of the other casino games. At blackjack, you must always be careful to establish yourself as a non-threatening loser, or risk being identified as a pro and thrown out.

1. Use a few "introductory plays" to become known to a casino before you go for a big score. If you are an unknown player in a casino, you must be more careful than if they know you and your past history and you seem "safe." Had I been a known player in either of the two incidents described above, and especially if the casino had recorded numerous plays with no inordinate wins, I may have passed muster with their game protectors. I'm sure that in both cases they would have studied the videos of my play to see if anything looked unusual, but a past history in their computer as just

a gambler is the best protection you can have to ensure that the welcome mat will remain out for you after a big win.

2. Size your bets in accordance with the other players in the casino. It is always more dangerous to bet at a level higher than the casino's regular customers. Even if they know you, you will be the person they will watch. It does not matter what the table limit signs say. Look around at the action on the tables before deciding if you want to play in any casino. If the casino has a high-limit room, go in and see what the action looks like in the high-limit room. It's rarely a good idea to be the biggest player in the house. Small to medium-sized casinos actually dislike it when a player bets more than their typical customer, despite the fact that they expect to win more on the bigger bets.

3. Move around to hide your wins. It's easier to hide the amount of your winnings in a big casino than in a small casino. In a big casino, you can move around from pit to pit. A small casino may have only one pit, and they may be closely tracking black (or even green) chips.

4. Bring your losses to the pit's attention. If you play for a while and lose any significant amount of money, be sure the boss sees it and gets it recorded. You want your overall playing history to show as many losses as possible.

5. Rat-hole chips if you can get away with it. Most pros learn the art of "going south" with chips. It is very easy to do this if you are moving from table to table, but not easy to do if you stay in one seat. It is easier to go south with chips if the table is crowded, and especially if other players are betting chips in the same denomination as you. If you are the only black chip ($100) bettor on a table, it is useless trying to hide your black chips. The floorperson will simply count the dealer's chip rack when you leave the table, and he will know what you walked with—assuming he counted the rack before you arrived. One extra benefit of rat-holing is that casinos will often comp losers more than they will comp winners.

6. Ask the pit boss what he shows for your play result. If you are a known player, and you have given the boss your player's card, you can ask him what the house has recorded

as your win or loss after each play, and after each trip if you are staying at a casino as a guest. It is a good idea to keep a record of your wins and losses so that you know what the game protection people are looking at the next time you arrive to play. It will not strike the boss as unusual for you to ask about this, as many players try to keep track of how much they're in for in order to estimate what they can ask for in comps. Also, do not hesitate to correct the amount if necessary. If the boss tells you that he has you in the computer for a loss of $400, it is absolutely fine to inform him that you lost $800.

7. Don't overstay your welcome on a winning play. If you are having an inordinate win on a session, do not sit there with a mountain of chips in front of you and keep playing. Sometimes, you just have to leave the best games.

If you win $20,000 on a slot machine, you'll probably get your photo taken, and the casino will hang your mug on the entryway wall with a big sign that says: Joe Blow Won $20,000 on Our Slots! If you win $20,000 on a blackjack table, they'll take your photo all right… and they'll be sending your mug shot around to all the other casinos in the vicinity, warning them that you may be a dangerous professional player.

Ah, blackjack… the only casino game where winning is hell.

How to Rat-Hole Chips

Rat-holing is an art form. It is extremely important that you never be observed going south with chips. This is a sign to surveillance that you may be a pro trying to hide your winnings. But if you don't hide your winnings, your career will likely be short. Here are some rat-holing tips:

1. Buy-in for $600 in black chips, then toss the dealer one chip and ask him to break it. Get three quarters, four nickels, and five silver. As you are casually placing your first bet, $25 to $100, take one of the black chips and place it in your pocket as you are reaching for your cigarettes or gum. With the multi-colored stack you have in front of you on the table, no one will notice that you are already short one black chip.

2. Later, when you go to the rest room, leave your chips on the table, but remove one more black chip and pocket it.

3. Later, when your cell phone rings and you stand up and turn away from the table to answer it, remove one more black chip.

4. Etc., etc., You get the picture. You just get one chip at a time. And you never stop.

5. Don't make the mistake of waiting until you see if you've won or lost to start rat-holing. You must rat-hole even when you are losing, as it will make your losses appear to be bigger losses.

6. If you lose the chips you have on the table, do not take rat-holed chips out of your pockets to continue playing. Buy in for more chips, even though you have chips in your pocket. If you pull rat-holed chips out of your pocket to continue playing, you may stage a comeback and end up sitting there with a win and no rat-holed chips. All of your early rat-holing went for naught.

7. For high-rollers who play on credit lines, it looks very bad if you are seen rat-holing chips when you are playing on a marker. In fact, the casino may think you are trying to pull a scam. If you get a blotch on your name with Central Credit, it may severely limit your credit options in the future. This is one reason why it is best for professional players to avoid playing on credit. I would not rat-hole chips at all if playing on a credit line.

8. Finally, don't immediately go to the cashier to cash out your chips after a play. Or, if you do, cash out only the chips you appeared to walk from the table with. You can cash out the rest later or have a friend do it.

"BARRED" VERSUS "BACKED OFF"

In Nevada and most other states, casinos are allowed to bar individuals from their games for almost any reason that would not fall into the category of a civil rights violation. This means that card counters and other professionals or suspected professionals can be excluded from the tables even though they may be breaking no laws. In New Jersey, casinos cannot bar players just for exhibiting intelligence; however, they may limit such players' bets in an attempt to make the game unprofitable.

But Isn't Barring Illegal Discrimination?

In the U.S., there are very strict federal laws against civil rights violations, and these laws protect Americans from being discriminated against in employment, access to public places, etc. To many card counters, it seems that the casinos should have no right to exclude them from the blackjack tables—which are open to the public—since they are breaking no laws. The civil rights laws, however, are very specific in defining the "protected" classes. You are protected from discrimination if that discrimination is based on your race, creed, age, nationality, sex, or mental or physical handicap. Unfortunately, intelligence is not within the definitions of the protected classes. Stupidity—which is a mental handicap—is protected. So, casinos must let stupid people play their games. But the casinos are fully within their legal rights to disallow smart people from playing at their tables. That's why they can tell card counters to take a hike.

Let's first define the terms. Barring is usually done by the shift manager or pit manager, and is most often done in the presence of another casino employee—usually a floor person or security guard. You will specifically be told that you are no longer allowed to play blackjack. Sometimes you will be read an official statement, such as a state's trespassing law, and notified that you are no longer allowed on the premises. Sometimes you will be told that you are welcome to play other games, but a barring is always a formal invitation to get lost.

If a floor person or pit boss approaches you alone, on the other hand, and simply tells you your action is no longer wanted, this is not a barring, but a backing off. This is an informal invitation to hit the road, and it is less serious.

Casinos rarely bar nickel bettors, even if they suspect them of counting cards. Such players are more often backed off informally. If you are backed off, it is usually safe to return to the casino on any shift when the boss who backed you off is not on duty. It is unlikely that your mug shot is hanging up in the surveillance room.

But if you have been barred from a casino and you have been playing at stakes high enough to concern that casino, then you should automatically assume that other casinos owned by the same parent company will have your name and photo on record as persona non grata. By "stakes high enough to concern that casino" I mean stakes that would be high enough to generate substantial comps in that venue. A $25 bettor may be a nobody in a swank carpet joint that regularly sees bets of multiple thousands, but such a player may be a big bettor in a sawdust joint that makes most of its money from twenty-five-cent slot machines. If your action is sufficient to get you a room and food where you play, then you are important enough to that casino to be watched.

On the other hand, if you are merely backed off from a casino, and if you were not playing at a level of action they might deem worrisome, then you probably are making some serious mistakes in what card counters call "comportment." You may seem too intense about watching the cards being dealt, and too serious and thoughtful about making your decisions.

If you are barred from a casino while playing at stakes high enough to concern just about any casino—average bets of multiple hundreds— then you may find that you will have problems at other casinos not even related by ownership to the casino where you were barred. Most casinos belong to a SIN—an appropriate acronym for Surveillance Information Network. These are informal networks of casinos in the same area that share (usually via fax or email) photos and names of suspicious players immediately. A high-stakes counter who is barred in one casino will often find that if he goes across the street to play at another unrelated casino, he will barely get a bet down on the layout before he is given the boot. That's a SIN.

Many casinos also subscribe to various blacklist agencies that provide monthly updates on "undesirables." Griffin Investigations and Biometrica are two of the most popular in operation today. If you are placing average bets under one hundred dollars, then you are unlikely to get your photo into one of these mug books. Black chip and higher bettors who are barred at multiple casinos stand a good chance of finding their action unwelcome almost everywhere.

As for whether or not you should try to play again where you have been barred, that depends on how serious you think the barring may have been to them. Many pit bosses have long memories. If you have a player's card, so they know who you are by name, then it would definitely not be safe to use your card in there again. You'll have to forego the comps. And remember, in Nevada and most other states, they can have you arrested for trespassing if you return after a formal barring. So, be careful.

Personally, I think smart people should be recognized as a minority group in this country so that our rights cannot be so easily trampled. The fact is, there are fewer smart people playing casino games than any other minority group. And in my opinion, as the smallest minority, we need the most protection.

CHEATING? AT BLACKJACK?

> In many societies it was a serious crime for anyone but the high priest to touch the instruments used to divine the will of the gods. This imbued the dice with a sacred quality. It also made sure no one could tell if they were loaded.
>
> — *David Johnston, Temples of Chance*

Yes, there are dealers who can and will cheat you in a blackjack game. Dealers are human beings and as such, some—despite their training—occasionally act human. Most casinos today prefer to take their profits from the house edge, rather than risk losing their customers due to a cheating scandal, or their license due to a conviction. But, let's be realistic. In recent years, we have seen quite a few major banks, investment companies, insurance companies, and others convicted of bilking the public in despicable scams. Blackjack dealers are no more honest than your banker, and casinos are no less dishonest than your average Wall Street investment firm.

There are a lot of crooks in this world, so let's learn to watch out for them at the blackjack tables.

BLACKJACK'S SORDID PAST

The game of blackjack, like three-card monte, was historically a popular game for traveling cheats. It was an easy game to cheat at, since a dealer who could control a single ace or 10 could obtain a dominant edge over the players. The game requires no equipment other than a deck of cards, and it's an easy game for players to understand.

Blackjack sleight-of-hand experts could rest assured that they could beat any player who came along. In fact, one of the arts of card cheating is letting the players win just enough so that they will not suspect cheating, so that they will keep coming back, thinking the game is on the level. A talented card cheater could pretty much assure himself of winning just about every single hand in a blackjack game. This might get the money very quickly, but it wouldn't look good from the players' perspective.

Some forms of cheating are easier to accomplish in a hand-held game than in a shoe game, but virtually any game can be crooked, and I have personally witnessed cheating in both hand-held and shoe games in casinos in Nevada as well as other states in the U.S. So, let's look at how it's done, what it will cost you, how to spot it, and how to protect yourself from cheating when you do spot it.

WHY CHEAT?

Obviously, for the money. But many casino players might then assume that games in major casinos would have to be honest, since no one would ever expect, say, the Hilton Corporation of hiring or training, or even allowing, its employees to steal from its customers. Let's look for a moment at the psychology of a dealer cheating in a casino, and how this differs from stealing and embezzling from other businesses.

If a bank employee takes money from the till, that employee is stealing from the bank. Similarly, if a casino dealer surreptitiously takes chips from his chip rack, he is stealing from the casino. Even if the surveillance cameras in the bank do not catch the bank embezzler, the bank employee still risks being caught when the discrepancy is later discovered in the employee's money count. This, in fact, is probably the major deterrent to bank tellers stealing from their employers.

But a cheating blackjack dealer has an option not open to the bank teller. The cheating dealer can keep the count on his chip tray looking "clean" if he simply manages to put back whatever he takes from the casino by stealing it from customers.

Let's say a bank teller has his buddy come in to make a $100 withdrawal five days a week, and each time he comes in, the teller gives him two extra hundred-dollar bills beneath the $100 on record. That's $1000 a week profit the teller can split with his buddy. But, even if that teller is a skilled sleight-of-hand artist, this scam will not last a week.

Each and every day, the teller's drawer will come up $200 short. Party over.

The casino dealer, on the other hand, may have an exact count on his chip tray when his shift begins, but every transaction is not covered by paperwork. At a crowded table, there may be five to seven players winning and losing various amounts every single minute. No audit of the chip tray will ever turn up a $200 discrepancy per day. But a discrepancy of $1000 a week, week after week, month after month, will probably be noticed eventually.

But, the casino dealer has an option not open to the bank teller. Whatever amount of money the casino dealer passes to his buddy every week, he can steal back from other players at his table in order to keep his total table win looking right over the long haul.

A talented cheater could be working in any casino. Although some crooked dealers might look for little mom'n'pop casinos out in the middle of nowhere, most crooks do tend to gravitate toward wherever the money is. It's hard to get away with $1000 a week in a little sawdust joint. The big casinos have players betting that amount and more on a single hand every night of the week.

WHAT WILL IT COST YOU?

Asking what a cheater can cost you is like asking you how much a pickpocket can steal from you. How much money do you have in your pocket? The cheat wants it all, and he will take as much of it as you let him take.

When Ed Thorp visited the

> **CHEATER'S SLANG:**
> Sub: a hidden pocket on a dealer's apron used to filch chips. All casino dealers wear aprons, the purpose of which is to keep dealers from having any access to their pockets. A sub foils the purpose of the apron and allows the dealer to steal chips without using an accomplice to get them off the table.

Nevada casinos in Las Vegas and Reno prior to the publication of *Beat the Dealer* in 1962, he found cheating in almost every casino he played in. As Nevada offered mostly hand-held single-deck games at that time, one of the most common techniques he ran into was the "seconds" dealer. This is a dealer who peeks at the top card so he always knows what the next card to be dealt is, then either delivers that card or holds it back and deals the unknown card beneath it (the "second") as he prefers.

Many years later, Thorp published a mathematical analysis of what this technique might cost the player. His results showed that if the dealer was capable of peeking at every top card, and was playing against a single player at the table, the dealer would win 95 percent of the time. At a full table, the dealer would win 90 percent of the time.

So, the potential damage a cheating dealer can do to your bankroll is huge.

PAYOUT "ERRORS"

The most common way that a dealer will cheat is by mispaying hands. This method of cheating is attractive to a crooked dealer because there is no sleight of hand required, and if caught the mispay appears to be an honest error. A dealer can "test" a player by underpaying one hand, and if the player doesn't notice, he can continue to underpay in similar situations.

There are five ways a dealer can cheat you with a mispay:

1. He can underpay your winning hand.
2. He can claim your winning hand is a "push."
3. He can claim your winning or tie hand is a loser.
4. He can underpay you when you are buying in for chips.
5. He can underpay you when he is "coloring up" your chips when you quit.

Definition:
Coloring up chips is casino lingo for exchanging lower denomination chips for higher denomination chips. When a player is about to leave a table, a dealer will often ask, "Can I color those up for you?" motioning to the player's chips. If the dealer exchanges three black ($100) chips for the player's twelve green ($25) chips, then the dealer has colored up the green to black.

All of these mispay methods require a player who is simply not paying close enough attention to the game. I have seen dealers make a seven-card 22 on their own hand, quickly say, "Twenty-one," and start collecting all of the players' bets. I have seen dealers deal a player a six or seven-card 21, say, "Twenty-two," and quickly pick up the players' cards and money.

You must watch the game, and if the dealer ever attempts to settle your hand and your bet before you have finished adding up the totals, stop him. And don't be slow about it. Put your hand out and say, "Wait a minute, what does that add up to?" If the dealer's total is correct, no problem. I guarantee you that no one at the table will be irritated with you for slowing down the game. If a dealer is continually trying to settle bets too quickly, and you continually have to stop the game, then find another table. Do not decide that you will just have to start trusting the dealer since he appears to always be right. Never allow a bet to be settled if you are unsure of the hand totals.

When you buy in or cash out, always verify that you are getting the correct amount of chips. This is true at both the tables and the cashier's cage. Dealers and cashiers are trained to line up chips in specified size piles in order to facilitate counting. Black chips get stacked in fives; green chips get stacked in fours; red chips get stacked in fives.

I once had a dealer stack my green chips into five stacks of five, then give me $500 in blacks for the greens. As I was leaving the table, he called me back. "I'm sorry, sir," he said. "I owe you $125 more. I did this wrong." He then showed me the green stacks five high, took one chip off of each stack, made a sixth green stack four-high, and dropped the extra chip on the table beside the pile.

This, obviously, was an honest dealer, as honest as a dealer could be. And I—despite decades of experience at the tables, and even knowing what I should be watching for—hadn't noticed the mis-stacking of my chips and the underpayment of $125 that had resulted. But this illustrates why mispays are among the most popular form of cheating. These types of underpayments do occur as simple mistakes, and even experienced players don't always notice them, especially if a lot of chips are involved.

Be especially wary of any dealer who colors up your chips when he is simply paying a winning hand. For example, if you bet $15 and win, be careful of any dealer who pays this bet by taking away two of your nickels and giving you a quarter. In fact, the payout in this example is correct, since you end up with one quarter and one nickel, or $30, the same as if he had just paid your three nickel bet by sliding three more nickels beside it.

But dealers who pay bets like this can be dangerous. In some casinos, dealers are instructed to pay bets by coloring up lower denomination chips. These casinos seem to think that this

DEALER SLANG
Barber pole: a player's bet stacked with multiple-denomination chips.

will encourage players to bet the higher denomination chips. But dealers who color up bets when paying them off can easily underpay player blackjacks or weird barber pole bets.

Payout errors can occur in both hand-held and shoe games, which is another reason why many cheating dealers prefer this method of theft. It doesn't matter which table the dealer is assigned to. There is no time or effort required for setting up the play. No accomplice is needed to pull it off. And if the dealer is careful in evaluating players and choosing his spots, he will rarely be caught.

Three Simple Rules To Avoid Payout Errors
1. Total your hand and the dealer's before the cards are swept away.
2. Verify the correct payout, being extra careful on blackjack payouts.
3. Be extra careful if a dealer colors up your chips during the payout.

CHEATING IN SINGLE-DECK GAMES

There are many ways a competent sleight-of-hand expert can manipulate cards in a single-deck game to cheat the players. Let's look at a few of the most common.

Dealing Seconds

As mentioned above, a blackjack dealer who can peek at the top card and deal the second can have a devastating advantage over players. One sign that a dealer may be dealing seconds is if two cards come off as he is attempting to deal one. I would advise leaving the table if you ever encounter a dealer who accidentally deals two cards instead of one. I myself would not play another hand on such a table. I realize this could have been an honest accident, but it is a very bad sign.

If you've ever studied card magic, one of the common sleights that can be used in many tricks is retaining the top card in order to produce it later. There are two main ways of keeping the top card on top when it appears you are dealing the top card. One is to pull it back at the moment when you are striking the deck with the thumb of your dealing hand, so that the card beneath it is struck and dealt instead. The other is to actually push two cards off the top, then pull the second card out from beneath the top card by holding down the top card when dealing the second.

Card mechanics call these two methods of dealing a second the strike second, and the push-off second. It takes many hours of practice to learn to deal either type of second smoothly. One problem that you will have when attempting to deal a strike second is that you will not pull back the top card far enough and hold it down tightly enough, and both the top card and the second will be dealt. Or, you will pull back the top card but the cards beneath it will fan out, and you will deal the second and third cards.

The push-off second is even more difficult to deal smoothly. Just pick up a deck of cards if you have one handy, and try pushing off the top two cards. It's easy to push off the top card, but the top two? There's a trick to it. One problem you'll have when attempting to push off two cards, so that you can grab the card beneath the top card to deal it, is that you will accidentally push off three or four cards, and more than one card will come out when you attempt the deal.

Note that in all cases, the big problem you'll have when trying to deal a second is that you will deal more than one card. Now try this test. Take a deck of cards and try to deal the top two cards at once, without attempting to deal the second card from the top. It is almost impossible to deal two cards from the top with a normal dealing style.

So, when I am in a hand-held game and I see two cards come off the deck when the dealer is attempting to deal one, I'm out of there. This may just be some rookie dealer who somehow managed to deal two cards at once, but I'm not going to bet my money on it.

The main problem with a good seconds dealer is that he will never deal two cards at once. You will never be able to see an expert dealing a second. For this move, the hand really is quicker than the eye.

In fact, the eye is exactly what you have to watch for if you think you may be up against an expert.

Dealing the second is useless if the dealer hasn't peeked the top card. The only way to see if an expert is dealing seconds is to watch his eyes. A dealer who continually looks down at his deck hand may be peeking at the top card. There is no reason for a dealer to look at the deck while dealing or while waiting for a player to make a decision. There are various methods sleight-of-hand experts use to "bubble" the corner of the top card in order to see the index when their hand is angled properly, but unfortunately you will not be able to see what the dealer sees unless your eyes are where his eyes are. But you can watch the dealer's eyes, and if you see that he keeps looking at the deck in hand at inexplicable moments, get out. There is no reason for the dealer to look at the deck when dealing. In fact, it's very unnatural to do this. There's nothing else you can do but leave the table.

> **CHEATER'S SLANG:**
>
> Bubble Peek: a surreptitious method of peeking the top card by pushing it into a slight arch over the card beneath it so the corner with the index can be glimpsed.

There are some dealers who entertain players by predicting the next card to be dealt. If the dealer is always getting it right, this is a dealer who is peeking. You will never see the peek, and the predictions seem astonishing to most players. In my opinion, these dealers are probably unlikely to be cheaters. They are just showoffs who have studied card magic. Why would a seconds dealer ever blow his cover this way? Still, I will leave the table fast when any dealer starts showing off in this fashion. A dealer who wants to brag about how dangerous he could be if he wanted to might decide he wants to take advantage of his skill at any time.

One thing you can do if you run into one of these "psychic" dealers is to watch his eyes. By playing at the table minimum, you might get an education on what the peek looks like, the timing on it, etc. Dealers who peek try to do so at moments when their hands are naturally engaged in some normal activity, like inserting their hole card, delivering a card to a player, straightening a player's bet or the chip rack, etc.

One telltale sign of many seconds dealers is that they seem inordinately interested in knowing what your cards are. If a dealer is continually asking you what cards you have while you are trying to make your decisions, or is frequently leaning forward to see them, be suspicious. A seconds dealer cannot make an informed decision on what to do with the top card unless he knows what you have. He may have a 6 on top of the deck that he would deliver to your total of 16 to bust you, but would hold back if you had a total of 14 or 15, as this would give you a 20 or 21.

I have a card-counting friend who once became suspicious that a dealer was dealing seconds in a double-deck game solely because the dealer continually asked him what his hand was, sometimes craning his neck to try and see his cards. He was losing, but the game seemed good, and he didn't want to leave unless he was sure. He never saw the dealer peek, and nothing else about the dealing style seemed unusual.

On one hand, he was dealt a hard 12, and mumbled, "Shit, another stiff."

The dealer asked him what he had.

It struck him that if the dealer was dealing seconds and had a 10 on top, it wouldn't matter what he had, since the 10 would bust any stiff. But if the dealer had a card that would bust some stiffs, but not others, he might be interested in knowing what his hand totaled. So, without showing his cards to the dealer, he said, "Another rotten sixteen," as he scratched the felt for a hit.

The dealer delivered him an 8.

When he tucked his cards to stand, the dealer looked at him curiously but said nothing.

The dealer turned over his hole card, an 8, and the player's 20 had beaten him.

The dealer chuckled, then said, "I thought you said you had sixteen."

My friend stood up, deciding it was time to leave. "I just wanted to make sure you gave me that eight," he said.

In telling me the story, he said, "I didn't really know for sure that he was dealing seconds until I said that to him. I saw a chill run through him. He not only realized that I knew what he was doing, he actually thought I knew the top card was an eight! Of course, I didn't know that. I just acted like I did."

Stacking a Blackjack

An alert dealer who is competent at legerdemain can stack himself a blackjack pretty easily in a single- or double-deck game. Locating a single ace and 10, then manipulating these cards into position (essentially separated by a single card) is the first step. The second step is the part that makes most players feel the first step is a waste of time, even if a dealer had the ability to accomplish step one.

Four Simple Rules To Avoid Seconds Dealers:
1. Don't play against a dealer who keeps looking at the deck.
2. Don't play against a dealer who "entertains" you by predicting the next card.
3. Leave the table if two (or more) cards are dealt as one.
4. Be wary of any dealer who is overly interested in what your cards are.

After the shuffle, the player gets to cut the deck. Even if the dealer has stacked himself a blackjack, wouldn't the player's random cut nullify the dealer's handiwork?

Yes, it would… assuming the dealer didn't nullify the cut.

How do you nullify a cut? There are many ways to do this. In casino games, most dealers give the player a cut-card to make the cut, then the dealer separates the deck in two at the point where the player placed the cut card, and completes the cut by placing the cards above the cut card below the cards beneath the cut card. It's as simple as can be.

I sat down to play at a single-deck game at a major Las Vegas Strip casino, and I was with a partner who writes for *Blackjack Forum* under the name "Radar O'Reilly." Radar stood beside me at the table, not playing, waiting to see if the game was any good.

The table minimum was $25, so I placed a $25 bet. The dealer shuffled the cards, I cut, and he dealt me a 20 and himself a blackjack. Radar leaned over and said, "Let's leave." I made a friendly comment to the dealer that it just didn't look like my lucky day, and after that one hand, we left.

"Why did you call off the play?" I asked Radar.

"He didn't cut the cards," Radar said.

> ### CHEATER'S SLANG:
>
> **High-Low Pick-Up:** an old cheating method in which the dealer would sort the used cards on the layout while picking them up into alternating high-low values. A false shuffle would then retain the high-low order, enabling the dealer to deal seconds without peeking as he would simply know that the next card to be dealt would more likely be high or low. This type of pick-up procedure cannot be used in modern regulated casinos. Any card-sorting today is usually limited to setting up a single hand. A crooked dealer today is more likely to look for a small set of cards that is already on the table in correct position—say an ace and 10 separated by a single card—so that he can manipulate these cards to where he wants them during the shuffle, without any visible sorting having occurred during the pick-up procedure.

"I cut the cards," I said.

"Yes, but after you placed the cut card into the deck, he didn't cut there. He took the top part off, like he was going to cut it to the bottom, but he placed it right back on top. It wasn't even that fast. He did it pretty slowly."

"I didn't even see it," I said.

"How could you see it? He was talking to you when he did the move, and you were looking at his face. I don't think anyone would see it if they weren't looking for it. They could probably watch him from the overhead cameras and never see it in surveillance. He separates the two halves at the cut card, then puts them back together. The motion looks exactly the same as an honest cut; he just didn't put them back together the way he was supposed to."

You are unlikely to see a dealer stack himself a blackjack. You may be able to see a cut nullified if you watch for it. But, unfortunately, there are other ways a dealer might accomplish this dirty deed. By placing a crimp or bend in a card, many dealers can get a player to cut exactly where he wants the cut to be. Some dealers can accomplish this by having a confederate at the table who will cut to his crimp or bend with 100 percent assurance.

> **CHEATER'S SLANG:**
>
> **Hopping the Cut:** a method of nullifying a player's cut in the old hand-held games, before cut cards were used, when players physically cut the deck on the table and the dealer completed it. A dealer who hopped the cut appeared to be completing it, but he actually hops the cut portion back into its pre-cut position. It is virtually impossible to detect this move when performed by an expert.

A better guideline for protecting yourself against this type of move is to simply bear in mind the mathematics of the game.

According to the odds, a dealer will deal himself a blackjack on the first hand after a shuffle (approximately):

- One time: every 20 rounds
- Twice in succession: every 400 rounds
- Thrice in succession: every 9,000 rounds
- Four times in succession: every 200,000 rounds
- Five times in succession: every 4 million rounds

So, if I see three first-round blackjacks in a row, I realize that I might just be the nine thousandth person to play against that dealer since the last time this occurred, but I'd probably elect to leave the table.

Marked Cards

Although marked cards have surfaced in casino blackjack games, marked cards are more likely to be found in a poker room today than in a blackjack pit. In a hand-held game, marked cards are much more dangerous for a cheater to use than peeking, because the cards themselves can

> **Three Simple Rules To Avoid Blackjack Stackers:**
>
> 1. Watch the cut carefully to be sure the dealer completes it properly.
> 2. Watch out for an accomplice at the table who may be cutting to a crimp.
> 3. If you see three first-round dealer blackjacks in a row, quit the table.

be used as evidence against the cheater. Since peeking is not that difficult, and accomplishes the same end, marked cards are not very popular with cheats today.

If you ever suspect that another player at a blackjack table is marking cards, possibly by nicking or scratching them in order to identify them later, get out of the game fast. If you suspect marked cards may be in use because of unusual or extraordinary plays in a high-stakes game, get out of the game. You will not be able to see the marks on a professionally marked deck.

Other Peeking Scams

There are dozens of different ways a dealer might cheat if he simply knows the top card, and many do not involve dealing seconds. In *How to Detect Casino Cheating at Blackjack*, former Nevada Gaming Control Agent Bill Zender describes a method used in an Indian reservation casino, where the dealer in a heads-up game would simply peek at the top card at the end of each round after the first three rounds had been dealt. If the top card was an ace or 10, the dealer would shuffle the deck. If it was a low card, he would deal the next round. This assured that the player would not get any ace or 10 as his first card after the third round of play, and he would play an inordinate number of rounds late in the deal with a poor starting card.

Cheating expert Sam Case, in a 1982 *Blackjack Forum* article, described a move he called the "Laughlin layaway," as he first saw it used by a dealer in Laughlin, Nevada. At the end of each round, this dealer would peek at the top card. If it was an ace or 10, she would use it to scoop up the cards on the layout, then put it into the discards with the scooped up cards. If it was a low card, she would just pick up the discards normally, and deal the card to the first base player on the next round.

This is a case where she would affect the result of the first base player drastically, though other players at the table would have a normal expectation on the game. Essentially, she is removing a few tens and aces from play in each deck, but they are all cards that should naturally have gone to the same player. Because she was peeking at the top card before making her decision, she would definitely be considered to be cheating in the state of Nevada, though it would be very difficult for cheating to be proven against her. From the perspective of anyone watching her, including the eye in the sky, she would simply appear to be burning one extra card on some rounds, and there is no law or regulation against dealers burning extra cards during the game.

In fact, in the state of Nevada, there are legal ways for a casino to effectively remove high cards from play, employing a common practice known as preferential shuffling.

Preferential Shuffling

Finally, let's discuss a cheating method that many casinos use in their hand-held games that has been ruled legal in the industry. Preferential shuffling is when the dealer counts cards, then shuffles when the remaining deck has excess high cards, but continues dealing when the remaining deck contains excess low cards.

The effect of preferential shuffling is similar to the effect of simply removing a few tens and aces from the deck. It would be illegal for a casino to remove cards from a deck, but it is not illegal for them to employ a dealing style that will accomplish the same end.

Card counters never have to worry about preferential shuffling because they can see very clearly when it is being employed. The count goes up; the dealer shuffles. The count goes down; the dealer deals another round. So, counters just leave the table after a short play.

Preferential shuffling is primarily a method casinos use to get a higher advantage against non-counters who aren't aware of it. Casinos like it because it chases the counters away from their tables in the first place, then gives the house a stronger advantage against the non-counters. Computer simulations show that preferential shuffling adds about 1.5 percent to the house advantage. This means that the house would have about a 2 percent advantage against perfect basic strategy players.

But you don't have to be a card counter to protect yourself from casinos that use the preferential shuffle.

Three Simple Steps To Avoid Preferential Shuffles:

1. Be careful in any game where the dealer continually seems to deal different amounts of the cards between shuffles—sometimes very few rounds, sometimes more.
2. If you see this, watch to see if the dealer's shuffles always seem to come after rounds where excess low cards (2 through 6) are dealt.
3. If so, leave the table.

CHEATING IN MULTI-DECK SHOE GAMES

Shoe games were initially introduced in order to eliminate many of the common hand-held cheating possibilities. And, as a matter of fact, they have accomplished this. It is usually more difficult for a dealer to cheat when dealing cards from a shoe than when controlling the cards in his own hands. Although shoes have been designed that allow dealers to peek and deal seconds, gaffed equipment like this is unlikely to be found in major casinos, or any casinos where there is strict gaming control. This type of equipment might be used on a cruise ship, in an unregulated Indian reservation game, or in a foreign country where gaming control is more lax. If you play in these types of venues, then you should be aware that gaffed equipment exists and is available on the black market. Other devices out there would include marked cards, loaded dice, magnetic roulette balls, etc. Magnetic dice have even been used in private high-stakes backgammon games. If you play blackjack in unregulated, and especially private or illegal games, then my advice to you would simply be to not play for big money. Professionally marked cards or a gaffed shoe would be almost impossible for any player to detect because there are so many different ways such devices could be used to cheat you.

So let's look at the ways that crooked dealers in more regulated areas can cheat you.

> **CHEATER'S SLANG:**
>
> Gaffed: rigged for the purpose of cheating, said of gaming equipment so altered. A gaff is a common magician's term for any device of trickery.

The Short Shoe

A short shoe, essentially, is a shoe that has cards missing. Assuming the house is trying to cheat the players, those missing cards would be tens and aces. Setting up a short shoe would require a crooked boss and dealer working together. The dealer would not be able to pull this off alone.

It is not difficult to set up a short shoe. In new unopened boxes, the cards are set up in alternating suits, ace to king, ace to king, then king to ace, king to ace. Because the aces and ten-valued cards come clumped together, it is very easy to leave a few of these high cards in the box when removing them. In most casinos, the boss removes the cards from the boxes, quickly fans through each deck himself to see that they are all there, then gives the decks to the dealer. Before shuffling the decks together, the dealer is required to fan the cards on the table, one deck at a time, front and back, making sure all cards are there and that there are no misprints or imperfections.

A short shoe is set up by a boss who purposely leaves high cards in one or more of the boxes. Since he knows that cards are missing, the dealer then very quickly goes through the motions of checking the decks and quickly goes into the washing and shuffling procedure.

In order to accomplish this, there must be no players sitting at the table during the dealer's fanning procedure. This is not a problem if the table being prepared is not yet in operation. Also, if the table is not yet open, there will be no surveillance on it, as surveillance doesn't watch closed games.

Once those short decks are shuffled together in the shoe, it's smooth sailing. Subsequent dealers on that table won't even know they're dealing from short shoes. As long as that shoe is in action on the table, all players will be playing against a higher house edge than normal. No sleight-of-hand is required. The shoe itself does all the dirty work, and it can last for as long as eight hours.

A short shoe is considered a more dangerous way for a casino to cheat, because—unlike the single-deck methods we've been discussing—with a short shoe there is physical evidence of cheating on the table. If anyone were to take out all of the cards in the shoe, the scam would be discovered. Also, if anyone were to examine the supposedly empty card boxes that the boss has stored in the cabinet at the pit podium, they would discover aces and tens left in the boxes.

Yet, major casinos in Las Vegas have employed this scam. The fact is, no one ever does go through the cards in the shoe to see if they are all there. And no one ever looks in the boss's card boxes at the podium. Why would they?

In addition to a closed table to enable the set-up, and a dealer and boss working together, this scam also requires a clean-up operation. Unless some other boss is in on this scam, that same boss who set up the shoe must take the cards from the table himself when it is time to introduce new decks into play. He'll have to get those used cards into the boxes they belong in, along with the cards that were purposely left in the boxes, so he can date and initial the boxes.

The short shoe is particularly devastating to card counters because the absence of some of the high cards means that excess low cards will continually be dealt. This will cause the count to rise throughout the shoe, shoe after shoe, but the counter will never see the high cards he is betting on. He will be continually betting big into garbage.

> **CHEATER'S SLANG:**
>
> **Cooler:** a deck or shoe with the cards prearranged to cheat either the players or the house. The use of coolers is rare in modern casinos because it entails switching an entire deck or shoe out of the game to get the cooler into the game, not easily accomplished with modern camera surveillance. Short shoes, though dangerous, are not nearly so difficult to set up.

MY EXPERIENCE WITH SHORT SHOES

A couple of years ago, I was working with a group of players who were training for a shuffle-tracking team in Las Vegas. There were a couple of dozen easy shuffles in town at that time, and we would send players into these easy games to get experience following the high cards through the shuffle.

One player called me, having lost about $1500 tracking one of these shuffles at an off-Strip casino. He insisted that the shuffle was exactly as we had described it in our training session, and it did not seem difficult to follow in the casino, but after half a dozen shoes, he had never once been able to locate the high cards.

> **Definition:**
>
> Shuffle tracking is a technique of visually following where slugs of high cards go during a shuffle. The tracker can then bet big in this portion of the next shoe, even though a traditional card counter would not have a high count at this point.

I went to the casino with Radar O'Reilly, the best slug tracker I knew, to sit in on the game with the player. I figured that between the two of us we could figure out what the trainee was doing wrong.

On the first shoe (six decks), the count went up to +14 by the end. This was ideal since it meant that the high cards were all located in the one-deck portion of the shoe that was unplayed. The dealer broke this one-deck piece in two, and plugged these cards into two different locations in the discard stack before shuffling, a fairly common pre-shuffle procedure.

I visually followed one portion of these cards through the shuffle, and Radar followed the other. To our astonishment, no excess high cards appeared in either area of the following shoe where they should have appeared! In fact, the count again ended up high, this time +12.

Again, we each followed one portion of these supposed high cards through the simple shuffle, and again, the high cards were not there in either location. Instead, once again, the count on the shoe ended in double digits.

We were so stunned to find a short shoe in a Las Vegas casino that we tracked the shuffle several more times to be absolutely sure—each time with the same result.

We pulled the player out of that casino, and stopped sending trainees there. They were irrefutably dealing from short shoes. We learned from talking to the trainee that the half-dozen shoes he had tracked before calling us had all been similar. He had never actually seen a high-card slug to track. He simply kept getting a high count by the end of each shoe, and had been attempting to track the cards that hadn't been dealt and that should have contained the high cards.

We later had a similar experience with yet another casino in Las Vegas, this one a bigger casino on the Strip. Shuffle trackers are probably the only players who can verify beyond a doubt that a short shoe is in use, without going through the cards to count all of the denominations. But non-trackers, and especially card counters, can still protect themselves from this scam.

> **CHEATER'S SLANG:**
>
> **Flat Store:** a casino that is cheating on many, if not all, games. Also called a bust-out joint. If a casino has a house policy of cheating the players, they are said to be running flat.

Two Simple Rules To Avoid Being Short-Shoed:

1. If possible, sit and watch the introduction of new decks into a game. You will not be short-shoed because you will see that all of the cards are there.
2. A major sign of a short shoe for card counters is a count that is always high at the end of the shoe. Leave the table if this continually occurs.

Cutting the High Cards Out of Play

This is a method that a crooked dealer can employ in shoe games on his own, without any accomplices in on the scam, and it has the same effect as the short shoe. By watching for big clumps of high cards that come out during the deal, then paying attention to where this group of cards is in the discard tray, the dealer will attempt to control this group of cards during the shuffle to an area that will be cut out of play. Once these cards are cut out of play, the dealer's job is easier. He always knows where these high cards are—behind the cut card—so he can continually control them to be cut out of play.

To accomplish this, a dealer must be fairly skilled at doing a variation on the house shuffle that looks enough like the standard house shuffle to pass for the house shuffle if anyone in the house is watching. This is much more difficult than it sounds, but crooks spend a lot of time practicing.

Getting a player to cut in the right place to get the high cards out of play is the easy part. Players tend to be creatures of habit, and a player who cuts in the center once will likely cut there again. The dealer will offer the cut to a player who will cut where he wants the cut. Note that the dealer does not need a highly precise cut to accomplish his deed. He just wants to get a fairly large segment of cards removed from play.

The effect of this phony shuffling procedure is identical to the effect of the short shoe. The only difference, in fact, is that the cards are literally missing from a short shoe, instead of just being behind the cut card. From the player's perspective, it makes no difference. Depending on how many high cards are cut out of play, you will lose at a faster rate than if playing in honest decks. From the cheater's perspective, there is a big difference. With a short shoe, there is always that nerve-wracking evidence until the clean-up operation is done. There is no physical evidence of any wrongdoing if the high cards are simply behind the cut card.

The way that card counters can tell that this ploy is being used is that the count is always high at the end of the shoe, and those high cards never seem to come out.

What If the Dealer Cheats to Help You?

Yes, this happens. Here's one recent incident that I encountered.

I was at a major Las Vegas Strip casino, again with Radar O'Reilly. We had just sat down at a two-deck game in the high-limit room. It was a $100 minimum table and there were no other players on the game. I came off the top with two bets of $100 each, and Radar placed a single $100 bet along with a $5 toke bet for the dealer.

The dealer said, "Wait till the next hand to place that bet for me."

Radar said, "Sure," cast me a glance that said "Weird," and pulled back the nickel.

We lost all three bets on that round.

On the next hand, Radar placed another $100 bet with the nickel bet for the dealer. Radar was dealt a blackjack.

Weird.

The dealer had a 10 up. On one of my hands I had a pair of nines and stood. On the other hand, I had a 9-7, hard 16. I showed the hand to the dealer, then tucked my cards to stand.

The dealer peeked under his 10, then said to me, "You should hit." Note that the dealer had already used the auto-peek device on the table to determine that he did not have a blackjack. This was a physical peek he accomplished by bending up the corner of the card the way dealers used to peek under tens in the old days.

I had a very strong feeling that he was giving me good advice, especially after having seen Radar's blackjack. But I didn't hit. I didn't touch my cards, but waved my hand across them the way you signal a stand in a face-up game and said, as matter-of-factly as I could, "No, I've been busting this hand all day." In fact, I was imagining what it would look like up in surveillance if a player tucked his cards, the dealer physically peeked under his upcard, then the player picked up his cards again and signaled for a hit, and hitting turned out to be the correct play!

Extra weird.

As it turned out, the dealer had a pat 17, so I won one hand and lost one, that hard 16 I wouldn't hit. We played until the cut card came out. Radar put out another toke bet for the dealer, and the dealer said, "Thanks." On the first hand after the shuffle, Radar was again dealt a blackjack. After that hand, we left. This game was way too dangerous.

A dealer this blatant about trying to help players is rare. He didn't even have the talent to peek his hole card surreptitiously. And he was advising me to replay a hand I had already tucked! How did this guy get onto a $100 minimum table in the high-limit room of a Strip casino?

I will not play against any dealer who exhibits skill, even if he is attempting to help me. Let's say this dealer knew his hole card, without blatantly peeking under his 10, and before I had tucked my cards, he said, "You should hit that hand."

Although this would look clean for the cameras, if I believed the dealer was giving me advice because he knew his hole card or the top card, I would still leave the table after that round. Players who make their living by cheating casinos call this playing with the help. No matter how tempting it might be, don't do it. Professional blackjack is a high-risk occupation as is. But you should be risking only money, not a felony conviction and prison sentence.

What If You Suspect You've Been Cheated?

You have a number of options if you suspect you've been cheated in a casino. You can complain to the pit boss, and if you don't get satisfaction, you can go over his head. If you still don't get satisfaction, you can go to whatever state entity serves as gaming control for that jurisdiction. But unless you have collected irrefutable evidence (highly unlikely), you are probably wasting your time trying to get justice. If you lost money, so be it. There is probably nothing you can do about it.

I will tell you honestly that no professional player I know would bother to report cheating. That's not only because it's so hard to prove. If you report the matter to Gaming Control, they will require you to provide your name and identification. You cannot anonymously report cheating to a gaming board. If you are a professional player, this is obviously a bad move. Your name will go to the casino where the incident occurred, and you will be labeled, at best, a troublemaker. If you lost money, the casino will claim you're just a poor loser trying to get your money back. The surveillance videos will show nothing. The boss will stick up for the dealer. Your name may get spread around to other casinos as a shot-taker.

Even if your complaint seems valid, you will be labeled intelligent. The videos of your play may be studied to see if you may be a card counter or other advantage player of some sort. This is the last thing you want anyone in the casino industry to think about you. Casinos do not want smart people at their blackjack tables.

If you get cheated in a department store, or ripped off by an auto mechanic, by all means, complain. Do whatever it takes to get your money back, and if you're in the right, you may have a good shot at getting your money back. But a casino is a different kind of business. The customers are not trusted. The gaming control boards are not set up to protect the customers, but to protect the state's tax income.

Your accusation is threatening not only a dealer, but the reputation and license of a casino and the state's tax revenues. Believe me, unless you have the whole play on video, the gaffed equipment, and a signed confession from one or more of the parties involved, you probably don't want this kind of trouble. There's one absolute rule you must follow whenever you suspect cheating. Get out of the game!

THE EYE IN THE SKY

> The best technology is no match for the devious human mind and I don't think the casinos will ever understand this.
> — *Cellini, The Card Counter's Guide to Casino Surveillance*

There are probably more professional blackjack players today than at any time in history. Making money in a casino has never been so easy. There are many reasons for this. One, the incredible expansion of the industry over such a short period of time has created thousands of jobs in pit supervision and surveillance, making game protection a wide-open field for the inexperienced job seeker willing to accept the low pay in hopes of advancing. Game protection has not always been an entry-level job. When the mob ran the casinos, they knew they needed "talent" to protect their games, and they paid for it. Surveillance became a low-end, dead-end job when the corporate accountants, who were more used to running hotels than casinos, classified it as a non-revenue-generating department, like maintenance and house-keeping.

Second, because there are few people working in surveillance who really understand game protection, the job of game protection has become increasingly technology-based. It is much easier to fool a machine than a human being. This is because machines do as they are told, look for what they are told to look for, and act as they are programmed to act.

Many casinos now depend on "facial recognition" software to help them find unwanted players whose mug shots are in computer photo files. The software doesn't work very well. Every surveillance operator I've ever talked with about this software tells me that it is all but useless. It attempts to identify persons against photos by measuring the distances between the eyes and the nose. It will pull up hundreds of possible matches that meet the criteria. Men, women, old people, young people, giants, midgets, black people, white people, Chinese—all come up as possible matches. Sometimes the operators run the software just to laugh at the results.

Al Francesco, a legendary blackjack pro and Blackjack Hall of Famer, told me he walked into a Nevada casino about ten years ago, and within minutes was approached by the pit boss and told he had been barred there in the past and was not allowed to play blackjack. Al told me that he had indeed been barred there, but more then twenty years earlier, at which time he was skinny and had a full head of dark hair, but that he had never been in that casino since. This boss who barred him still recognized him.

Those days are over.

The old time bosses learned first-hand what card-counting plays looked like, as well as big player teams and hole card plays; they could smell trouble at their tables. Today, there are computers analyzing the blackjack players' strategies. You don't have to fool a pit boss or an old con. You just have to play in such a way that the computer doesn't recognize what you're doing. And if you come up with any slightly new twist, the computer can't see it.

THE IMPORTANT THINGS TO KNOW ABOUT SURVEILLANCE

The surveillance department is always understaffed. In most of the big casinos, there will be anywhere from one to three surveillance monitors watching the video screens. They have minimal training in game protection. The job attracts voyeurs who enjoy watching people from hidden cameras in a dark room, zooming in on sexy women. They get bored and play games to see who can find the ugliest person in the casino, the girl with the skimpiest outfit, stuff like that.

They basically wait for phone calls from the pit, requesting that they pay attention to some specific player who may be a card counter, or just a big bettor who is unknown to the pit personnel. They will watch this person's play and attempt to figure it out. They have minimal card-counting skills, but most can keep a simple count and watch to see if the player's bets are moving up and down with the count. After making a determination on the player, they call the pit with their decision.

If they are unsure, or if the player is winning a lot, they may have to take the video of the play and input all of the player's bets and play decisions over a period of thirty to forty minutes of play into a computer program designed to identify card counters. This is very tedious work and is generally assigned to the lowest level surveillance employee. The poor quality of the videos often make the work difficult. The focus is not good, nor is the camera angle ideal. It is not always easy to read the card values. It is difficult to ascertain how tall a player's stack of chips is from overhead. Much of the data that goes into the computer is guesswork. The newer casinos have newer camera systems that work better.

Surveillance is often called to watch a player simply because he is a "refusal."

Every professional player has to decide how to handle the identification/refusal issue. Many pros never give a name. This way there is never any documentation on them connected to a name. Some pros use false identification, feeling that it looks more natural for a big bettor to get a player's card, plus there is the added value of the comps.

> **Definition:**
>
> A refusal is a player who failed to provide identification to the pit. In some cases, the floor person may simply ask a player if he has a player's card, or would like to be rated. He is basically asking the player if he would like to have his action credited toward complimentaries. If a player says no, he is a refusal and is under suspicion.

It's true that being a refusal is suspicious in itself, and having a player's card immediately sets the game protection personnel at ease. If you give them your ID, it appears that you don't mind if they collect data on your play, which they will do. But there are other considerations.

Should You Be a Refusal? The Pros and the Cons:

Pros:

1. They can never look up your prior play history in their computer files. They can't insert "white male, about 40," and get a play history.

2. They can't send your name out to other casinos for their reports on you, and the other casinos won't have any reports on you anyway.

Cons:

1. It looks suspicious to be refusing to give your name and ID when you could be earning comps.
2. Those comps have a real dollar value.

Should You Get a Player's Card?
The Pros and the Cons:

Pros:

1. The pit personnel will not immediately be suspicious of you.
2. You will earn comps, and these could have substantial value if you play big.

Cons:

1. They will be able to look up your play history and send information about you to other casinos.
2. You may have to change IDs often, as you burn out your name(s).

In fact, there are a few pros who have played successfully for many years under their own names. They generally accomplish this by using various methods of appearing to have lost money in a casino, and getting these losses documented, in order to keep their play histories looking good wherever they play. It comes down to fooling the computer system by controlling the information that gets entered into it. Other pros get into using false identification and getting new IDs as necessary.

The refusals never have to hassle with false ID. They reason that even a false ID is an ID, and the name on that ID will get entered into the casino's records. Casinos may never get a "real" name on a player using false ID, but they will acquire a record on his aliases, and often his aliases will be connected.

If you are not intending to play professionally, but you are a card counter, then you should probably play primarily as a refusal, unless the comps are very valuable to you. In this case, you take your chances on burning out your real name, then decide whether you want to get into the whole fake ID game.

It is illegal to possess a fake ID that appears to be issued by a government agency, such as a passport or driver's license. Other types of IDs may be used providing they are not used for illegal activities. For instance, if you obtain a credit card in a fake name to check into a hotel, and you pay your hotel bill when the bank sends the credit card charge to you, no crime is committed. If you refuse to pay the hotel bill, claiming not to know who the person is with that name, that is fraud, and you will be prosecuted.

Four Tips to Keep the Eye From Identifying You As a Pro

1. Do not play for long periods of time at the same table. If they're going to run a computer analysis of your play, don't give them an easy time of it.
2. Never meet with another card counter in a casino, even in a restaurant or coffee shop. Many pros have been busted as a result of associating with other players.
3. Don't call other counters or teammates room to room in the casino hotel, if these are supposed to be players unknown to you. Use your cell phone.
4. Spread your play around to many different casinos, and to different shifts within the same casino.

The bigger the money you play for, the more you have to be concerned with surveillance and game protection threats. If all your bets are $50 or less, you have few worries. Even if you get kicked out of a casino for being a card counter, you're not likely to have your name and photo being spread around to other casinos. The game protection squad in any casino looks at four things:

1. How you are playing right now, on this trip
2. Your prior history as a player, if you have one
3. Any known suspicious associates you may have
4. Any reports on you obtained from other casinos or surveillance services

If you can keep all of these factors looking good to them, you're a welcome customer. If any one of these factors looks bad to them, you will have problems.

This is where the real fun of blackjack comes in, a type of fun you cannot have in any other casino game. The blackjack pit is the casino's war zone. Here, you may legally act out all of your James Bond and Ninja-warrior fantasies, and with a big money payoff if you're good at it.

Though it's just a game, you can't take it lightly, because casinos can get dead serious about it if you're not careful. If you really hit them for a big score, and they discover you're a card counter, depending on the level of advancement of their security department—which generally runs from Neanderthal to Cro-Magnon—you could be evicted politely or rudely, threatened with physical harm, taken against your will into a back room, handcuffed, pushed around, have your chips confiscated, your photo taken, your body searched...

Most pros avoid filing lawsuits when their civil rights are violated because they don't especially want the publicity. But that's another issue, and beyond the scope of this book.

> **Professional Gambler's Rule #11:**
>
> You're not just playing against the percentages, you're playing against people.

Remember: Casinos don't just dislike smart people. They hate smart people.

It's the job of surveillance to find the smart players and get rid of them. If you're a card counter, that's you. You are the enemy.

And that's what makes blackjack exciting.

TEAM PLAY

There are phenomenally profitable options available for a group of two or more players with skill at blackjack.

— *Ken Uston, Million Dollar Blackjack*

I know of blackjack teams that have been composed of as few as two players and as many as one hundred-fifty. A big team might have players playing simultaneously in casinos in different cities, different states, and even different countries. There are three main functions of a blackjack team: 1) The team approach allows players to combine their bankrolls and bet bigger, increasing everyone's potential win in dollars; 2) The team approach smoothes out bankroll fluctuations; and 3) The team approach allows players to camouflage their playing skills by having different players take different roles in applying the playing and betting strategies.

Let's look at how each of these functions works.

WHY FORM A BLACKJACK TEAM?

1. The team approach allows players to combine their bankrolls and bet bigger. If I have two friends and each of us has $5,000, if we agree to combine our funds into one $15,000 bankroll, then we can each play on this larger bank, bet bigger, and play with a real dollar expectation that's three times as big as if we were each playing on our separate $5,000 bankrolls. That's three times as much win

potential for each of us, with no more investment of time or money.

2. A team approach levels out the bankroll fluctuations.
Because there are three of us playing on the same bankroll, in addition to having a much higher expectation in dollars won, we will also be getting three times the number of hands played in the same amount of time. This gets us into the long run much faster and smoothes out the fluctuations in capital. One player's losses on a session will often be compensated for by wins of another player.

3. The team approach allows players to camouflage their playing skills.
We can also use our combined skills to hide our strategy from the casinos. One of us can count cards and bet small, signaling another player who appears to be paying little attention to the game to bet big or enter the table at opportune times.

These are a few of the arguments in favor of forming a blackjack team. There are also a number of arguments against the team approach. Consider these.

WHY NOT FORM A BLACKJACK TEAM?

1. Players of lesser skill may draw down the win rate of a talented player. You may have practiced counting until you're sure of your skill, but do you really know how well your buddies play? Have they devoted the same time and effort to learning to count that you have? Do they even have a legitimate win expectation? If you team up with other players, you might just be winning money for them, while they're getting a free ride on your skills.

2. A dishonest player could steal money from the team bank. How well do you trust your friends with your money? Are these friends that you would go into business with, and with whom you would have a joint checking account where you all have free access to the funds? That's what a blackjack

team is. A larcenous player on a team can steal without anyone ever being sure of any wrongdoing. If he says he lost $3,000 in the casino last night, how can you be sure he didn't?

3. It can be stressful thinking that other players may be losing your money. Even if you trust your friends' skill and honesty, some people are just not comfortable with having their money at risk when they are not there watching over it. What if you are having winning trips, but your buddies are having losing trips, one after another? Can you be cool about this? If you have won a total of $7,000 on your last three trips, and your teammates have lost a total of $9,000 on their last three trips, will this depress you? Because that is what team play is all about—smoothing out those fluctuations. Unfortunately, in this case, your wins smoothed out their negative fluctuations while their losses smoothed out your positive fluctuation. Many players just like to feel responsible for their own money and their own results.

GUIDELINES FOR FORMING A TEAM

If the team idea appeals to you, then here are some general guidelines to get you started:

1. Start small. Work with two to five players at most for your initial effort. Some of the best teams are husband/wife or boyfriend/girlfriend teams.

2. Only team up with players you trust completely with your money. If this limits you to your brother and your mother, then that's your team.

3. Put all team rules in writing. You must produce a handbook for all team members that explains exactly who is investing what, the terms of withdrawing any investment, and how wins and losses will be divvied up, and when.

4. All players must test each other's skills, and be able to pass the team's tests before being allowed to play. There should also be testing before each playing trip to make sure no player's skills have gotten rusty.

5. Each time a team issue arises, there should be an agreement on how to handle it in writing. Such issues would include: how much players are allowed to bet, how travel expenses are handled, which games can be played, toking policies, how and when wins and losses on playing sessions are reported, who will keep the books for the team and exactly what will be entered, etc.

Many teams break up over arguments about misunderstandings. Someone didn't report a loss, or bet too much, or kept missing signals, or paid for a meal with team funds. As you might expect, most team breakups occur when the team has suffered losses. When a team is winning, everyone forgives infractions and may become lax about team rules and agreements. As soon as a big loss occurs, all hell breaks out.

So-and-so didn't do this. We said we were going to do that. No, I told you that we should do this other thing. Hey, if it's all down in writing, there's no arguing. Everyone knows what they're supposed to do, and if any member of the team has committed infractions, then you've got to decide what to do about it. The big teams often have big handbooks.

Some small teams manage to operate successfully without written handbooks, but I would advise against this. These teams are usually composed of professional gamblers who have known each other for years and who live by the code that a gambler's word is his bond. None of them ever do violate any of their verbal agreements, and they don't forget what those agreements are. A husband/wife team could probably use this approach, and possibly a team composed of brothers or very old friends. But be careful! It's better to iron out difficulties in writing before arguments occur, than wish you had done so later.

HOLE CARDS, DEVICES, SHUFFLE TRACKING, AND NEVADA-STYLE "JUSTICE"

To the public at large, one of the most incomprehensible things about professional blackjack strategies is hole-card play. Hole-card play is not a single strategy, but a whole range of strategies. The one feature that can be found in all of these strategies is that the player either knows the dealer's hole card, or has valuable information about that hole card, whether it's a paint or not. To most casual blackjack players, this seems absolutely incredible and impossible, unless there is some sort of cheating going on. But it's not impossible, and in fact, most hole-card strategies are perfectly legal.

In the Spring 2003 *Blackjack Forum*, Richard W. Munchkin, author of *Gambling Wizards*, interviewed "RC," one of the most successful hole-carders of modern times. In introducing us to RC, Munchkin writes, "For every one hour spent on the table playing, the hole-card player may spend ten hours scouting… Most players, even if shown a dealer who is flashing, would not be able to spot the hole card anyway. Hole-carders spend hundreds of hours training their eyes to see something that flashes by in a fraction of a second, often cast in shadow."

James Grosjean's *Beyond Counting* (now out of print, though a second edition has been announced) is widely regarded as the hole-carder's bible. A meticulous mathematician, Grosjean was the first person to accurately figure out the hole-carder's edge at blackjack with perfect reads and perfect play (just over 13 percent), and in addition to his work on blackjack, he provided some of the first detailed hole-card analyses of games like Three-Card Poker, Let It Ride, and Caribbean Stud Poker.

Hole-card players speak their own language and have their own heroes. Most consider card counting too weak to be worth the trouble. Many quickly attain notoriety in the casinos and a degree of fame among other pros that appreciate the rare skills they have developed. But let's look at some of the forerunners of today's players, describe some of the most common hole-card strategies, and get a historical overview of this type of legal strategy.

In 1980, Stanford Wong published a book, *Winning Without Counting* (now out of print), with an initial price tag of $200. To pros, the book was well worth it. Wong discussed many methods of hole-card play for the first time and provided the only detailed description and analysis of "warp" play ever in print.

What is warp play? In the old days, dealers used to manually peek under their tens and aces to see if they had a blackjack before satisfying the players' hands. This constant bending up of the corners on the tens and aces tended to put a warp into these cards if the casino did not change its decks frequently. An observant player could see the arc in a dealer's hole card created by hours of bending the corners of the tens and aces. Warp play was simply using this information to make strategy decisions.

Then, Ken Uston's *Million Dollar Blackjack* was published by SRS Publishing in 1981. In addition to everything Uston wrote about card counting and team play, Uston went into more detail about two of the hole-card techniques Wong had revealed the year before in *Winning Without Counting*: "spooking" and "front-loading." Uston, in fact, had become quite adept as a hole-card player after his first book, *The Big Player*, was published in 1977.

What is front-loading? A front loader is simply a sloppy dealer who flashes his hole card as he is placing it beneath his upcard. It's actually a pretty descriptive term, since one common way that such a dealer inadvertently flashes the hole card is by tipping the face of the card up toward the "front" of the table as he is "loading" it. A player who sits in a seat that provides him a view of this card is said to be "front-loading."

Spooking is something else again. It used to be standard procedure for dealers to manually peek under any 10 or ace to see if they had a blackjack, in which case they would immediately turn up the card and collect all bets without playing the hands. Some dealers, in peeking, angled the card in such a way that a person standing behind them, or sitting at another table on the other side of the same pit, could glimpse the card also. It wasn't long before players started working in teams to take advantage of such dealers. The guy behind the dealer was called the spook. He would signal his buddies playing at the table with whatever information he could get on the hole card. Dealers don't peek this way anymore, and this is one of the reasons why.

THE PEEK FREAKS WIN
IN A NEVADA COURT

In 1984, a Las Vegas district court found that two players—Steve Einbinder and Tony Dalben—who were taking advantage of a downtown blackjack dealer who was inadvertently flashing his hole card, broke no state laws in exploiting this information to play their hands. The court ruled that it was the dealer's job to hide his hole card, not the players' job to refrain from looking at it. No Nevada court has since ruled otherwise. Although this was a lower court decision and is not binding on any other court in the state, the Einbinder/Dalben decision is widely regarded as the law in Nevada, as the logic is so clear and irrefutable. With the Einbinder/Dalben decision, for the first time, hole-card players knew that their strategies were legal to use in the casinos.

A word about the precise strategy Einbinder and Dalben were using…

Pros call it first-basing, because the player seated at first base is the one who glimpses the dealer's hole card. The dealer, in this case, is not a front-loader, because the first-base player glimpses the hole card only when the dealer is peeking under his tens and aces, not while the dealer is loading the hole card. Technically, the first-base player is spooking the dealer, not from behind, but from the side seat at the table while playing himself.

BUT "VIDEO FRONT LOADING" GETS THE SHAFT

On April Fools Day, 1984, two players in Las Vegas were arrested at the Marina Casino for using a concealed video camera to peek at the dealer's hole card. This device was yet another of Keith Taft's inventions. One player, Keith's brother Ted, wore the miniature camera in his belt buckle, while the other player, Rodney Weatherford, a Lockheed Engineer, sat in the casino parking lot in the cab of a dump truck that had been fitted with a satellite receiving dish. Rodney's job was to watch the video images picked up by the table-top-level camera, in order to electronically signal Ted at the table with the value of the dealer's hole card.

I was sworn in as an expert witness in their defense and attended the whole trial, but did not get to testify. Here's what happened:

For a few days, the prosecution paraded before the judge and jury all of the electronics, the video tapes, and the communication devices. They even took us all down to the courthouse garage to examine the old truck with the satellite receiving dish in it. And this was a 1984 satellite dish, nothing like your home model Direct-TV dish today. It was huge! It looked like a battleship radar scanner!

Throughout all of this, I'm thinking, Wow, this is really cool! I liked Keith. He was undeniably brilliant, and, in fact, was one of my heroes. He was the classic mad scientist, inventing in his basement laboratory high-tech devices the likes of which James Bond would be proud to own. He just wanted to take as much money out of the casinos as he possibly could, and I fully supported his right to do this by any legal means. Remember, there were no anti-device laws at that time, and the Einbinder/Dalben decision that legitimized front-loading as a legal strategy in Nevada had already been rendered. Also, I was openly advertising and selling Keith's concealable "David" blackjack computers in my magazine, *Blackjack Forum*, and I had written the operating manual for "David."

After the prosecution finished presenting the state's case—and they had all kinds of gambling experts and gaming agents take the stand to describe the way the whole thing worked—I met with the defense attorneys to discuss my testimony. To my surprise, the attorneys had decided not to put either of the defendants on the stand, nor did they want to put me on the stand. They had decided to present no witnesses, but to simply present their closing arguments. The attorneys, John Curtas and Stephen Minagil, were the same attorneys who had just successfully represented Einbinder and Dalben.

John Curtas, Ted's attorney, explained his legal strategy to me. First of all, he did not see any reason to refute the evidence as presented. In fact, the defendants had done exactly what the prosecution said they had done. So, there was no argument about any of the prosecution's case. The only argument to be made was that the defendants never committed the crime of cheating according to the Nevada cheating statutes. Why should Curtas and Minagil argue with the gaming agents' descriptions of the equipment and its usage? The defendants had the law on their side. Curtas had prepared a closing argument in which he intended to acknowledge that the defendants had done exactly what the prosecution had said they had done. Then, he intended to read to the jury all of the Nevada cheating statutes, one at a time, and simply point out that what the defendants in this case had done did not violate a single statute on the books.

He read the statutes to me, and he was right. Technically, no crime had been committed.

However, before the closing arguments, the attorneys had to meet with the judge in his chambers. When Curtas came back from the judge's chambers, he was steaming mad. The district court judge, the Honorable Donald Mosley, had asked both sides to give him a briefing on their proposed closing arguments. When Curtas described his closing argument to the judge, the judge told him that he would not allow it. Curtas pled with the judge; he simply wanted to read the law to the jury. The jury, he argued, were not legal experts, and they did not know the wording of the Nevada laws against cheating. According to Curtas, the judge said, "I used to be a blackjack dealer, and I know what cheating is. Your client was cheating."

So now, as the defense had forgone their opportunity to present any witnesses, the case was closed. The only defense Curtas was allowed to present in his closing argument was to inform the jury that the Nevada law books would be available to them in the jury room, and that they had the right to read the law for themselves.

The players, needless to say, were convicted of felony cheating.

And the state of Nevada, needless to say, realized that it needed a law that would make the use of such devices illegal in casinos, and it needed this law fast. These players had been railroaded to prison without a fair trial, and the state knew it. There was always a possibility that some jury in a similar case in the future would actually read the law and realize that a defendant accused of using a device to aid him in making decisions at a gaming table violated none of the cheating statutes.

The Anti-Device Law is Tried and Found... Vague

In 1985, the state of Nevada passed its first "anti-device" law, making computer play, hidden video camera play, etc., illegal for blackjack players. This law was immediately criticized by attorneys as being unconstitutional due to its "vagueness."

When a blackjack player by the name of Philip Anderson was busted for using a concealed computer in a Las Vegas casino shortly after the anti-device law went into effect, the law was challenged in court. And it was challenged on the basis of its being unconstitutional precisely because it was too vague. To no one's surprise, the player won his case. The judge acknowledged that the law was simply too vague to be legitimate.

What do we mean by "vague?" The law simply states that no player may use a "device" as an aid in making betting decisions in a casino. But it doesn't define what it means by "device." Therefore, according to this Nevada law, a rabbit's foot could be construed as such a device, and having one on your person at the gaming tables could be construed as felony cheating. *The Daily Racing Form* could be illegal to read in the casino's race book, because it's a device used in making betting decisions. Roulette and baccarat players could be forbidden to write down past results, as such players have traditionally done, as the pens and paper could be construed as "devices" that were being used to aid in their decision-making. As the law was worded, no distinction was made between computer devices, electronic devices, intelligent devices, hidden devices, or any other types of devices. All "devices" used in the casino for aiding a player in betting decisions were simply declared cheating devices. These were the types of arguments made by Philip Anderson's attorney, and the judge agreed and threw out the case.

The state appealed the verdict to the Nevada Supreme Court. And guess what? The Nevada Supreme Court refused to make a ruling on the anti-device law's constitutionality. Why? Let's see... If the supreme court ruled that the law was unconstitutionally vague, then the law would have to be removed from the books. Players would again be allowed to use concealed computers, communication devices, high-tech electronic devices, etc. Keith Taft would be back in business. But if the court ruled that the law was not unconstitutionally vague, then the judges would have to explain the logic of their decision, and such a decision defied all logic.

So, the court stated that it simply would not rule on the constitutionality issue, and the law still stands. Many attorneys to this day believe that a serious court challenge could quash the Nevada law as written (and many other states have copied Nevada's anti-device law verbatim into their statutes). But few players have much desire to take a stand in court and face a possible prison sentence.

Let's just say the Nevada justice system is somewhat biased toward the casinos' side of the issues. A cynic might believe that this is because judges are elected in Nevada, and the casinos provide the majority of the funds for the judges' election campaigns. A judge who rules against the casinos in any big case might find his campaign fund a bit thin when the next election rolls around.

MORE NEVADA JUSTICE

In 1986, I got a late night phone call from a Las Vegas card counter and tournament pro I knew named Ed. He was upset. Two of his friends—Allan Brown and Barry Finn, also players I was acquainted with—had been beaten up and hospitalized by security guards at Binion's Horseshoe.

The Horseshoe surveillance agents had determined that the two players were using the same hole-card technique for which Einbinder and Dalben had been acquitted of cheating charges in a Nevada court the previous year. First-basing was not well known at the time Einbinder and Dalben were arrested. Within a year, however, it was very well known, not because their case was widely publicized, but because Lyle Stuart published *Ken Uston on Blackjack* in 1986. Uston provided an extensive discussion of first-basing in this book, and many pros began using it. So, the Horseshoe guards apparently decided to take the matter into their own hands.

Ed was calling me to get the name of an attorney who would represent players against casinos, and it was not easy to find such attorneys in Nevada. I suggested various Las Vegas attorneys who were known to take cases for players back then—Andy Blumen, Les Combs, Richard Wright—and both Andy and Les took the case.

As the beating was so severe that both players had been hospitalized— Brown with a ruptured spleen—the players sued. Within a few weeks, however, the Horseshoe offered to settle out of court, and the players accepted the offer. The amount was never disclosed, but, needless to say, it was substantial.

The casino was hoping that this would end the incident, but it was too late. The district attorney had already proceeded with the state's criminal case against the Horseshoe, and the players' settlement did not automatically relieve the Horseshoe guards and managers of the state's criminal charges against them.

But, then, it's never too late in Nevada. As it turned out, the jury found for the defendants, but the judge overturned the jury's verdict. The DA tried to appeal the case, but the court records all mysteriously disappeared (darn!), so that the state had to drop its charges against the Horseshoe. Don't you just hate it when that happens? Only in Nevada…

"TELL" PLAY TESTED IN A RENO COURTROOM

A player and dealer were also arrested in Reno for cheating by collusion at Harold's Club in 1984. Because of the unusual way the player, Yip, played his hands, and because he always won whenever he played against this particular blackjack dealer, Yang, the casino called Gaming Control, and gaming agents viewed videos of the play. They had both the player and dealer arrested for felony cheating by collusion. The state claimed that despite the fact that the videos had no sound track, the videos proved beyond any doubt that the dealer had to be verbally telling the player her hole card whenever she peeked under her 10 or ace. Whenever the dealer peeked, the player made the correct strategy decision, indicating that he knew what she had.

I was hired as an expert witness for the defense. Here's the story.

The defense attorney, Ron Bath, told me he absolutely believed his client, Yang, was innocent. Although gaming officials felt that the player and dealer were involved in some sort of Asian conspiracy to cheat Harold's Club, the fact was that not only did they not know each other, but they did not even speak the same language. One was Korean, the other Chinese. I watched the surveillance videos in Ron Bath's office. And as it turned out, the player was simply reading dealer tells, another hole-card method pros had been using for years that was not widely known.

Ironically, Harold Smith, Sr., founder of Harold's Club in 1935, had mentioned tell play at blackjack in his 1961 autobiography, *I Want to Quit Winners*, and said that he always had to be on the lookout for dealers who were exhibiting subconscious mannerisms, as they were exploitable by smart professional players. This, in fact, is the oldest mention of tell play at blackjack in print. Unfortunately for Harold's Club, the founder of their casino who (literally) wrote the book on their game protection concerns was long dead and gone. And unfortunately (for the casino), some of Harold Smith's wisdom had died with him.

> The term tell comes from poker. A tell is simply some unconscious physical mannerism that indicates to a perceptive observer whether you are feeling strong or weak. If a poker player has a tell, another poker player can often read him, and know whether or not he should call, raise, or fold. Ian Andersen briefly discussed tell play at blackjack in his 1976 book, *Turning the Tables on Las Vegas*, but provided little information on the methods. Blackjack dealers with tells, however, are often just as readable as poker players. Because their mannerisms are subconsciously driven, they are unaware that they are displaying any readable information. Note that tell play at blackjack only worked in the old days when dealers still manually peeked under their tens.

I testified as an expert witness in the State of Nevada v. Yip and Yang, and was astonished to learn that the casino and gaming personnel who testified were totally oblivious to the possibility of tell play! As an expert witness, it was not difficult for me to explain the techniques of tell play to the jury, since the prosecution had entered some twenty-two hours of video tape into evidence! The tapes told the story. After checking under her tens, the dealer's body language almost always indicated whether she was pat or stiff, and these tells were readable whether the player who had beaten her was playing at her table or not. She was a classic example of the perfectly readable dealer.

In the courtroom, within twenty minutes of my explanation of what to look for, the entire jury started calling out the dealer's hole card each time she peeked. They could all read her like a book! It was amusing to say the least. Even the judge could read the dealer. I knew, right then and there, that these two were going to be found not guilty (and indeed they were). The case proved to be an embarrassment for the industry experts, because all of them had insisted that the dealer must have been verbally telling the player what she had under her tens and aces, since they had spent hours watching the videos and could see no signals!

I published Steve Forte's *Read the Dealer* that same year, the first book to deal exclusively with playing dealer tells. Steve, in fact, had taught me everything I knew about tell play. Within two years, however, most casinos in Nevada were using auto-peek devices for dealers to check their hole cards. The auto-peekers work in such a way that the dealers cannot see the value of the hole card under their 10 unless it is an ace. The hole-card craze had gotten to be too much for the casinos. The tell players, the spooks, the first-basers. Whoever invented that auto-peek device must have made a bundle. So much for dealer peeking!

Hole-card play, however, is still a strategy used by professional players. Many of these older techniques are obsolete, but many other techniques work just as well. Far be it from me to publish any secrets here, as the casinos read the same books that the players read. The pros are the players who stay a few steps ahead of the casinos and the books. Suffice it to say that there are still front-loaders out there, and there are various mathematical methods based on shuffle-tracking techniques that can also reveal a dealer's hole card.

Just don't get caught using a "device" in a Nevada casino, unless you've got the money and desire to fight constitutional challenges to a vague law.

SHUFFLE TRACKING

Finally, since we're covering advanced techniques here, let's say a few words about shuffle tracking. This is an advanced card-counting strategy. Years ago, when shuffles were fast and simple, I suspect numerous card counters independently discovered the most accessible form of shuffle tracking for the solo player—slug location.

You're sitting in a shoe game, watching the count climb ever upwards, and just when it reaches what must be an all-time high, the shuffle card emerges. As your spirits sink, you stare at the undealt portion of the deck—the cutoffs—that must contain nearly every paint and faint in the shoe. For some inexplicable reason, you continue to stare at that glorious slug of high cards, even as the dealer slaps it on top of the discards to begin his shuffle routine.

To your joy and amazement, when the dealer finishes shuffling and hands you the cut card, you're still staring at that slug! True, it's somewhat dispersed, but most of it's right there in the bottom third of the six-deck stack of cards in front of you. So you cut this segment to the top of the pack and the cards soon verify exactly what your eyes had seen. For the next two decks, tens and aces just pour out of that shoe. From the very first round of play, the count enters the nether regions of negativity, but you just keep betting big, knowing there's more to come.

For blackjack players, this is how shuffle tracking was born. It was a purely visual thing. It had nothing to do with voodoo, guesswork, or advanced mathematics. It was simply a logical extension of card counting. Shuffle tracking, however, has numerous advantages over traditional card counting:

1. You don't seem to be betting with the count, and in fact, you'll often be able to bet big off the top.

2. You'll often appear to be misplaying your hands. If you know you're in a slug of high cards or low cards, you'll play accordingly. You'll be making strategy deviations in shoe games that a counter would normally only make in one-deckers. When you stand on your hard 15 versus a dealer 10, right off the top of the shoe, when the table is painted in tens, or better yet, take insurance on your 20 at this time, the counter catchers will label you a typical idiot.

3. This seemingly unintelligent betting and playing pattern also allows you to utilize a larger betting spread without raising suspicions.

4. Unlike traditional card counting, shuffle tracking is immediately obvious to you when you are doing it correctly. The results are right before your eyes. With normal card counting, if the count goes up, you raise your bet. But on the next round, and the one after that, and the one after that, the big cards don't necessarily come out. They might actually be located somewhere later in the deck—maybe behind the cut card. With shuffle tracking, when you put your big bet on the table, the big cards come out. They always come out. They have to come out because you know where they are.

Card counters have been tracking shuffles ever since the casinos introduced the multiple-deck shoe games to foil counters. Shuffles used to be very simple and easy to track. When computers were legal, prior to the anti-device laws that were passed in the mid-'80s, many of the big teams used tracking computers. Keith Taft devised numerous models, his most successful design using a program he called "Thor." Mickey Lichtman, another pro player of that era, also developed a tracking computer. And "Rats Cohen," a former employee of Taft's, bootlegged Taft's Thor computer and was selling it as "No-Rand."

Tracking computers were especially popular in Atlantic City because the games there were ideal. To hand-shuffle eight decks, very fast and simple shuffle procedures were required. But when the Atlantic City casinos discovered that tracking computers were in use, they began making their shuffles more complex. These godawful shuffles soon spread to Las Vegas. When computer play was finally outlawed in Nevada and New Jersey, the complex shuffles remained.

So these days, just like card counting, hole carding, and other advantage play techniques, shuffle tracking is more difficult than it used to be. Very little was in print about shuffle tracking until 1994 when I published a series of three articles on the subject in *Blackjack Forum*. The methods in that series were primarily geared toward tracking the simpler shuffles, many of which still existed and quite a few still do. As the shuffles continued to grow more complex, however, the methods described in that series weakened.

About five years ago, I met a tracker named "Radar O'Reilly," who was successfully tracking some of the most complex shuffles in Las Vegas, Atlantic City, and elsewhere—shuffles that every other professional tracker I knew considered unbeatable. Radar had realized that smaller slugs were where the value was, and had worked out methods for tracking much smaller slugs than were possible with the methods I knew. But Radar had no idea what the player's advantage was with these techniques, only that they worked.

I worked out the math and was astonished to discover that the small slugs of six to thirteen cards that Radar was tracking had a huge value. In 2003, I added some of Radar's techniques to the shuffle tracking material I'd published earlier, along with the first mathematical analyses of casino shuffles based on the sizes of the trackable slugs, and published the material as a book titled *The Blackjack Shuffle Tracker's Cookbook*.

Like hole carding, shuffle tracking is an advanced technique that is not easily accessible to casual players. If you are interested in attempting to use any of these advanced methods, I'd suggest that you first study the literature available on them. For warp play, front-loading, and spooking, see Stanford Wong's *Basic Blackjack*. Ken Uston goes into more detail on front-loading and spooking in *Million Dollar Blackjack*, and he describes first-basing in *Ken Uston on Blackjack*. If you can find a copy of James Grosjean's *Beyond Counting* (it goes for an arm and a leg on eBay), you'll find more comprehensive and accurate mathematical analyses of various types of hole-card techniques than anywhere else. Also, you can read Richard Munchkin's interview with the great hole-carder "RC" at: www.blackjackforumonline.com. Steve Forte's *Read the Dealer* is the only in-depth treatment of tell play in print, though it's hard to find dealers who peek under their tens anymore. For shuffle tracking information, you'll find some basic training in my own *Blackbelt in Blackjack*, and a comprehensive treatment in my *Blackjack Shuffle Tracker's Cookbook*.

SECTION FOUR:

ODDS, ENDS, AND OTHER WEIRD STUFF

THE BLACKJACK HALL OF FAME

> After taking stock of my life, I find my most valuable acquisition is the wisdom I've learned through gambling.
>
> — *N. M. "Junior" Moore, The Crossroader*

In January of 2003, I had the honor of being inducted into the Blackjack Hall of Fame. If you've never heard of the Blackjack Hall of Fame, that's probably because it didn't exist prior to 2003. The brainchild of Max Rubin—author of *Comp City*, professional player, and host of the annual Blackjack Ball in Las Vegas—the Blackjack Hall of Fame may just be the most bizarre casino promotion ever conceived.

I have remarked in various publications in years past that it would be appropriate for the city of Las Vegas to erect a statue to Ed Thorp for bringing the casinos more business than all of the industry's marketing moguls combined. Unfortunately, the Las Vegas Convention and Visitors Bureau never took me seriously. Perhaps they should have. Now Vegas has been one-upped by an Indian reservation casino a few hundred miles west.

How did this come about?

Max Rubin, a consultant for the

Barona Casino in Lakeside, California, somehow convinced the casino bigwigs that a hall of fame for the world's best blackjack players and most respected experts on beating the game would be good for business. Some say Max could sell sand in Egypt. I'm trying to imagine Max pitching this idea to Barona's execs…

"Here's the plan, gentlemen. Barona builds a monument to honor all of the blackjack players that they won't allow on their tables. You have bronze plaques made with their faces, and you put them all in a museum where gamblers can come and admire them."

"Wait a minute, Max," says Joe Barona. "Are you talking about card counters?"

"Not just any card counters," says Max. "These are hall of fame card counters. We'll open the voting to the public, and you'll get the cream of the crop. Famous old-timers like Thorp and Uston will be in there, but you'll also get the biggest threats around today, players like Tommy Hyland!"

Says Joe: "What are you smoking, Max? We've got Tommy's mug shot hanging on a wanted poster up in the surveillance room. He's not even allowed in the parking lot!"

"But think of the PR on this, Joe," says Max. "A casino honoring its most fearsome opponents. It's never been done before!"

"Right... Are we paying you by the hour for this consultation, Max?"

"I'm on retainer this week, Joe. But I haven't gotten to the best part yet. Think about this. You give all of the hall of famers lifetime comps at the Barona!"

"Comps to what?"

"Everything. Luxury suites. Room service. The steak house. The golf course. Booze. Whatever they want. For the rest of their lives—as long as they stay off your tables. It's an advantage play for you, Joe! Talk about a win-win situation! You can write off the comps as a game-protection expense."

"Okay, Max, that settles it. Whatever you're smoking, I want some. But you can't toke up any more when you're on the clock. Now take the rest of the day off and come back tomorrow."

Try as I might, as I weave my fantasy of this discussion, I just can't seem to get to the part where the Barona marketing exec says, "Sure, Max! Great idea! How much money do we need to build this museum?"

In any case, in the winter of 2002, a diverse selection of twenty-one blackjack experts, authors, and professional players were nominated. Voting was open to the public for about a month on the Internet, and the final voting was completed at the 2003 Blackjack Ball in January, an event open only to the top professional players.

THE BLACKJACK HALL OF FAME

The seven chosen Blackjack Hall of Famers (in alphabetical order) were:

Al Francesco
Peter Griffin
Tommy Hyland
Arnold Snyder
Edward O. Thorp
Ken Uston
Stanford Wong

You may be familiar with some of these names. Knowledgeable card counters are familiar with all of them. Griffin, Snyder, Thorp, Uston, and Wong are primarily known to the public through their writings. Francesco and Hyland are primarily known to professional players (and casino game protection personnel!) for their relentless and highly successful "team" attacks on the casinos.

The following year, at the 2004 Blackjack Ball, two more inductees were added, again with primary voting done by professional gamblers at the Ball. The two added members included Keith Taft, a brilliant inventor who has spent more than two decades milking the casino blackjack games with his high-tech electronic devices, and (are you ready for this?) Max Rubin! Then at the 2005 Blackjack Ball, Julian Braun and Lawrence Revere were inducted into the hall of fame, bringing the total membership to eleven.

In 2004, the Barona Casino actually created a physical hall of fame, similar to the Binion's Horseshoe's "Wall of Fame" for great poker players. Each inductee has a plaque with his photo and a few words about his contributions and accomplishments. There is also a museum of cheating devices, which is probably more interesting to the public than a bunch of old photos. There are marked cards, computer shoes, hold-out gizmos for card-switching, and all kinds of cool stuff.

To whatever extent the Barona Casino is "sponsoring" the Blackjack Hall of Fame, I must admit that this membership and lifetime comp is definitely the strangest thing I've ever won from a casino. I've been thinking of calling around the casinos of Vegas to see if I can get similar terms. Any interested casino managers who would like to match the Barona's lifetime comp offer, please contact my agent, Max Rubin, to work out the terms.

In any case, let's look at the eleven current Blackjack Hall of Fame members, and explain why they were chosen by professional players for this honor.

JULIAN BRAUN

Julian Braun died in 2000 and his only book, *How to Play Winning Blackjack*, is long out of print. For ten years in the early days of card counting, he did a vast amount of the computer work for some of the top authors. He did the programming for the second edition of E.O. Thorp's *Beat the Dealer*. His programs were used to develop all of Lawrence Revere's systems, as well as the Hi-Opt systems. Of the "pre-Stanford Wong" professional players (the pros playing before the first edition of Wong's *Professional Blackjack* came out in 1975), most were using either Thorp's Ten-Count, Thorp's Hi-Lo, Hi-Opt I, Hi-Opt II, Revere's Point Count, Revere's +/-, or Revere's Advanced Point Count. These were the most popular and widely disseminated systems in use for about ten years, and Julian Braun's programs were used to develop all of them!

AL FRANCESCO

Al is one of the most highly respected blackjack players in the history of the game. This is the guy who literally invented team play at blackjack and taught Ken Uston how to count cards. Ken once said to me, "I owe everything to Al, Arnold. He really might be the greatest blackjack player there ever was, and he's also a real gentleman."

Al is primarily known to the general public through Ken Uston's books as the mastermind who created the big player (BP) team concept. Al started his first blackjack team in the early 1970s, and until Uston's first book, *The Big Player*, was published in 1977, Al's teams were completely invisible to the casinos and extracted millions of dollars from them.

Virtually all of the most successful blackjack teams that came after *The Big Player* was published—the Hyland team, the MIT team, the Czech team, the Greeks—used Al's BP concept to disguise their attacks, and that approach is still being employed profitably by teams today.

Professional players know Al for his highly inventive approaches to beating the casinos, though all of his methods cannot be written about because they are still in use by players. An in-depth interview with Al Francesco appeared in the Summer 2002 issue of *Blackjack Forum* and can be found in the BlackjackForumOnline.com Library.

PETER GRIFFIN

Peter was the math genius who first proposed using the mathematical shortcuts developed by statisticians for estimating answers to highly complex problems in analyzing and comparing blackjack card-counting systems. He was the first to break down the potential gains available from any card-counting method to two prime factors: the betting correlation (BC) and the playing efficiency (PE). These two parameters facilitated highly accurate estimation of any system's potential win rate in any game using any betting spread, without extensive computer simulations. He described how these methods could be used to evaluate the differences between single-level and multi-level counting systems, as well as the value of using multi-parameter methods (keeping more than one count). This book was a milestone for system researchers, developers, and players as the most important analysis of card-counting systems since Thorp's *Beat the Dealer*.

Blackjack researchers have been using Griffin's methods ever since. Any proposed counting system, regardless of its level of simplicity or complexity, can quickly be broken down to its BC and PE, and its comparative value to other systems and methods can be determined.

Over a period spanning twenty years, Griffin published dozens of technical papers in mathematical journals and at academic conferences, all gambling related. Even in his most technical writing, wit and off-the-cuff quips are the hallmarks of his style.

Griffin authored two books, *The Theory of Blackjack: The Complete Card Counter's Guide to the Casino Game of 21* (1978, revised many times since, published by Huntington Press); and *Extra Stuff: Gambling Ramblings* (1991).

Peter Griffin died in 1998 at the age of sixty-one.

TOMMY HYLAND

Tommy started playing blackjack professionally in 1978 while still in college. That was also the year he started his first informal "team." He's never looked back. For more than twenty-five years, he has been running the longest-lasting and most successful blackjack team in the history of the game. He and his teammates have played in casinos all over the U.S., Canada, and the world. He has used big player techniques, concealed computers (when they were legal), and had one of the most successful "ace location" teams ever. He has personally been barred, back-roomed, hand-cuffed, arrested, and even threatened with murder at gun-point by a casino owner he had beaten at the tables. Every year, the Hyland team players take millions of dollars out of the casinos. And even though Tommy has had his name and photo published in the notorious Griffin books more times than any other player in history, he continues to play and beat the games wherever legal blackjack games are offered. He has also fought for players' rights by battling the casinos in the courts.

Despite his fearsome reputation, Tommy is polite, soft-spoken, and always a gentleman. He is as loved by players as he is feared by the casinos. In an interview conducted by Richard Munchkin in 2001, Tommy said, "If someone told me I could make $10 million a year working for a casino, I wouldn't even consider it. It wouldn't take me five minutes to turn it down... I don't like casinos. I don't like how they ruin people's lives. I don't think the employment they provide is a worthwhile thing for those people. They're taking people that could be contributing to society and making them do a job that has no redeeming social value."

You can read the complete interview with Tommy in Munchkin's book, *Gambling Wizards* (Huntington Press, 2002), or in the BlackjackForumOnline.com Library.

LAWRENCE REVERE

Lawrence Revere was both an author and a serious player. He died in 1977. His only book, *Playing Blackjack as a Business*, initially published in 1969, is still in print. If you look at the "true count" methods being employed pre-Revere, you will see why Revere was inducted into the hall of fame. The earlier methods were cumbersome and mentally fatiguing to use. In the second edition of *Beat the Dealer*, in which Thorp first proposed the Hi-Lo Count, he mentioned a simplified method of using the count, though he failed to develop it as a full system. Revere had a leap of brilliance that led him to come to the conclusion that the simplified method of obtaining a "true count" that Thorp had mentioned could be fully developed and employed with the most powerful of point count systems. Revere's method was so simple compared to the alternatives, it has been employed by virtually every serious balanced point count system developer since, including Stanford Wong, Ken Uston, Lance Humble, Bryce Carlson, Arnold Snyder, and others. As a serious player, Revere's knowledge of the game included such esoteric techniques as shuffle tracking and hole card play.

MAX RUBIN

Max is the author of *Comp City*, first published in 1994, with an expanded second edition published in 2002. In this groundbreaking book, Max exposed techniques even non-counting players could use to get an advantage over the casinos by exploiting weaknesses in the casinos' comp systems. Max's inside information came from his years of experience in the industry as a dealer, pit boss, and casino manager. Max still does consulting work for the Barona Casino in California.

The initial manuscript for *Comp City* included advanced comp-hustling techniques that could be used by professional card counters, but the editors at Huntington Press decided to delete this section from the book in order to appeal to the wider market of recreational players. These excluded portions were published in *Blackjack Forum* in June 1994, and can be found now in the BlackjackForumOnline.com Library.

In the mid-1990s, he started hosting the Blackjack Ball, a secret annual event for professional players, where he serves as Game Master as many of the top pros compete for the Blackjack Cup and the title of World's Best Blackjack Player.

Now, as a host of the Game Show Network's World Series of Blackjack, Max has become one of the most visible public advocates of professional players.

ARNOLD SNYDER

I would characterize myself as a pro blackjack player who has been writing about casino blackjack for about twenty-five years. My first book, *The Blackjack Formula* (1980), revolutionized the ways professional card counters attacked the games by pointing out, for the first time, the relative importance of penetration over rules or counting system to a card counter's win rate. My advice has since been borne out by numerous independent computer simulations. In fact, it's pretty common knowledge among card counters today that penetration is the name of the game, and many find it hard to believe that for the first two decades of card counting, players did not know this. I also went against the grain in the early 1980s by recommending that players start using highly simplified sets of strategy indices based on data from Peter Griffin's analyses, and by recommending numerous other simplifications, including rounded indices and simple unbalanced counts. I refrained from publishing a lot of what I'd figured out about blackjack for many years, to preserve opportunities for players, but in my 2003 *Blackjack Shuffle Tracker's Cookbook* (Huntington Press), I revealed a number of discoveries on some of the most powerful techniques for beating casinos today.

From 1981 to 2004, I was the publisher and editor of *Blackjack Forum*, a quarterly journal for professional players (now published online at www.blackjackforumonline.com). And I am proud to say I have twice made it to the "final table" at Max Rubin's annual Blackjack Ball.

KEITH TAFT

Keith is not well known to the general public, but among professional players he is revered as an electronics genius who has spent more than thirty years devising high-tech equipment—computers, video cameras, and communication devices—to beat the casinos. Blackjack was his initial target, and always remained his prime target. His first blackjack computer, which he completed in 1972, weighed fifteen pounds. Over the years, as computer chip technology developed, his computers became smaller, faster, and lighter. By the mid-1970s, he had a device that weighed only a few ounces that could play perfect strategy based on the exact cards remaining to be dealt.

If it were up to Keith, his son Marty's name would be right along his in the Blackjack Hall of Fame, as the two have worked as partners since Marty was a teenager. For thirty years they have jointly created ever-more-clever hidden devices to beat the casinos, trained teams of players in their use, and have personally gone into the casinos to get the money. Keith and Marty may, in fact, have literally invented the concept of computer "networking," as they were wiring computer-equipped players together at casino blackjack tables thirty years ago in their efforts to beat the games.

When Nevada outlawed devices in 1985, it was specifically as a result of a Taft device found on Keith's brother, Ted—a miniature video camera built into Ted's belt buckle that could relay an image of the dealer's hole card as it was being dealt to a satellite receiving dish mounted in a pickup truck in the parking lot, where an accomplice read the video image, then signaled Ted at the table with the information he needed to play his hand.

An in-depth interview with Keith and Marty Taft was published in the Winter 2003-04 *Blackjack Forum*, and is available in the BlackjackForumOnline.com Library.

EDWARD O. THORP

Edward Oakley Thorp is widely regarded, by professional players as well as the general public, as the Father of Card Counting. It was in his book, *Beat the Dealer*, first published in 1962, that he presented his Ten-Count system, the first powerful winning blackjack system ever made available to the public. All card-counting systems in use today are variations of Thorp's Ten-Count.

When Thorp's book became a best seller, the Las Vegas casinos attempted to change the standard rules of blackjack, but their customers would not accept the changes and refused to play the new version of the game. So, the Vegas casinos went back to the old rules, but switched from dealing hand-held one-deck games to four-deck shoe games, a change that the players would accept. Unfortunately for the casinos, in 1966 Thorp's revised second edition of *Beat the Dealer* was published. This edition presented the High-Low Count, as developed by Julian Braun, a more powerful and practical counting system for attacking these new shoe games.

In 1961, Thorp and C. Shannon jointly invented the first wearable computer, a device that successfully predicted results in roulette. Thorp has an M.A. in Physics and a Ph.D. in mathematics, and has taught mathematics at UCLA, MIT, NMSU, and U.C. Irvine, where he also taught quantitative finance.

For many years Ed Thorp wrote a column for the now-defunct *Gambling Times* magazine. Many of these columns were collected in a book titled *The Mathematics of Gambling*, published in 1984 by Lyle Stuart.

KEN USTON

Uston burst onto the scene in 1977 with the publication of *The Big Player*, co-authored with Roger Rapaport. In this book, Uston exposed the secrets of Al Francesco's big player teams. The book caused a falling out between Al and Ken that lasted for years, as Al felt Ken had betrayed his trust as well as his teammates.

But there is no denying that this book caused an upheaval in the world of card counting, changing the ways that professionals looked at the game and attacked it. Three of the most successful international blackjack teams—the Tommy Hyland team, the MIT team, and the Czech team—all were founded in 1978, the year after Uston's book was published.

Al and Ken later patched up their relationship and Uston went on to start many blackjack teams of his own. He was a personality on a grand scale, who legally challenged the casino industry in the courts of both New Jersey and Nevada. His playing career spanned two decades of play at the highest levels, and included card counting, BP teams, hole card techniques, and concealed computer play.

Ken is also the author of *Two Books on Blackjack* (1979), *Million Dollar Blackjack* (1981), and *Ken Uston on Blackjack* (1986).

Uston died in 1987 at the age of fifty-two.

STANFORD WONG

Stanford Wong self-published his first book, *Professional Blackjack*, in 1975. It was later published by the Gambler's Book Club in Las Vegas, then revised and expanded numerous times and published by Wong's own company, Pi Yee Press.

Wong is widely regarded as one of the sharpest analysts of systems and methods for beating the casinos. In *Professional Blackjack*, he described a never-before-revealed table-hopping style of playing shoe games, a method of play now known as wonging. *Professional Blackjack* had a profound impact on serious players because it provided card counters with an easy yet powerful method for attacking the abundant four-deck shoe games that had taken over Las Vegas. Many pros still think of card-counting opportunities as "pre-Wong" and "post-Wong."

In his second book, *Blackjack in Asia*—a book priced at $2,000 and one of the rarest gambling books sought by collectors today—Wong discusses the unique blackjack games he had discovered in Asian casinos as a professional player, along with the optimum strategies he had devised for beating them. The book also included underground advice for exchanging currencies in these countries on the black market, as well as an account of his own hassles with customs officials when he attempted to leave the Philippines with his winnings. Of all of Wong's books, this is my personal favorite, as it reveals more of his anti-establishment personality than any of his later books.

In 1980, Wong published *Winning Without Counting*, priced at $200, and again, on a personal note, this is my second favorite book by Wong (and another collector's item if you can find one). He not only discusses many hole card techniques that had never before been mentioned in print—front-loading, spooking, and warp play—but he also delved into many clearly illegal methods of getting an edge over the house, including various techniques of bet-capping, card switching, card mucking, etc. He was widely criticized by those in the casino industry for the amusing way in which he discussed and analyzed such techniques, but anyone with half a brain could see that he was merely informing players with a tongue-in-cheek sense of humor.

Wong subsequently published *Tournament Blackjack* (1987), *Basic Blackjack* (1992), *Casino Tournament Strategy* (1992), *Blackjack Secrets* (1993), and since 1979 has published various newsletters including *Current Blackjack News*, aimed at serious and professional players.

TWENTY-ONE
QUESTIONS

> Circus Circus is what the whole hep world would be doing on Saturday night if the Nazis had won the war... Right above the gambling tables the Forty Flying Carazito Brothers are doing a high-wire trapeze act, along with four muzzled Wolverines and the Six Nymphet Sisters from San Diego... The madness goes on and on, but nobody seems to notice...
>
> — *Hunter S. Thompson, Fear and Loathing in Las Vegas*

Question #1: How many states in the U.S. have legal casinos with blackjack?

A: Twenty-seven states: Arizona, California, Colorado, Connecticut, Florida (cruise ships off the coast only), Illinois, Indiana, Iowa, Kansas, Louisiana, Massachusetts (cruise ships off the coast only), Michigan, Minnesota, Mississippi, Missouri, Nevada, New Jersey, New Mexico, New York, North Carolina (video blackjack on Indian reservations only), North Dakota, Oregon, South Carolina (video blackjack parlors only), South Dakota, Texas, Washington, and Wisconsin.

Question #2: How many professional blackjack players are there?

A: That depends on your definition of "professional." If we define a professional player as anyone who makes money from the game, then there are many thousands in the U.S. alone. Many of these players, however, are occasional players who count cards and make money on gambling trips, but otherwise make a living from another occupation.

If we define a professional player as someone who makes a substantial portion of his income from blackjack, then there are maybe a thousand all total in the U.S. Many of these players, however, are young team players, often college students, who get a job working with one of the big teams. Some are just young players trying out the life of a gambler, who will not last more than a few months to a year, either because they lack the acting ability to pull it off, or they simply find it too difficult. Blackjack is a substantial portion of the income of many of these young players simply because they are students, or just out of school, and they don't really have all that much income.

If we further narrow it down to defining a professional as someone who makes most of his income from blackjack, has done so for at least two years, and considers this his profession in life, then we're really down to a relative handful, maybe one hundred to one hundred-fifty players in the U.S.

Question #3: If you play solid basic strategy, what percentage of hands will you win, lose, and push (tie)?

A: Win: 43 percent. Lose: 48 percent. Push: 9 percent.

Question #4: What percentage of hands will an expert card counter win, lose, and push?

A: Generally, about the same. Depending on the number of decks and the level of penetration, he will win some fraction of a percent more hands, and more still if he avoids playing at negative counts. The major difference, however, is that the card counter will be betting more money on the hands that he wins, and less on the hands that he loses.

Question #5: What percentage of hands does the dealer bust?

A: If the player is playing basic strategy, heads up with the dealer, the dealer will bust about 28 percent of the time. The more players at the table, however, the higher the dealer's bust percentage. Why? The reason the dealer only busts 28 percent of the time against a single player is that the player must play his hand first, and if the player busts, the dealer doesn't complete his hand. With each additional player at the table, there is a greater chance of at least one hand being in action, forcing the dealer to complete his hand.

Question #6: What percentage of hands does the player bust?

A: A basic strategy player busts about 16 percent of the time. The player's bust percentage is lower than the dealer's precisely because the player stands on such a large percentage of his stiffs, whereas the dealer must hit to a total of 17.

Question #7: What's the simplest blackjack card-counting system?

A: The simplest published system may be Ed Thorp's "fives count." This system was initially proposed by Thorp in a mathematical paper prior to the publication of *Beat the Dealer*, and it can be found in his book. This is a single-deck strategy where the player simply counts the fives as the deal progresses, and whenever all four fives are gone from the remaining portion of the deck, the player alters his strategy according to a chart Thorp provides, and raises his bet. This strategy would not be useful in today's single-deck games because of the generally poor penetration.

The simplest published counting system that would be of some value is probably Ken Uston's Ace-Five count, published in his book, *Million Dollar Blackjack*. With this system, the player starts a running count at zero at the beginning of each deck (or shoe), and counts each 5 seen as +1, and each ace seen as -1. The player bets more when the count is positive and less when negative. In a single-deck game with at least a 75 percent shuffle point (thirty-nine of the fifty-two cards dealt), using a 1 to 5 betting spread, the player could get about a 0.5 percent advantage over the house. The problem is that single-deck games with good Las Vegas rules, dealt out this deeply, don't exist anymore.

In modern single-deck games, the system may get you over the break-even point, but you would likely be quickly identified as a card counter. In shoe games, a system like this might lower the house advantage by a fraction of a percent, but you won't get over the break-even point without a very large betting spread.

Question #8: What's the most complicated blackjack card-counting system?

A: I'll vote for the Hi-Opt I system, which counts tens as -1 and 3 through 6 as +1, with side-counts of the twos, sevens, eights, nines, and aces. That's a running count plus five separate side counts!

355

Not only that, but you have about one hundred-fifty strategy index numbers for altering your play from basic strategy, and you have to adjust these index numbers based on your individual side counts for different decisions. The late Peter Griffin used this system—in fact, Griffin devised the side-count charts himself—but I doubt it was ever used by a player betting serious money. Griffin was a mathematician and played for nickels just to enjoy the challenge.

Question #9: What's the most unusual blackjack game ever invented?

A: Since we've seen such weird games as Double Exposure and Blackjack Switch actually enter real-world casinos, I'll have to go with a theoretical game invented by Peter Griffin. Remember, Double Exposure was just a theoretical game invented by another mathematician, Richard Epstein, years before it appeared in a real casino, so maybe Griffin's "Woolworth Blackjack" will someday show up (but I sincerely doubt it).

In Woolworth blackjack, the only cards used are the fives and tens, specifically, a single deck with twenty fives and thirty-two tens. Since you can't actually make a total of 21 with only tens and fives, 20 is the best hand, but there is no 3 to 2 payout for a "blackjack," which doesn't actually exist in this variation of the game. The basic strategy is very simple: Always double down with a total of 10, and always stand on a total of 15. That's it. You follow this strategy regardless of the dealer's upcard. The house edge against the player following this basic strategy is 0.63 percent.

Don't expect this game to appear any time soon at a casino near you.

Question #10: Are the blackjack odds the same on video blackjack machines as they are in live casino games?

A: If all of the rules and payouts are identical to the casino game you are comparing the video game to, and if the video game is dealt honestly (randomly) from standard fifty-two-card decks, then the answer is yes. There is no difference. But let's look at what's really out there.

First, regarding the payouts, there are many video blackjack games that state: Blackjack Pays 2 for 1. This is a confusing statement for many blackjack players who believe that it means that they are getting paid more for their blackjacks, when in fact they are getting paid less. The term "2 for 1" is not the same as "2 to 1." A 2 for 1 payout is an even money payout. This is the type of terminology that is used in slot devices, but not on table games. 2 for 1 means that you have bet one unit and if you get a blackjack you will get your bet back, plus one extra unit; that's considered 2 for 1 among slot players. If you play a machine like this, you may not even notice the underpay. Since the machine deducts one credit from your account when you place the bet, when you get a blackjack, you will see two credits added back. But that's just your initial bet, plus one more unit. Also, some machines disallow all pair splits, simply because of the space allotment on the video screen. So, if you see a video blackjack machine and you want to play it, check to see that the rules, payouts, and options really are the same as a regular blackjack game.

Regarding the prospect of the game being honestly dealt from standard fifty-two-card decks, this would not be a concern in the state of Nevada. Gaming laws in Nevada specify that video slot devices that deal card games must deal them from standard decks, using a random number generator to select each card dealt. Gaming Control must approve the device and the software used to deal the cards.

In other states, however, these laws may not exist. They may also not exist on cruise ships, in foreign countries, on Indian reservations, etc. Many of the big slot manufacturers in Japan (Sega, for instance) make computer chips that allow the casino operator to "set" the house advantage from 1 percent to 20 percent, regardless of what the rules and payouts are on the machine. The machine simply deals the cards needed to obtain this edge over the player, regardless of the player's strategy. So, if you are playing perfect basic strategy, and expect that the house has only a 0.5 percent advantage over you, the house may actually be retaining 5 percent or more, depending on their setting.

Note that this is not considered "crooked" in most of the world, as casinos typically are allowed to set the payout percentage on other slot devices. In many states and countries, a video blackjack or video poker device is just another slot machine.

Question #11: Are the blackjack odds the same in Internet casinos as in casinos in Las Vegas or Atlantic City?

A: The answer here is identical to the above, with one stipulation. Most Internet casinos are physically located in countries where there are no gaming controls. So, any Internet blackjack game could be set to provide the house with a set percentage, just like a video slot device, and this would not be illegal. If an Internet casino claims on its Web site that all card games are randomly dealt, then you will have to decide if they are telling the truth. If there is no governing body that examines and tests their software to verify their claims, then they cannot be prosecuted for fraud. Most Internet casinos are honest and use random software, but some have stolen money from their customers by using cheating software, or simply disappearing with their customers' deposited funds. For lists of both reputable and disreputable Internet casinos, see my website at: www.blackjackforumonline.com.

Question #12: When did casinos first start dealing multiple-deck games and why?

A: Casinos in Europe were dealing baccarat and trente-et-quarante from multi-deck shoes for centuries. They dealt and banked these games from shoes because it eliminated many of the easiest forms of cheating. When blackjack became a house-banked game in the U.S., it was dealt from a single deck right from the start. The popularity of the game in the U.S. attracted the attention of the European casinos, and they decided to offer it to American travelers. They converted it to a shoe game, for their own protection. A few casinos in Nevada did offer blackjack games dealt from four-deck shoes as far back as the 1950s, probably for the entertainment of European customers. But note that blackjack was not that popular of a game even in the U.S. at that time. In 1953, the most popular casino games in Nevada, in order, were: slot machines, craps, roulette, blackjack, and bingo.

Question #13: Can a player beat casino blackjack in the long run without card counting?

A: The most common way that professional players beat casino blackjack, without counting cards, is hole card play. This is simply taking advantage of a sloppy dealer who flashes his hole card either when pulling it off the deck or while loading it beneath his upcard.

This strategy has been found to be legal in the Nevada courts, because it is the dealer's job to hide the hole card, not the player's job to avoid looking in that direction.

Question #14: What was Ken Uston's biggest selling book?

A: Trick question! Uston's best-selling book was *Mastering Pac-Man*, which sold an estimated three million copies in 1982. Uston became addicted to playing the video game while in Atlantic City, and ultimately figured out a strategy for beating the machine, allowing the player to play forever on a single quarter. Bally's, the manufacturer of the Pac-Man device, heard about the book before it was published, and actually threatened to sue the publisher if the book was published, claiming it would ruin their business on the machine. The book was a huge success and Bally's never sued.

Question #15: What are the most highly valued "collector's items" for those who prize card counting books and historical paraphernalia?

A: This would be a difficult list to put in order by dollar value, but these items would all be on the list:

1. Stanford Wong's Blackjack in Asia, published in 1979, hard bound, sold for $2000 per copy for about a year, then was taken off the market by Wong after about a dozen were sold, never to be republished. Because of the high retail price, which was never lowered, and the few copies in existence, this may be the highest priced book sought after by collectors of gambling ephemera.

2. Advantage Playing by Steve Forte, published in 1983 by the author, twenty-four pages photocopied and stapled, not copyrighted, almost impossible to find. The booklet was used by Forte in private lessons to teach card counting, shuffle tracking techniques, and various types of hole card play. Because of the inexpensive reproduction technique, it would be very difficult to prove authenticity. If you were one of the fortunate few who got a copy from Steve, see if you can get him to sign it!

3. *Playing Blackjack to Win*, by Baldwin, Cantey, Maisel, and McDermott. Published in 1957, spiral bound, M. Barrows and Co., the first book to provide an accurate basic strategy

for blackjack, and to describe a valid (though weak) card-counting system.

4. The *Beat the Dealer* Computer, 1966, the first concealable blackjack "computer" ever devised. Ed Thorp worked on its development with Dr. Tom Bean, who sold it via mail order. It was a small plastic device with dials that the player could turn as tens and non-tens were removed from a single deck. The device was meant to be used in the player's hand, and the player could read the count by feeling tiny bumps on the dials.

5. *Playing Blackjack as a Business* by Lawrence Revere, self-published, 1969, thirty-six-page spiral-bound edition. Very rare.

6. *Beyond Counting* by James Grosjean, published in 2000, 223 pages, large format soft cover. Incredibly, this book is already a collector's item after only five years in print. Here's why: I had the honor of publishing this book, and the initial printing was one thousand copies. When those copies had been sold, the author requested that no other copies be printed. Ever. It is one of the most advanced texts on professional play in print, and the last time I looked, copies were going on eBay for $500 each. Grosjean tells me that he is planning to bring out a second edition of his book in the Fall of 2005, but that it will be made available to professional gamblers only, through referrals, and will be priced appropriately for this small, high-end market.

Question #16: What was the first book to describe blackjack?

A: The game was most likely first described as vingt-un in the old Hoyles. Exactly when the oldest reference was made, I do not know. Steve Forte owns an 1845 Hoyle that describes vingt-et-un. Regarding Hoyle: Edmund Hoyle was an eighteenth century English lawyer, whose first book was titled *A Short Treatise on Whist*, a popular card game in the mid-seventeen hundreds. He later expanded the book to include discussions of two other now-extinct card games, Piquet and Quadrille. Since then, virtually any book describing the rules of games may be called a Hoyle. There have probably been a thousand different Hoyles published in the centuries since Edmund Hoyle's death in 1769, by hundreds of different publishers in dozens of languages. The popular phrase, "according to Hoyle," has little meaning since the various Hoyles often disagree with each other.

Also, the games described in any Hoyle depend largely on the year of publication. It's probable that Edmund Hoyle had never even heard of vingt-un. Edwin Silberstang's 1996 Encyclopedia of Games and Gambling: A Modern Hoyle for Sophisticated Gamers, on the other hand, not only provides proper blackjack basic strategy, but describes newer casino games like video poker, and is the only Hoyle I know of with comprehensive rules and procedures for playing strip poker! (What exactly qualifies as an article of clothing? Can an undergarment be removed prior to a shirt or skirt?) Silberstang spells out the rules of strip poker in detail, though the proper old barrister, Edmund Hoyle, would probably turn over in his grave if he saw his name on this book!

The oldest book I have seen that calls the game "blackjack" is the *Handbook on Percentages* by Charles E. Shampaign. It was initially published in 1928, then was revised in 1930 and published by Joe Treybal Sporting Goods in St. Louis, Missouri. Sometime in the 1970s or '80s, the Gamblers Book Club in Las Vegas reissued it in a spiral-bound format.

Question #17: Can a casino put a bad player at the table, who will play so poorly that it changes the odds of the game so a good player cannot win?

A: No, not unless the dealer is doing something with that player to cheat. For instance, if the dealer is peeking and dealing seconds, using this player to draw off cards that would either hurt you or help the dealer, then this would have an effect. But no player can affect the long run odds of other players just by playing poorly, no matter how bad that player is.

But this does not mean that some casino boss wouldn't try this ploy. There are many casino management personnel who do not understand the math of the game. If you saw the movie, *The Cooler*, with William H. Macy, it was about a guy who was supposed to be so unlucky that the casino owner would send him down to tables just to stand there whenever a big player was winning in order to reverse the odds. This movie was based on reality. Although most modern casinos do not employ "coolers," there are still some old casinos in Nevada where coolers are on the payroll. Note that this employee does not deal or play at a table; he just stands there to give off bad vibes and cause winning players to start losing. You wouldn't think any business could be so superstitious in this day and age, but a few coolers still exist.

Question #18: Is a pat hand (total of 17 to 21) always a better hand for the player than a stiff hand (total of 12 to 16)?

A: No. A pat hand is always better than a stiff hand when the dealer has a low card (2 through 6) showing. But when the dealer has a high card showing (7 through ace), a player sometimes has a better shot at winning when he has a stiff. As an example, if the dealer shows an 8 or 9 upcard, and your hand totals 17, you are in very bad shape. You would have a better chance at winning if you had a total of 12 or 13 than you do with a 17. In fact, the only dealer upcard your 17 will have a positive expectation against is a 6. If the dealer upcard is any card from 2-5, your 17 will lose more than it will win.

Question #19: If I make a total of 21 (not a blackjack), what card would I most prefer the dealer to show as an upcard?

A: This is one that just about every player would guess wrong. You have your highest win percentage (96.3 percent) against a 10 up. The dealer's best chance to beat your 21, where your edge is only 88.2 percent, is when he shows a deuce. Incredibly, if you've made a total of 21, the dealer is better off with any upcard of 2 through 6 than any upcard of 7, 8, 9, 10, or ace.

Question #20: If I have a promotional coupon book from a casino, with a coupon that pays me an extra $5 with a $5 bet, and the coupon stipulates that it is for even money bets only, how much difference will it make if I play the coupon on a single-deck game or a shoe game, and how much difference will the rules make?

A: It makes extremely little difference, not more than a few cents to the coupon's value. But you should be aware that you may be able to get more value from the coupon if you play it at baccarat, or even craps, as opposed to blackjack. In some casinos, when a coupon specifies "even money bets only," the house interprets this to mean that if you are dealt a blackjack, you will be paid even money, not 3 to 2. This raises the house edge over you on blackjack by more than 2 percent.

At baccarat, you can bet the banker bet against a house edge of only 1.1 percent, and at craps, against a 1.4 percent total house advantage.

Question #21: Do casinos have camera surveillance everywhere on their property?

A: Casinos are forbidden from having camera surveillance inside the guests' hotel rooms and in the public restrooms. Other than that, they do have cameras everywhere. The newer casinos have cameras that can follow a customer from one end of the property to the other, including inside the restaurants, in the elevators, in the hotel lobby and hallways, and even in the parking lot.

POETRY (WITH APOLOGIES)

What? A blackjack book with a poetry section? Ha! Whoever said gamblers ain't got no culture! Like all gambling experts, I only plagiarize from the best.

A VISIT FROM ST. WHO?
(For Kenny Uston, with apologies to Clement Clarke Moore)

'Twas the night before Christmas,
And all through the pit,
Not a player was betting,
Not even one chip.

The dealers stood waiting
With frowns all around,
In hopes that some high-roller
Soon would sit down.

The house chips were nestled
All snug in their racks,
With visions of buy-ins
For reds, greens, and blacks.

The lights on the crest
Of the new dollar slots
Gave the lustre of riches
To all the have-nots.

The boss in his bow tie,
The waitress, the shill,
Had all settled in
For a long night of nil.

When out in the lobby
There rose such a clatter,
The boss sprang to his phone
To see what was the matter.

Then what turned his Visine-soaked
Eyes into gawkers,
But a high-rolling drunk
With eight gaudy streetwalkers!

A ten-buck Havana
Cigar in his lips,
The smoke it encircled
His arms full of chips.

His belly was full
From far too much feasting,
And it shook when he laughed
Like a chorus girl's g-string.

The shift boss grinned,
In his heart felt a rush.
He knew in an instant
It must be some lush!

"On dealers! On floormen!"
He called them by name,
"On runners and doormen,
Let's hustle this lame!"

The drunk spoke no word
But went straight to a table,
And filled all the spots
To the max he was able.

Then laying a finger
Aside of his toke,
He won every hand
'Til that table went broke.

The boss's face went white
As some new fallen snow,
Not once, but three times,
He saw that rack go!

The gray-haired old guard
Watched it all with a grin.
"That's no drunk!" he said,
"That's the ghost of Saint Ken!"

"He comes back each year
On this eve for a scuffle,
To clean out some bastard
Who gave him the shuffle!"

And that spectre exclaimed
As he split with his crew,
"Merry Christmas to all
Who can count down a shoe!"

ACES (OR 42.08%)
**(For James Grosjean who figured it out,
with apologies to Joyce Kilmer)**

I think that I shall never face
a poem as lovely as an ace.
As my first card, so confident,
it gives me fifty-two percent.

That one lone spot they call the faint
rejoices with the slap of paint.
For then my lowly bet as such
gets paid with half again as much.

But when the dealer shows that ace,
my hand lies still in weak disgrace.
For then my only safety net
is found in the insurance bet.

And if the ten-card doesn't snap,
my hand is still a piece of crap.
I hit my stiffs! It's so unjust!
A dealer's ace-hand rarely busts!

Like a stealthy big-game hunter,
aces humble every punter.
Poems are writ by fools in haste,
but only Bee can make an ace.

CHARGE OF THE COUNT BRIGADE

(For the Craps, Inc. blackjack team,
with apologies to Alfred Lord Tennyson)

Half the bank, half the bank,
Half the bank plundered,
Into the Valley of Debt,
Betting six hundred.
Forward the Count Brigade!
"A marker again!" he said.
Into the Valley of Debt,
Betting six hundred.

Forward the Count Brigade!
Was there a hand misplayed?
Not though the BP knew
Someone had blundered.
Theirs not to show alarm,
Theirs to turn on the charm,
Theirs but to bet the farm,
Into the Valley of Debt,
Betting six hundred.

POETRY (WITH APOLOGIES)

Cameras to the right of them
Cameras to the left of them
Cameras in front of them
Panning for one nerd.
Griffin behind the wall,
Boldly they stack it tall,
Into the Jaws of Debt,
Negative flux and all,
Betting six hundred.

Flashed all the cameras there,
Flashed mug shots everywhere,
Survey Voice analysts
Studied and wondered.
Glared at and shuffled on,
BPs just hit and run,
Act like they're having fun,
They who have lost a ton,
Clamped by the Jaws of Debt,
'Til all the bank that's left
Is a measly six hundred.

Where did their bankroll go,
They who were in the know,
while surveillance wondered?
Some will say, "That's the flux!"
Others cry, "This game sucks!"
Regardless, they lost big bucks,
All but six hundred.

DO NOT GO GENTLE INTO
THAT BACK ROOM
(For the LVHCM, with apologies to Dylan Thomas)

Do not go gentle into that back room,
Just because they snapped you with the Biometric zoom;
Do not surrender into that sure ruin,
Rage, rage, against the spying Griffin goons.

Do not go calmly into that black book,
They say you're a cheater, call you a crook,
Peddle your mug shot, it's libel, just look,
Litigate, litigate, throw the left hook.

Do not go meekly to show your ID,
Tell them to charge you with some felony,
They don't have a case, they've no right to hold
Your license, your passport, your MasterCard Gold.

Do not go easy when they confiscate
The chips that you won when the hour was late,
They can't take the winnings your system achieves,
Sue them, screw them, they are the thieves.

Do not run scared when your teammates get caught,
Do not give up when the pit heat gets hot,
When they read you your rights, do not leave town,
Show up next door with your hat brims turned down.

Do not waste time at Caribbean Stud,
When they fix all their dealers and blackjack's a dud,
When the one-card poker is too much to fight,
It's time to go gentle into that dark night.

THE GRIFFIN

(For Tommy Hyland, with apologies to Edgar Allen Poe)

Once upon a midnight dreary, while I counted weak and weary,
Over many a poorly chosen game of six-deck, deal four,
While I nodded, nearly napping, suddenly there came a tapping,
As of someone gently rapping, slapping 'til my shoulder's sore.
"'Tis some silly host," I muttered, "Tapping 'til my shoulder's sore."

Only this and nothing more.

Ah, distinctly I remember, it was in the bleak December,
I became a slot club member for the coupon books and more.
Eagerly I wished the morrow; vainly I had sought to borrow
Tickets to see Cher or Charo—Charo whom I do abhor.
But no ticket comps could gain me entrance through the showroom
door—

For Charo who was such a bore.

So that now as I sat counting, never with the true amounting,
On the plus side to a favorable five or even four,
Came that tapping at my shoulder, which was growing ever bolder,
Tapping with an urgent finger, tapping I could not ignore.
"'Tis some host," I sat repeating, "Maybe Cher has open seating—

Cher! For her I do adore!"

Presently I toked for cover, turned to see which host did hover,
Fawning with that sycophant demeanor that I so deplore.
"Sir," said I, "I'm feeling woozy, need a room with a Jacuzzi;
Can you get my airfare if I play a little more?
I've been losing, all my boozing"—here I turned to see the whore—

Just a boss, and guards galore.

Deep into his eyes now peering, long I sat there wondering, fearing,
Doubting, thinking thoughts all counters dare to think when heat's in
store.
Did the clanging slots go quiet? Was it time to try the Hyatt?
Spoke the boss just one word, a word I did deplore;
This he whispered with a snarl as he motioned toward the door—

Spoke the boss, "Nevermore."

"But" said I, "I'm RFB here; check my average bet, you'll see here,
That my action justifies my status in this store.
I've got thousands with the cashier; don't do anything so rash here;
Surely there is some mistake; admit you've made mistakes before."
But his lips stayed pursed in anger like a soldier's lost in war;

Spoke the boss, "Hit the door."

Then I saw the book he showed me, I suppose he felt he owed me,
Something of a reason for performing his distasteful chore.
Black as night and far more evil was this cause for my upheaval,
Now I learned that I was entered into Griffin, Volume Four.
There's my mug upon the flyer, labeled "Counter, Don't Ignore."

Quoth the Griffin, "Nevermore."

Ah, distinctly I remember, it was in the bleak December,
My career went down the tubes without a prayer I might restore.
In that black book my dreams fizzled, for my face had now been chiseled,
Into memories of every eye in every pit from shore to shore.
So I donned a mustache and continued as before—

"Screw the Griffin, evermore."

And finally…

PROWL
(For Pennie Ruchman, with apologies to Allen Ginsberg)

I saw the best grinds of my generation
destroyed by bad bets,
barred, hysterical, stakeless,
dragging themselves through the Reno streets at dawn,
looking for some promo chips…

Stop! That's all the poetry I can take! There is no way I'm going to satirize all twenty pages of Ginsberg's "Howl," when only one gambler in a million has ever even read the thing! (Pennie is that one…) Frankly, I'm just hoping the rest of you remember "The Night Before Christmas." That's enough culture for one book.

BLACKJACK REALITY VERSUS BLACKJACK HYPE

> The best hustler is not necessarily the best player among hustlers. He has to be a very good player, true, but beyond a certain point his playing ability is not nearly so important as his skill at various kinds of conning.
>
> — *Ned Polsky, Hustlers, Beats, and Others*

When you first enter the world of gambling, you only see what this world pretends to be. You see casinos touting their "loose slots" and their "liberal blackjack games" and their "big winners." You see system sellers promoting their "professional secrets," sure to change your life and your tax bracket. In the world of gambling, it seems everyone's trying to give you money.

That's the hype.

The reality is that this world is after your money. The casinos brag about their winners for the sole purpose of bringing in more losers. The system sellers tell you they're giving you the keys to the vault, but when you get to the vault, you find a combination lock. Funny, they never mentioned the combination.

Some of the con men are easy to spot. They take out slick newspaper and magazine ads and promise you $500 or $1000 a day, no work required.

But others are more difficult to identify. They drape their books or advice with lots of complex-looking math and false claims of experience at the tables. Their books may even be endorsed by well-known, reputable experts who didn't have the time to actually read the books before providing their endorsements, or who lacked the expertise to validate the books' claims.

How do you spot this type of con artist?

He tends to provide a lot of scholarly citations, but few details of practical application based on his personal observation and experience at the tables. No matter how complicated the system, the phonies always say, "It's easy." They use a lot of jargon meant to confuse beginners. Their writing is often deliberately hard to understand, designed to make you feel that your lack of understanding is your fault.

When Ken Uston wrote about team play, you know he did it. You can feel it on the page. When Stanford Wong wrote about tournament strategies, you know he played in these tournaments. When Charles Lund wrote about beating the slots, you know he spent many hours playing and figuring out these machines. All of these authors fill their books with a hundred problems they've had in attempting to execute their strategies. They discuss how difficult it is to get everything right. Real professional players always give lots of clear warnings to beginners. They tell you what it's like when the casinos become suspicious, when the play goes wrong, and what kinds of mistakes you will make. They've been there, done that.

Many intelligent people flock to the con artists because they don't really play themselves. The purpose of the groups formed around such "experts" is to foster a sense of elitism among their members, who all want to be perceived as experts, though they're not willing to test their expertise at the tables. They don't care if you don't win, or even if you lose, because they don't risk their own money at the tables and they don't know how it feels. To them, blackjack has nothing to do with putting their financial positions on the line; it's just a mutual admiration society.

Nobody succeeds at blackjack because he is the best at doing what authorities tell him to do. He succeeds because he is able to think on his own.

On the other hand, if all you want to do is talk blackjack instead of beat it, these groups are fine for you. If you pat the right people on the back, they'll soon be patting you, and there's no money lost in that.

Anyway, I hope you get something out of this book. I do want you to know that there really is such an animal as a professional blackjack player, but if this is your goal in life, you've got to be careful. I know better than anyone that you can succeed, but it's a jungle out there. Though some players do make a lot of money at this game, most never acquire all the skills needed to win over the long haul. I don't know what's more dangerous to your bankroll—the casinos, the system hawkers, or the Internet "experts" and phony "pros."

The world of professional blackjack is a Darwinian survival-of-the-fittest world. Ultimately, your success will depend less on your bankroll than on your decisions. Whom are you going to trust? What do you really need to know?

Where will you rank in the gambling food chain?

Let's hope you'll be one of the predators and not the prey.

— *Arnold*

APPENDIX

COMPREHENSIVE BASIC BLACKJACK STRATEGY
FOR ANY NUMBER OF DECKS

	2	3	4	5	6	7	8	9	X	A
STAND										
17	S	S	S	S	S	S	S	S	S	S
16	S	S	S	S	S	H	H	H	H1	H
15	S	S	S	S	S	H	H	H	H	H
14	S	S	S	S	S	H	H	H	H	H
13	S	S	S	S	S	H	H	H	H	H
12	H	H	S	S	S	H	H	H	H	H
A7	S	S	S	S	S	S	S	H	H	S2
DOUBLE DOWN										
11	D	D	D	D	D	D	D	D	D3	D4
10	D	D	D	D	D	D	D	D		
9	D5	D	D	D	D					
8				D5	D5					
A8					D5					
A7		D	D	D	D					
A6	D5	D	D	D	D					
A5			D	D	D					
A4			D	D	D					
A3			D5	D	D					
A2			D5	D	D					
SURRENDER (late)										
17										¢6
16								¢7	¢	¢8
8-8										¢9
15									¢10	¢6
7-7									¢5	¢9

S = Stand   H = Hit   D = Double Down   ¢ = Surrender

1 = Stand with 3 or More Cards
2 = Hit in Multi-Deck, or if Dealer Hits S17
3 = European No-Hole Hit
4 = Multi-Deck or European No-Hole Hit
5 = Single-Deck Only
6 = With Hit Soft 17 Only
7 = Single Deck Hit
8 = Single Deck, X-6 Only
9 = With Hit Soft 17 in Multi-Deck
10 = Excluding 8,7

COMPREHENSIVE BASIC BLACKJACK STRATEGY
(CONTINUED)

PAIR SPLITS

	2	3	4	5	6	7	8	9	X	A
NO DOUBLE AFTER SPLITS										
AA	$	$	$	$	$	$	$	$	$	$1
99	$	$	$	$	$		$	$		
88	$	$	$	$	$	$	$	$	$1	$1
77	$	$	$	$	$	$				
66	$2	$	$	$	$					
33			$	$	$	$				
22		$2	$	$	$	$				
WITH DOUBLE AFTER SPLITS										
AA	$	$	$	$	$	$	$	$	$	$1
99	$	$	$	$	$		$	$		
88	$	$	$	$	$	$	$	$	$1	$1
77	$	$	$	$	$	$	$2			
66	$	$	$	$	$	$2				
44			$2	$	$					
33	$	$	$	$	$	$	$2			
22	$	$	$	$	$	$				

INSURANCE: NO
SURRENDER (EARLY)

	2	3	4	5	6	7	8	9	X	A
17										¢
16								¢	¢	¢
8-8									¢	¢
15									¢	¢
14									¢	¢
7-7									¢	¢
13										¢
12										¢
7										¢
6										¢
5										¢

$ = Split   ¢ = Surrender
1 = European No-Hole Hit
2 = Single Deck Only

SPANISH 21 BASIC STRATEGY

	2	3	4	5	6	7	8	9	X	A
18+	S	S	S	S	S	S	S	S	S	S
17	S	S	S	S	S	S	S6	S6	S6	¢
16	S5	S6	S6	S	S	H	H	H	H	¢
15	S4	S5	S5	S6	S6	H	H	H	H	H
14	H	H	S4	S5	S5	H	H	H	H	H
13	H	H	H	S5	S4	H	H	H	H	H
12	H	H	H	H	H	H	H	H	H	H
11	D4	D5	D5	D5	D5	D4	D4	H	H	H
10	D5	D5	D6	D	D	D4	H	H	H	H
9	H	H	H	H	D3	H	H	H	H	H
8	H	H	H	H	H	H	H	H	H	H
A9	S	S	S	S	S	S	S	S	S	S
A8	S	S	S	S	S	S	S	S	S	S
A7	S4	S4	D4	D5	D6	S	S4	H	H	H
A6	H	H	D3	D4	D5	H	H	H	H	H
A5	H	H	H	H	D4	H	H	H	H	H
A4	H	H	H	H	H	H	H	H	H	H
A3	H	H	H	H	H	H	H	H	H	H
A2	H	H	H	H	H	H	H	H	H	H
Pair Splits										
AA	$	$	$	$	$	$	$	$	$	$
99			$	$	$		$	$		
88	$	$	$	$	$	$	$	$	$	¢
77	$	$	$	$	$	$				
66			$	$	$					
33		$	$	$	$	$				
22		$	$	$	$	$				

INSURANCE: NEVER

S = Stand   H = Hit   D = Double Down $ = Split   ¢ = Surrender

3 = hit if hand contains 3 to 6 cards
4 = hit if hand contains 4 to 6 cards
5 = hit if hand contains 5 or 6 cards
6 = hit if hand contains 6 cards

SUPER FUN 21 BASIC STRATEGY										
	2	3	4	5	6	7	8	9	X	A
18+	S	S	S	S	S	S	S	S	S	S
17	S	S	S	S	S	S	S	S5	S5	¢5
16	S	S	S	S	S	H	H	H	¢4	¢4
15	S5	S5	S	S	S	H	H	H	H	¢4
14	S5	S5	S5	S5	S5	H	H	H	H	H
13	S4	S4	S5	S5	S5	H	H	H	H	H
12	H	H	S4	S4	S4	H	H	H	H	H
11	D4	D4	D4	D4	D4	D4	D4	D4	D4	D4
10	D4	D4	D4	D4	D4	D4	D4	D4	D3	D4
9	D3	D4	D4	D	D	H	H	H	H	H
8	H	H	H	H	H	H	H	H	H	H
A9	S5	S5	S5	S5	S5	S5	S5	S5	S5	S5
A8	S5	S5	S5	S5	D5	S5	S5	S5	S4	S5
A7	S3	D4	D4	D4	D5	S4	S4	H	H	H
A6	D3	D3	D4	D4	D5	H	H	H	H	H
A5	H	H	D3	D4	D4	H	H	H	H	H
A4	H	H	D3	D4	D4	H	H	H	H	H
A3	H	H	D3	D	D	H	H	H	H	H
A2	H	H	H	D	D	H	H	H	H	H
PAIR SPLITS										
AA	$	$	$	$	$	$	$	$	$	$
99	$	$	$	$	$		$	$		$
88	$	$	$	$	$	$	$	$	$	$
77	$	$	$	$	$	$	$		¢	¢
66	$	$	$	$	$	$				
44				$	$					
33	$	$	$	$	$	$				
22	$	$	$	$	$	$				
INSURANCE: NEVER										

S = Stand   H = Hit   D = Double Down $ = Split   ¢ = Surrender
3 = hit if hand contains 3 to 5 cards
4 = hit if hand contains 4 or 5 cards
5 = hit if hand contains 5 cards

APPENDIX

DOUBLE EXPOSURE BASIC STRATEGY

	4	5	6	7	8	9	10	11	12	13	14	15	16	17	18	19	20	AA	A2	A3	A4	A5	[A6]
21	S	S	S	S	S	S	S	S	S	S	S	S	S	S	S	S	S	S	S	S	S	S	[S]
20	S	S	S	S	S	S	S	S	S	S	S	S	S	S	S	S	H	S	S	S	S	S	[S]
19	S	S	S	S	S	S	S	S	S	S	S	S	S	S	S	H	H	S	S	S	S	S	[S]
18	S	S	S	S	S	S	S	S	S	S	S	S	S	S	H	H	H	S	S	S	S	S	[S]
17	S	S	S	S	S	S	S	S	S	S	S	S	S	H	H	H	H	S	S	S	S	S	[S]
16	S	S	S	H	S	S	S	S	S	S	S	S	S	H	H	H	H	S	S	S	S	S	[H]
15	S	S	S	H	H	H	S	S	S	S	S	S	S	H	H	H	H	S	S	S	S	S	[H]
14	S	S	S	H	H	H	H	S	S	S	S	S	S	H	H	H	H	S	S	S	S	S	[H]
13	S	S	S	H	H	H	H	H	S	S	S	S	S	H	H	H	H	S	S	S	S	S	[H]
12	S	S	S	H	H	H	H	H	S	S	S	S	S	H	H	H	H	H	H	S	S	S	[H]
11	D	D	D	D	D	D	H	H	D	D	D	D	D	H	H	H	H	H	D	D	D	D	[H]
10	D	D	D	D	D	H	H	H	D	D	D	D	D	H	H	H	H	H	H	D	D	D	[H]
9	H	D	D	H	H	H	H	H	D	D	D	D	D	H	H	H	H	H	H	H	H	H	[H]
8	H	H	H	H	H	H	H	H	D	D	D	D	D	H	H	H	H	H	H	H	H	H	[H]
7	H	H	H	H	H	H	H	H	H	H	D	D	D	H	H	H	H	H	H	H	H	H	[H]
6	H	H	H	H	H	H	H	H	H	H	D	D	D	H	H	H	H	H	H	H	H	H	[H]
5	H	H	H	H	H	H	H	H	H	H	D	D	D	H	H	H	H	H	H	H	H	H	[H]
AT	S	S	S	S	S	S	S	S	S	S	S	S	S	S	S	S	S	S	S	S	S	S	[S]
A9	S	S	S	S	S	S	S	S	S	S	**D**	**D**	**D**	**D**	S	S	H	S	S	S	S	S	[S]
A8	S	S	S	S	S	S	S	S	**D**	**D**	**D**	**D**	**D**	S	S	S	H	S	S	S	S	S	[S]
A7	**D**	**D**	**D**	S	H	H	H	H	H	D	D	D	D	D	S	H	H	H	H	H	H	H	[S]
A6	D	D	D	H	H	H	H	H	D	D	D	D	D	H	H	H	H	H	H	H	H	H	[H]
A5	H	D	D	H	H	H	H	H	D	D	D	D	D	H	H	H	H	H	H	H	H	H	[H]
A4	H	H	D	H	H	H	H	H	D	D	D	D	D	H	H	H	H	H	H	H	H	H	[H]
A3	H	H	D	H	H	H	H	H	D	D	D	D	D	H	H	H	H	H	H	H	H	H	[H]
A2	H	H	H	H	H	H	H	H	D	D	D	D	D	H	H	H	H	H	H	H	H	H	[H]
AA	$	$	$	$	$	$	$	H	$	$	$	$	$	H	H	H	H	$	$	$	$	$	[$]
TT	S	S	S	S	S	S	S	S	S	$	$	$	$	S	S	S	H	S	S	S	S	S	[S]
99	$	$	$	S	$	$	$	S	$	$	$	$	$	S	$	H	H	S	S	S	$	$	[S]
88	$	$	$	$	$	S	S	S	$	$	$	$	$	H	H	H	H	S	S	S*	S	$	[$]
77	S*	$	$	H	H	H	H	H	$	$	$	$	$	H	H	H	H	S	S	S	S	S	[H]
66	$	$	$	H	H	H	H	H	$	$	$	$	$	H	H	H	H	H	H	S	S	S	[H]
55	D	D	D	D	D	H	H	H	D	D	D	D	D*	H	H	H	H	H	H	D	D	D	[H]
44	H	H	H	H	H	H	H	H	$	$	$	$	$	H	H	H	H	H	H	H	H	H	[H]
33	H*	H*	$	H	H	H	H	H	$	$	$	$	$	H	H	H	H	H	H	H	H	H	[H]
22	H*	H*	$	H	H	H	H	H	$	$	$	$	$	H	H	H	H	H	H	H	H	H	[H]

Use bracketed [A6] column only if dealer hits soft 17. If dealer stands on soft 17, use the 17 column.

S = stand   H = hit   D = double if allowed (otherwise hit)

D (bold) = double if allowed (otherwise stand)   * = double if doubling after splits allowed

$ = split   Note: Player A2, A3 means any soft 13, soft 14, etc.

BLACKJACK SWITCH BASIC STRATEGY FOR MULTIPLE DECKS										
	2	3	4	5	6	7	8	9	X	A
STAND										
17	S	S	S	S	S	S	S	S	S	S
16	S	S	S	S	S	H	H	H	H	H
15	S	S	S	S	S	H	H	H	H	H
14	H	S	S	S	S	H	H	H	H	H
13	H	S	S	S	S	H	H	H	H	H
12	H	H	H	S	S	H	H	H	H	H
DOUBLE DOWN										
11	D	D	D	D	D	D	D	H	H	H
10	D	D	D	D	D	D	D	H	H	H
9	H	H	H	H	D	H	H	H	H	H
A8	S	S	S	S	S	S	S	S	S	S
A7	S	S	S	D	D	S	S	H	H	H
A6	H	H	H	D	D	H	H	H	H	H
A5	H	H	H	H	D	H	H	H	H	H
A4	H	H	H	H	H	H	H	H	H	H
A3	H	H	H	H	H	H	H	H	H	H
A2	H	H	H	H	H	H	H	H	H	H
PAIR SPLITS										
AA	$	$	$	$	$	$	$	$	$	$
99		$	$	$		$	$			
88	$	$	$	$	$	$	$	$	$	$
77		$	$	$	$	$				
66		$	$	$						
33			$	$	$					
22			$	$	$					
INSURANCE: NO										
	S = Stand		H = Hit		D = Double Down			$ = Split		

Acknowledgments and References

Much of the more recent history of blackjack has been recorded in *Blackjack Forum* magazine, a quarterly journal for professional gamblers that I have had the honor of editing since 1981. Up until 2004, the magazine was printed as a hard copy publication, but it is now strictly an online publication, which is available free to the public at www.blackjackforumonline.com. The online library contains hundreds of articles from back issues of the magazine, so that any interested player or researcher can easily look up many of my sources.

Regarding the history of blackjack and card counting, you will find in our online library interviews with, and articles by, many of blackjack's most renowned characters. In addition to my interviews with Julian Braun and Ken Uston, you'll find Richard W. Munchkin's interviews with Tommy Hyland, Al Francesco, MIT mogul Johnny C, computer/ electronics wizards Keith and Marty Taft, legendary card counter Darryl Purpose, and the notorious hole-card expert "RC."

You'll also find Russell Barnhart's description of his 1962 trip to Nevada with Ed Thorp and Mickey MacDougall, as well as Allan Schaffer's article about the legendary pre-Thorp 1950s card counter, Jess Marcum. There is a section on cheating, with many articles by Sam Case, as well as by Steve Forte, Howard Collier, Joel Friedman, Allan Pell and others. In any case, I'm not going to reproduce the contents of the library here, as it is open to the public and available free of charge to anyone who can surf the Web.

I am indebted to countless authors, experts, players, mathematicians and computer programmers for the various strategies presented herein. My primary reference for the standard blackjack game was Peter Griffin's *Theory of Blackjack*. I believe Frank Scoblete published the first accurate Spanish 21 strategy in his book, *The Armada Strategies for Spanish 21*. The first Super Fun 21 strategy I ever saw was on Michael Shackleford's www.wizardofodds.com website, where you can find accurate strategies for just about any casino games. My double exposure basic strategy came from *Stanford Wong's Professional Blackjack*. The Blackjack Switch basic strategy is another one I first saw at Michael Shackleford's site. The switching strategy for Blackjack Switch, however, is my own device, so to whatever extent it errs, you can blame me. In compiling the history of blackjack, I owe much to Howard Schwartz at the Gamblers Book Shop in Las Vegas, and Steve Forte for making materials from his library available to me. Bits and pieces of blackjack's history came primarily from the materials below. — A.S.

Andersen, Ian, *Turning the Tables on Las Vegas*, Vanguard Press, New York, 1976.

Anners, Henery F., *Hoyle's Games,* Brown, Bazin & Co., 1845.

Asbury, Herbert, *Sucker's Progress,* Dodd, Mead & Co., New York, 1938.

Baldwin, Cantey, Maisel, & McDermott, *Playing Blackjack to Win,* Barrows & Co., New York, 1957.

Barnhart, Russell T., *Gamblers of Yesteryear,* GBC Press, Las Vegas, 1983.

Chafetz, Henry, *Play the Devil: A History of Gambling in the United States, 1492-1955,* Bonanza Books, New York, 1960.

Chambliss, C.R., and Roginski, T.C., *Playing Blackjack in Atlantic City*, GBC Press, Las Vegas, 1981.

Cohen, Sam, *The Automat: Jess Marcum, Gambling Genius of the Century,* self-published, 1993.

Cotton, Charles, *The Complete Gamester,* London, 1674.

Culbertson, Ely, Morehead, & Mott-Smith, *Culbertson's Hoyle,* Greystone Press, New York, 1950.

Culbertson, Ely, Morehead, & Mott-Smith, *Culbertson's Card Games Complete,* Greystone Press, New York, 1952.

DeArment, Robert K., *Knights of the Green Cloth,* University of Oklahoma Press, 1982.

Demaris, Ovid, *The Boardwalk Jungle,* Bantam Books, New York, 1986.

Drago, Harry Sinclair, *Notorious Ladies of the Frontier,* Dodd, Mead & Co., 1969.

Dixon, Adams & King, *Playing the Cards That Are Dealt,* University of Nevada Oral History Program, Las Vegas, 1992.

Eisler, Kim Isaac, *Revenge of the Pequots,* Simon & Schuster, New York, 2001.

Epstein, Richard A., *The Theory of Gambling and Statistical Logic,* Academic Press, San Diego, 1977.

Florio, John, *The World of Wordes,* London, 1611.

APPENDIX

Gardiner, Alexander, *Canfield: The True Story of the Greatest Gambler,* Doubleday, Garden City, NY, 1930.

Goodman, Robert, *The Luck Business,* Free Press, New York, 1995.

Grosjean, James, *Beyond Counting,* RGE Publishing, Oakland, 2000.

Humble, Lance, and Cooper, Carl, *The World's Greatest Blackjack Book,* Doubleday & Co., New York, 1980.

Jacoby, Oswald, *How to Figure the Odds,* Doubleday, Garden City, NY, 1940-47.

Jacoby, Oswald, *Oswald Jacoby on Gambling,* Hart Publishing, New York, 1963.

Johnston, David, *Temples of Chance,* Doubleday, New York, 1992.

Lewis, Oscar, *Sagebrush Casinos,* Doubleday, Garden City, NY, 1953.

MacDougall, Michael, *Gamblers Don't Gamble,* Garden City Publishing, New York, 1939-40.

MacDougall, Michael, *Danger in the Cards,* Ziff-Davis, New York, 1943.

MacDougall, Michael, *MacDougall on Dice and Cards,* Coward-McCann, New York, 1944.

Marks, Dustin, *Cheating at Blackjack,* Index Publishing, San Diego, 1994.

Messick, Hank and Goldblatt, Burt, *The Only Game in Town,* Thomas Crowell & Co., New York, 1976.

Munchkin, Richard W., *Gambling Wizards,* Huntington Press, Las Vegas, 2002.

Munting, Roger, *An Economic & Social History of Gambling in Britain & the USA,* Manchester Univ. Press, UK, 1996.

Nelson, Walter, *The Merry Gamester, or Games Through the Ages,* Merchant Adventurers Press, 1996.

Ortiz, Darwin, *Gambling Scams,* Lyle Stuart, Secaucus, NJ, 1984.

Parlett, David, *The Oxford Guide to Card Games,* Oxford University Press, UK, 1990.

Puzo, Mario, *Inside Las Vegas,* Grosset & Dunlap, New York, 1977.

Reid, Ed & Demaris, Ovid, *The Green Felt Jungle,* Simon & Schuster, New York, 1963.

Richardson, Sir Philip, *Systems and Chances,* G. Bell & Sons, London, 1929.

Rose, I. Nelson, *Gambling and the Law,* Gambling Times, Inc., 1986.

Rose, I. Nelson, and Loeb, Robert A., *Blackjack and the Law*, RGE Publishing, Oakland, 1998.

Rubin, Max, *Comp City,* Huntington Press, Las Vegas, 1994.

Scarne, John, & Rawson, Clayton, *Scarne on Dice,* Military Service Publishing Co., Harrisburg, PA, 1945.

Scarne, John, *Scarne on Cards* (Updated, Enlarged), Crown Publishers, New York, 1974 (orig. 1945).

Scarne, John, *Scarne's New Complete Guide to Gambling,* Simon & Schuster, New York, 1961-74.

Scarne, John, *The Odds Against Me,* Simon & Schuster, New York, 1966.

Scarne, John, *Scarne's Guide to Casino Gambling,* Simon & Schuster, New York, 1978.

Scarne, John, *Scarne's Encyclopedia of Card Games,* Harper Perennial, New York, 1973-83.

Shampaign, Charles E., *Handbook on Percentages,* Treyball Sporting Goods, 1928-30.

Sheehan, Jack, *The Players: The Men Who Made Las Vegas,* University of Nevada Press, Reno, 1997.

Silberstang, Edwin, *Silberstang's Encyclopedia of Games & Gambling,* Cardoza Publishing, New York, 1996.

Skolnick, Jerome H., *House of Cards,* Little, Brown & Co., Boston, 1978.

Smith, Harold, Sr., *I Want to Quit Winners,* Prentice-Hall, New York, 1961.

Snyder, Arnold, *The Blackjack Formula*, RGE Publishing, Oakland, 1980.

Snyder, Arnold, *Blackbelt in Blackjack*, Cardoza Publishing, 1983, 1998, 2004.

Snyder, Arnold, *Blackjack Wisdom*, RGE Publishing, Oakland, 1997.

Stuart, Lyle, *Lyle Stuart on Baccarat,* Lyle Stuart, Secaucus, NJ, 1984.

Taylor, Rev. Ed. S., et al., *The History of Playing Cards,* London, 1865.

APPENDIX

Thackery, Ted, Jr., *Gambling Secrets of Nick the Greek,* Rand McNally & Co., 1968.

Thomson, David, *In Nevada: The Land, The People, God, and Chance,* Alfred A. Knopf, New York, 1999.

Thorp, Edward O., *Beat the Dealer,* Random House, New York, 1962-66.

Tilley, Roger, *A History of Playing Cards,* Clarkson N. Potter, Inc., New York, 1973.

Uston, Ken, and Rapoport, Roger, *The Big Player,* Holt, Rinehart & Winston, New York, 1977.

Uston, Ken, *Two Books on Blackjack,* Uston Institute of Blackjack, Wheaton, MD, 1979.

Uston, Ken, *Million Dollar Blackjack,* Gambling Times, Hollywood, 1981.

Uston, Ken, *Ken Uston on Blackjack,* Barricade Books, Fort Lee, NJ, 1986.

Wechsberg, Joseph, "Blackjack Pete," from *Collier's,* July 25, 1953, New York.

Wilson, Allan N., *The Casino Gambler's Guide,* Harper and Row, New York, 1965-70.

Wilson, Thomas (editor), *Pioneer Nevada,* Reno, 1951.

Wong, Stanford, *Stanford Wong's Blackjack Newsletters,* Pi Yee Press, San Diego, 1979-84.

Wong, Stanford, *Winning Without Counting,* Pi Yee Press, San Diego, 1978.

Wykes, Alan, *The Complete Illustrated Guide to Gambling,* Doubleday, Garden City, NY, 1964.

Zender, Bill, *How to Detect Casino Cheating at Blackjack,* RGE Publishing, Oakland, 1999.

[no author listed], *Hoyle's Complete Book of Games,* M. A. Donohue & Co., New York, 1927.

INDEX

INDEX

INDEX

WIN MONEY AT BLACKJACK! SPECIAL OFFER!

THE CARD'OZA BASE COUNT STRATEGY

Finally, a count strategy has been developed which allows the average player to play blackjack like a **pro**! Actually, this strategy isn't new. The Cardoza Base Count Strategy has been used successfully by graduates of the Cardoza School of Blackjack for years. But **now**, for the **first time**, this "million dollar" strategy, which was only available previously to those students attending the school, is available to **you**!

FREE VACATIONS! A SECOND INCOME? - You bet! Once you learn this strategy, you will have the skills to **consistently win big money** at blackjack. The longer you play, the more you make. The casino's bankroll is yours for the taking.

BECOME AN EXPERT IN TWO DAYS - Why struggle over complicated strategies that aren't as powerful? In just **two days or less**, you can learn the Cardoza Base Count and be among the best blackjack players. Friends will look up to you in awe - for you will be a **big winner** at blackjack.

BEAT ANY SINGLE OR MULTIPLE DECK GAME - We show you how, with just a **little effort**, you can effectively beat any single or multiple deck game. You'll learn how to count cards, how to use advanced betting and playing strategies, how to make money on insurance bets, and much, much, more in this 6,000 word, chart-filled strategy package.

SIMPLE TO USE, EASY TO MASTER - **You too can win!** The **power** of the Cardoza Base Count strategy is not only in its **computer-proven** winning results but also in its **simplicity**. Many beginners who thought card counting was too difficult have given the Cardoza Base Count the acid test - they have **won consistently** in casinos around the world. The Cardoza Base Count strategy is designed so that **any player** can win under practical casino conditions. **No need** for a mathematical mind or photographic memory. **No need** to be bogged down by calculations. Keep **only one numbe**r in your head at any time. The casinos will never suspect that you're a counter.

DOUBLE BONUS!! - **Rush** your order in **now**, for we're also including, **absolutely free**, the 1,000 and 1,500 word essays, "How to Disguise the Fact that You're an Expert", and "How Not to Get Barred". Among other **inside information** contained here, you'll learn about the psychology of the pit bosses, how they spot counters, how to project a losing image, role playing, and other skills to maximize your profit potential.

As an **introductory offer to readers of this book**, the Cardoza Base Count Strategy, which has netted graduates of the Cardoza School of Blackjack **substantial sums** of **money**, is offered here for **only** $50!

To order, send $50 by check or money order to:

Cardoza Publishing, P.O. Box 98115, Las Vegas, NV 89193

WIN MONEY PLAYING BLACKJACK!

MAIL THIS COUPON NOW!

Yes, I want to **win big money** at blackjack. Please **rush** me the Cardoza Base Count Strategy. I understand that the Double Bonus essays are included **absolutely free**. Enclosed is a check or money order for $50 (plus postage and handling) made out to:

Cardoza Publishing, P.O. Box 98115, Las Vegas, NV 89193

Call Toll-Free in U.S. & Canada, 1-800-577-WINS

Include $5.00 postage/handling for U.S. orders; $10.00 for Can/Mex; HI/AK and other countries $15.00. Outside U.S., money order payable in U.S. dollars on U.S. bank only.

NAME_____

ADDRESS_____

CITY_____ STATE _____ ZIP _____

Order Now to Win! 30 Day Money Back Guarantee! Big BJ 2012